# CONVERSATIONS WITH RICHARD PURCELL

To Nanette—
many Blessings!

Susan Lawlor

# CONVERSATIONS WITH RICHARD PURCELL

## THE ADVENTURES AND REFLECTIONS OF A SAN FRANCISCO RENEGADE PRIEST

Susan Casslan with Richard Purcell, OFM

Meandering Trail Press
San Francisco, California

Meandering Trail Press
San Francisco, California
www.meanderingtrailpress.com

ISBN: 978-0-9828941-1-8



Printed in the United States of America

# Contents

For Jay... wherever I might find him.
And, with gratitude, to the Aurora Dawn Foundation.

# PREFACE

Father Richard Purcell knew many people more intimately and for a longer period of time than he knew me. Although this book reflects my personal encounters with him, others will have their own impressions and recollections of this extraordinary man. In time, I know there will be multiple tales of Richard's life, so that he will continue to exist in the minds and hearts of those who knew and loved him. And for those who never met him, perhaps they will be inspired by these stories.

This is a work of nonfiction, although to protect confidentiality, many of the names have been changed. Richard contributed to this book, and I recorded numerous quotes by him verbatim. His suggestion for a title was *A Trail of Beauty*. Native Americans played an important role in his personal history, and he took this phrase from the American Indians. Richard believed that this phrase closely reflected his own existence, one that was filled with endless gifts and good fortune.

Richard's two decades with the Tooham O'odham and Akila O'odham Indians in Arizona had a significant impact on the way he viewed the world. Throughout the time I knew him, much of his heart remained with the Native Americans, and he requested that when he died, his ashes be left with the Akila O'odham, where they would be buried in the desert. Thus, he expected that this book would include a great deal about his time in Arizona, and he saw *A Trail of Beauty* as a fitting name for his life story.

Unfortunately, I never knew Richard when he lived in the desert, and any accounts of this period came to me second-hand. Since I knew him only in his later years, I felt inspired by, and most capable of writing about, that time. We knew each other in San Francisco – and thus the book's final title. This title seemed especially appropriate since my relationship with Richard coincided with my encounters with the Secular Franciscans of Most Holy Redeemer Church in San Francisco, and with several of the Franciscan priests and brothers from Richard's province. I was not only living in the city of Saint Francis, I was also surrounded by the friendship, love, and spiritual insights of many Franciscans.

Richard himself certainly stood out as a true Franciscan, even though he often criticized the Catholic Church. As much as possible in this modern world, Richard practiced what St. Francis taught. Richard prioritized love in his interactions with others, and he spent his life living and working with the poor. He also existed for the present moment, with little fear of the future. His practice of being present and surrendering fear was especially poignant when, due to amyotrophic lateral sclerosis (ALS), he slowly lost control of all of his bodily functions, including his ability to breathe. Even in that state, he exuded peace and optimism.

In the end, Richard encouraged me to write a book that reflected my own experiences of our time together. Again, others' perspectives of Richard may differ. Yet one thing is certain – Richard Purcell had a profound effect on many lives, and he is one human being that none of us will ever forget.

Susan Casslan
November 20, 2011

PART I

# FINDING RICHARD

"How difficult it is to be simple."[1]
– Vincent Van Gogh

## Marty's Place and Richard Purcell

Marty's Place, a homeless shelter for men with AIDS, was an aging, three-story Victorian located in San Francisco's inner Mission District. Over the course of several years, I frequently visited this building, and I eventually felt very much at home there. It had certainly been a home to many who had come before me. It had especially been home to the collection of faces that decorated its living room mantel – the photographs of men who had died there from AIDS, well before their time.

The house was named after Marty Purcell, whose picture also sat on the mantel. Marty was the brother of the shelter's founder, Father Richard Purcell, a Franciscan priest. With the help of volunteers, Richard had personally cared for Marty and all these men until they passed away.

In 2006, Richard discovered that he too was dying. He was diagnosed that year with amyotrophic lateral sclerosis, or ALS. Also known as Lou Gehrig's disease, ALS is a devastating and fatal illness. Its victims gradually lose the use of all their muscles, until they are entirely paralyzed. The last muscles to go are often respiratory. As these muscles deteriorate, the patient either suffocates or gets hooked up to a ventilator. Richard had ruled out the ventilator option. He insisted that he didn't want to be kept alive on a machine, and by early 2009, he asked to be put on home hospice care.

For as long as possible, Richard preferred to remain at Marty's Place with the kind of people who he had lived with for over two decades – mostly gay men with AIDS. And in an ironic turn of events, these men began to care for him.

After Richard's diagnosis, Aurora Dawn, the foundation which helped finance the shelter, put its work on hold. The men with HIV who lived at Marty's Place gradually moved out and found other homes. But many of these men continued to stay connected with the old Victorian.

The house became a center of sorts – a place for people to gather for fellowship and support. Those of us who physically cared for Richard called ourselves "The Circle of Care." We consisted of former Marty's Place residents, and other people whose lives Richard had touched.

In addition to his caregivers, an endless number of individuals came to visit Richard. People constantly wanted to spend time with him, and friends were frequently phoning from various parts of the globe. Richard reveled in this steady stream of callers. He enjoyed talking to people, and it was something he did very well. In fact, he may have survived longer and more comfortably than other ALS victims because he was able to continue his life's vocation years after he lost his ability to do other things. His special talent was to counsel others, and so as long as he could speak and listen, he was still highly functional.

Richard was a man of contradictions. He had been a friar his entire adult life, and he requested that he be dressed in his Franciscan robe at his wake. At the same time, he had distanced himself from the Catholic Church. This was because he felt that its hierarchal structure had strayed too far from the teachings of Jesus and from Richard's own spiritual values.

In further opposition to the Church, Richard stated openly that he was gay. And he felt that for anyone – gay, straight or even priests – sex was a healthy thing. However, Richard also extolled the virtues of celibacy, which he claimed could free a person for other purposes in life, including service to others.

Richard was a kind and caring person who was able to see beyond people's faults and love them unconditionally. But he was also adept at a kind of gossipy humor that took cutting swipes at people behind their backs. For instance, I heard him describe some individuals as creeps, idiots, and other unprintable epitaphs. He usually reserved these insults for those who abused power, and at times, such persons were government officials or members of the upper echelons of organized religions.

Right up until his last days, Richard remained a good looking man. He had white hair, a goatee, an Irish grin and rascally eyes that were often on the lookout for some good-natured mischief. Well into his disease, he had a muscular physique, and his right bicep revealed a faded and indecipherable tattoo. I initially wondered how a priest had ended up with a tattoo, and I surmised that behind the tat was a fascinating and probably amusing story.

Richard was full of stories, and I inevitably decided that I wanted to write down as many of these tales as possible before he passed away. I asked him if I could record some of his thoughts as well as his biography, and much to my delight, he agreed. He also gave me his journals, which he had begun to tape after he was diagnosed with ALS. I was pleased to be part of these interviews, as they gave me an excuse to spend more time with Richard. In fact, I told him that just being at Marty's Place lifted my spirits.

"Everybody says that," he replied, as if he were agreeing that it was raining outside or that it was Thursday. Richard had no doubts that the home he had created after his brother Marty's death meant so much to so many people. That was why he created it, and he hadn't done it alone. His energy ignited a whole community of people who were committed to the shelter's vision.

Knowing Richard and being part of this community touched my life in a unique and remarkable manner. This experience gave me something that is difficult to define, but it had much to do with inner peace, hope and healing.

In fact, most of us who cared for Richard in his final years weren't there for selfless reasons. We had each come to receive an incredible gift.

## 2002-2004

Richard and I both lived in the Lower 24th Street corridor of San Francisco's Mission District. I had moved to this city and neighborhood in 2002 to be with my partner, Rebecca. I had no regrets about moving; however it took me a while to adjust to San Francisco itself.

Despite its reputation as a beautiful and fascinating place, San Francisco had its own share of problems. It had a harshness to it, especially on our side of Market Street, where it was burdened with poverty and at times, shootings and armed robberies.

Our neighborhood was a mixed bag. It was slowly becoming gentrified, which caused some tensions between the whites moving in and our mostly brown neighbors. The inner Mission had been a Latino district for decades, but things were changing. Trendy art galleries and coffee shops were sprouting up and rents were rising. Many of the former residents couldn't afford to live there anymore, but others held their ground. Our barrio was colorful and interesting, but as a new arrival, I had trouble figuring out where I fit in.

My neighbors were Guatemalan, Mexican, Honduran, and many other nationalities. Some of the local whites appeared wealthy, and others were homeless and pushing shopping carts. And still others were the tattooed young hipsters, who hung out at cafés and clubs, or zipped through the 'hood on their skateboards.

It took me a while to settle into this place, and get a sense of who was there with me. And not only was I adjusting to a new home, I also experienced during those years, a terrible personal tragedy. My beloved brother Jay died. I found myself emotionally adrift, reaching out for anything to grab hold of. Rebecca was a tremendous help, but I needed more than she could give.

So I hooked up with a grief support group, and took some classes and joined a gym. Then there was Luz.

My story of Richard actually begins with Luz. She led me to the place where my path and his came together for a while. Luz also introduced me to the Mission District. She became a bridge into that community and into many other things.

Luz – a Spanish word that means light. Luz was Mexican-American, and when I met her, in her seventies. She had a round face, kind eyes, some excess pounds, and walked with a cane due to a bad hip.

Luz lived near me, and she was one of the first friends I made in my barrio. When I learned that she didn't have a car, I offered to drive her at times to the grocery store. We'd shop, and then afterwards, have coffee or lunch. In time our friendship deepened, and I learned about Luz's life.

Luz had stumbled upon some hardships in her years, which kept her consistently living under the US government's definition of poverty. Not that she minded. "I'm a Franciscan," she would tell me. "A follower of St. Francis."

Luz was a member of the Secular Franciscan Order (SFO) or the Third Order of St. Francis. The order was set up for Franciscans who wanted to live as lay persons – people who respected Franciscan values, but preferred to marry or live secular lives. In other words, they did not want to be brothers, nuns or priests.

Luz explained to me that in order to follow the teachings of St. Francis, one needed to live by his example. And to cherish, as St. Francis cherished, what he called "Sister Poverty." He believed that poverty held riches within its limitations. Luz believed this too, and she had personally discovered many. She didn't treasure the kind of poverty that caused suffering. She saw the need for social justice and she realized that all humans required certain necessities. But she also felt that there was beauty in living a life that was simple and unencumbered.

Luz always conveyed a sense of inner peace. That was one trait that Richard really admired about her.

"She's the real deal," he told me. He also said that even though Luz had repeatedly come to him for spiritual guidance, she was in many ways his teacher. He had tremendous respect for her and for the way she lived.

## 2005

I first met Richard in Luz's flat. He stopped by one afternoon while Luz and I were visiting, and Luz invited him inside. He looked at me with an open, curious face and extended his hand.

"This my friend, Richard," said Luz. She didn't introduce him as a priest, even though ironically, she and I had just been discussing Mass. Luz knew I'd been raised Catholic, and I was explaining to her why I no longer went to church. As Richard sat down to join us, Luz continued our conversation.

"Why don't you go to church?" Richard asked, as he listened to us talk.

"I can't get into it," I said. "I tried, but it just doesn't work for me."

"Me neither," he commented. "And I tried to get into it for 65 years."

Luz laughed, "And he ought to know."

"Why is that?" I wondered.

"Because he's a priest."

"What?"

That was how I learned Richard's story. I discovered that he was a gay Franciscan friar, and that he ran a homeless shelter for men with AIDS. I told him that my brother had died of AIDS, and he nodded with concern.

"I don't go to Mass, but I do say the rosary sometimes," I said. "It calms me down and helps me sleep."

"That'll put you to sleep," said Richard.

Luz laughed again, but I frowned. I still hadn't grasped Richard's endless penchant for humor and teasing.

"No, really," I insisted. "It's like meditation. Like Buddhist prayer beads. The rosary quiets my mind and helps me sleep."

Richard cringed. "I think I'd rather stay awake all night than say the rosary."

This was my introduction to Richard's total irreverence for all things Catholic. In time he would express his opinions in more detail. A few weeks later he invited me to Marty's Place. He showed me around and introduced me to some of the residents. Then we went into the dining room for cookies and tea. As we talked, he revealed more of his feelings toward the religion in which we'd both been raised.

"Truthfully," Richard explained, "99 percent of the Catholic faith is loony. Take communion, for instance." He held up a cookie as if it were a host. "We're eating the body of Christ? We lock it up in a golden box and say magic words over it? You and I grew up with those fairy tales, but for somebody looking at it from the outside – it's totally insane."

He dunked the cookie into his cup and took a bite. I must have looked bewildered. I had never heard any practicing priest talk like this.

"I don't get it," I said. "You make fun of the Church Richard, but you also say that you liked being a priest."

"I loved it," he agreed.

"And that you have no regrets."

"That's because I got away with so much. And in my province, I had some wonderful brothers who were in authority. I asked for unusual permissions – and God bless those men – they allowed me to follow my own heart. But honestly, any organized religion is so limiting – in terms of where it'll take you with spiritual growth."

Richard believed that most religions were based on a lot of superstition. "Not that there's always anything wrong with superstition," he said. "Sometimes myths are powerful images that relate to real things. But the trouble with many of these symbols is that they don't change. They don't evolve the way all of life evolves and changes. In the Catholic Church, people are still believing the same things or saying the same words that they've said for thousands of years. That just doesn't work for me anymore."

Richard had remained a priest for perhaps the same reasons that many priests did. He had invested decades in the Church and he was entitled to some benefits. For example, he had health insurance, and if he chose to live in community with other friars, he would get free room and board. But Richard had no income. Since he chose to live at Marty's Place, he survived on solicited donations and food from the local food bank.

One reason Richard remained a friar was because he loved his fellow Franciscans. "They are wonderful men," he told me. "And so many of us are queer. But that's the case with plenty of religious leaders of all faiths around the world."

"Do you think a lot of priests and brothers are gay?" I wondered.

"Does the pope live in Rome?" he replied. "And instead of seeing homosexuality as a detriment, you would think that those in authority would view it as a plus. They should be grateful that so many gay people are drawn to these vocations. But frankly, I've always suspected that a lot of the attacks on gays in the Catholic Church come from internalized homophobia. As they say, it takes one to know one."

Richard explained what he meant. "I have a theory," he said, "that some of the worst homophobes in the Church are themselves, closet queens."

Richard was not alone in his theory. In time, I would meet other gay men who were, or had once been, Catholic brothers or priests. Like with Richard, I met several of these men through Luz. And Luz had a compelling story of how she met these men herself.

## Most Holy Redeemer

Luz's parents were Mexican immigrant farm workers who had somehow made their way into San Francisco. There, they struggled to give their children a foothold in this country. Luz grew up in the inner Mission, and as a young woman, married. Unfortunately, her husband turned out to be an alcoholic. He left her with nothing but two daughters, and with little money, she worked hard to raise them alone.

Throughout these struggles, Luz often drew strength from the religion in which she'd been raised. But one day her faith was tested. This happened when she learned something about her oldest daughter, Daniela. Daniela had been spending a lot of time with a short-haired girl at her high school, and Luz had been watching the two of them with concern.

"You shouldn't spend so much time with Kathy," Luz warned Daniela. "I know about that girl. If you associate with her, people will think you're a lesbian."

"Well, they might as well," said the daughter.

"*Perdón?*" asked Luz. "Might as well what?"

"They may as well think that."

"*Qué?*"

"Because I am one."

"What?!"

That was that. Daniela walked away, leaving her mother suspended in shock and disbelief. Luz didn't know what to think or do.

After she recovered from this revelation, Luz found her way to a Parents and Friends of Lesbians and Gays (PFLAG) meeting. Many meetings later, Luz began to regain her footing. She felt at peace again. There was nothing wrong with Daniela, Luz decided. She had a wonderful daughter and there was no cause for concern. With this new-found awareness, Luz started volunteering at PFLAG. She worked as a translator, reaching out to Spanish speaking families of gay people, helping them also find peace.

After Daniela had grown, Luz continued going to these meetings. She went there for herself and for the LGBTs and their loved ones who still suffered from confusion or homophobia. And Luz found out something else through this work. She discovered that she really liked the gay and lesbian community. She felt at home there, perhaps because like her – a daughter of immigrants, who lived between worlds and borders – gays also seemed to exist on an invisible social edge. Luz could relate to their pain, humor, and need for connection.

So Luz started taking the bus into the Castro District. There, she began attending a new Catholic Church, Most Holy Redeemer, which was populated by mostly gay men. She also joined the Secular Franciscan Order of the Most Holy Redeemer Church.

Luz often invited me to join her for Mass, and at first, I refused. And I jokingly repeated what Richard had once said about churches. He called them "wind tunnels." I told Luz, that if he meant churches were giant hollow structures filled with hot air, then I had to agree.

After a while however, I became curious about Most Holy Redeemer (locally known as MHR). Luz had spoken highly of the parish, and I was drawn to the fact that it welcomed gays. So I eventually agreed to at least check it out, and I was actually quite impressed. The church was beautiful, and the chorus of predominantly gay male voices that filled the sanctuary with music was especially impressive. So was the parish's history.

MHR had once ministered to the Irish Catholics who had inhabited San Francisco's Eureka Valley District, (which later became the "gay Mecca" known as the Castro). As the gays moved in, the Irish left. And in the 70s, like a lot of Catholic churches all over the country, the ranks of parishioners at MHR began to dwindle. When the AIDS epidemic hit in the 80s, some of the MHR laity began to reach out to the gay men who were suffering in their midst. Consequently, a relationship evolved between the neighboring gay community and the aging faithful at MHR. In time, gay men began pouring into the church and eventually formed the bulk of the congregation.

From my perspective, gay people taking over the pews of a Catholic church was a real coup. When I was growing up, the Church had always been the center of the community. It was where people got married, baptized, and blessed before burial. To have these important occasions approved by the Church was a real symbol of their social acceptance.

Of course gays were never part of this system, and in the eyes of Catholicism, same-sex behavior is still considered a sin. The majority of churches do not marry gay couples, nor do they baptize the children of gay parents. In my own case, none of the good church-going people in my home town spoke up when my gay brother was being tormented right under their noses for his sexual orientation. But that's another story that I'll touch on later.

Despite all this, I still felt some connection with the Church. Although I had some serious complaints around growing up Catholic, there was also something comfortably familiar for me about the religion. I appreciated the beauty of its rituals, art and music, and the kindness I remembered from a few nuns and priests. The Church stirred up emotions in me, just as a Midwestern autumn or a thunderstorm might whenever I ventured back to where I was born. I can't say that Catholicism's good influences in my life overshadowed the negative, but the religion was in my blood.

As a young adult, when feeling defeated and alone in some unfamiliar place, I ventured into a few churches. I still hadn't forgotten the promise that I'd been given as a child. That maybe I'd find peace there, and some sort of community. I knew the prayers after all. I knew the drill. So I'd go inside and in every situation, felt like I didn't belong. People would sit through Mass, repeat some words, mumble a few songs, and then get in their cars and drive home. Nobody reached out to newcomers. And like a lot of religions, Catholicism appeared to be a support system for the nuclear family, which definitely didn't include me.

In time, I sought out alternative places of refuge, and some were healthier than others. My brother found crystal meth. Thus, it was no small thing for me to sit in MHR and hear gay men raise the rafters with their music. I knew why they were singing so joyful and loud. They had been welcomed home.

## The Secular Franciscan Order

In time, Luz brought me to her Secular Franciscan group, which convened in the parish hall at Most Holy Redeemer. There, I met some more gay men who were connected with the Church. Some of them had been Catholic brothers and a few had studied to be priests. They affirmed what Richard had told me – that many Catholic religious men and women were indeed gay. Their views were echoed by other sources, including Reverend Donald Cozzens in his book *The Changing Face of the Priesthood*, where he estimates that 25-50 percent of American Catholic priests are homosexual.

It made sense that gays would be drawn to this life. Historically, many gays have followed this path because they had no interest in marrying someone of the opposite sex. Perhaps freedom from marriage or children also left them more available for service. And LGBTs might have some special perspectives on the teachings of Jesus. After all, if Jesus cared about outcasts, gays certainly fit the bill.

Several of the men in Luz's fraternity had abandoned their vows because of the Church's homophobia, but they were still devoted to some form of spirituality. Especially the teachings of St. Francis.

In addition to these men, at that first meeting I also met the group's spiritual assistant, Father Louie Vitale. Father Louie's reputation had preceded our introduction, as he was well known around San Francisco. Louie was a social activist who had been to jail many times for protesting the government's military activities. And as the former pastor of St. Boniface's in San Francisco's Tenderloin District, he had an unusual way of running a church.

Louie saw a clear link between Christianity and social justice. In addition to his anti-war efforts, he opened his church to the homeless. He unlocked St. Boniface during the day so that the homeless could get some sleep on the church's empty pews. And every year he ceremoniously blessed the city's taxi drivers. According to the country's labor statistics, cabbies are in serious danger of being murdered on the job, so Louie saw blessing these guys as a priority. The homeless and taxi drivers – these were the kinds of people that Louie cared about.

Louie was a tall, lanky man in his 70s with white hair and a beard. The first time I met him, he was wearing his brown Franciscan robe and sandals. He arrived at our gathering on the bus, and refused to eat any meat during the evening's pot luck. He was quiet for most of the meeting, but after a while he delivered for us a profound soliloquy on God, faith and spirit. His words were moving, intelligent, and laced with a keen knowledge of the brutality of the world. Louie's faith was not naive. He understood that it was difficult to believe in any kind of God on this planet when there is so much human suffering. But he didn't ask us to believe. He merely set an example of how a Franciscan should live – simply, always spreading joy and love, and working toward peace.

Richard and Louie had known each other for decades. Louie had once been the provincial (head) of Richard's Franciscan order. Louie had helped Richard make some major decisions in his life, including where Richard would serve as a friar.

I knew Richard loved Louie, but he never spoke of him in the glowing and revered terms that so many people around San Francisco did. That was because Richard was never reverent about any person or thing. One of Richard's pet names for Louie was "Lou-Lou."

I was initially struck by the warmth and humor of these Franciscans. I was welcomed with open arms and immediately felt at home. I could see why Luz loved these men. They were very much like her – kind people who prioritized spirituality in their lives. I enjoyed the meeting and I was intrigued with the fact that the Secular Franciscan Order was based on the teachings of Saint Francis.

Saint Francis had always impressed me. He had given up the riches of his family to live with the poor. He saw a sacredness in nature and in animals, and he advocated peace and nonviolence. Rumor has it that some of his early followers joined his order to avoid being forced to fight in the Crusades. They may have been some of the original draft resisters.

I decided to return to this group, and by my second visit, I realized that I wanted to be part of the fellowship. I asked to join, and began what is known in the order as a period of inquiry.

Most of my adult life, I'd considered myself an agnostic, but that didn't mean I wasn't drawn to spirituality. It might have been hard for me to define what my own spirituality meant, but I'd always been searching. And for a time, the Secular Franciscans became part of that journey.

My initiation into the organization was very informal. Our discussions were extremely open and devoid of dogma. We also said some prayers and had a loose association with the worldwide Secular Franciscan community. To me, the prayers and the more formal design of these meetings were incidental. They were just rituals – things I had to go through in order to hang out with such good people. And I had no problem with rituals. I had been taught to pray as a child and I had learned how to meditate as an adult. I'd lived on a yoga ashram and I'd explored Buddhism. There were always "things" that one had to deal with in any spiritual practice. They took such forms as prayers, bells, bows, and songs. I viewed these things as mantras. And as Sogyal Rinpoche, a Tibetan Buddhist teaches, mantras protect us from our own mind.

I prayed aloud with the others in the group, and sat quietly through the occasional meeting. And I reveled in finding what I had sought and truly needed: fellowship and spiritual support.

Eventually Father Louie left San Francisco. After protesting the activities of The School of the Americas in Fort Benning Georgia, he was sent to prison. Richard took his place as our spiritual assistant, and that was when I really got to know him.

## 2006

Richard started coming to our Secular Franciscan meetings. He was officially called the spiritual assistant, but he never presented himself in that way. He just hung out with the rest of us and laughed and joked around as much as we did. In fact, he told us that the highest forms of prayer are laughing and crying.

Another thing he said was that we shouldn't just have these meetings. We should be helping others. I had heard the same thing in Catholic school: that faith without works is dead. All of us knew what Richard had done for people in his own life, and what he was still doing. We realized he was right. Some of us already did volunteer work, but we began to talk about what we could do together as a group.

One thing we cared about was the concerns of gay Catholics. We felt that a lot of gay people who were raised in the Catholic Church, or in other religions, were suffering. They felt alienated from their families, communities, and even themselves. We thought that maybe we could support these people, and at the same time deal with our own feelings of alienation. Jerry, one of our members, had started a website called The Gay Catholic Forum, and a few of us wrote for it. Others followed Richard to San Damiano, a Franciscan retreat house in Danville where he held workshops for gays.

Richard had been leading these workshops for years. He conducted weekend retreats for people with AIDS, and also led quarterly afternoon retreats for LGBTs and their families and friends. These retreats were called "Days of Dialogue." Richard also called them "Talking Circles," a term he had picked up while living with Native Americans in Arizona.

Our Talking Circles had no agendas. People would just get together and converse. During these gatherings I also heard Richard preach a little, and that's when I really got a sense of how thoughtful and funny he was.

Meanwhile, I got to know Richard socially. He was close to Luz, and the three of us occasionally got together. During this period, Luz started having some health problems. She had hip surgery, and she was also diagnosed with myeloma. She was in intense pain, and in and out of hospitals. Richard and I visited her, and it meant so much to her to see us. During these visits I watched Richard do what he did so well, which was lift the spirits of someone who was suffering.

One day Richard told me that he was having problems with his foot.

"What's wrong with it?" I asked.

"It doesn't work," he said. "I'm having trouble walking." Shortly after that he was diagnosed with ALS.

## July 1, 2009

Pinto, a black and white cat, crawled up onto Richard's lap. I was fascinated with the fact that both Pinto and Plumita, Richard's little white dog, seemed to know that Richard was not well. Plumita remained diligently by his side, and even independent Pinto wouldn't stray far from Richard's bedroom.

Richard's bedroom was on the ground floor of Marty's Place, and just outside his room was a lovely patio and garden. By the summer of 2009, Richard was no longer able to walk, and it became harder and harder for his caregivers to carry him up and down stairs. Luckily, when the weather was nice, we could still wheel him outside.

As Richard and I sat on this courtyard patio one afternoon, I conducted another one of our interviews. Richard seemed happy to see me, and as usual, willing to tell me anything I needed to know. I had brought along some lunch from a local deli, and I handed him a sandwich. He was losing coordination in his upper extremities, and his hands were shaking, but he still managed to feed himself.

Plumita had been at his feet, staring at Richard with imploring eyes, and Richard tossed her a few pieces of bread and roast beef. He would always share whatever he ate with his dog, and consequently, she had become an unabashed beggar. She would never let any of us alone when we were eating.

I watched them both for a while, then opened my notebook. "Richard," I began, "as a Franciscan, you must have been drawn to St. Francis. What do you think of him?"

"St. Francis?" asked Richard. "Frankly, I'm sick of him. When you talk to some Franciscans, it's like the whole world revolves around St. Francis."

I was a little taken aback, but I let him proceed.

"For God's sake," he said, "it's been 800 years. Lord have mercy, get a grip. All this messing around with ancient history and not coming into the present. Can we update things a little?"

Richard chewed and swallowed, then lowered his voice. "On the other hand, Francis was a great guy. He was an exceptional figure in the history of the world, although he was probably off his rocker. He made a radical shift in the Church. Before him, religious people were locked up behind walls. He felt we could serve God and still live in the world with other people. This idea was revolutionary. Of course, Rome got hold of what he was doing and twisted it all out of shape. Francis was in his 40s when he died, so he had only about 20 years to start this movement. He had thousands of friars following him in a very short time. But it all backfired on him; Rome ruined it."

"How so?"

"The way they ruin everything. Power-hungry people booted him out. It's the same thing today. We're still fighting the same battle."

"What battle?"

"The battle that exists in most religions and in most governments. The one that says that only select people can run the show. This wasn't what Francis had in mind when he started his brotherhood. He just wanted to live with and help the poor. But then Rome got involved and spoiled it. Anyway," he sighed, "it's all ancient history. It's not part of my own reality. It's the same with Jesus."

"What is?"

"Jesus is also part of the past. I don't stay that focused on something that has no relevance for my life today."

"It seems to me that much of what Jesus said is very relevant today," I protested.

"That's true," Richard agreed. "Or a lot of things that they claimed he said. If Jesus existed, I'm sure he was a great man. But what parts of the New Testament are really the words of Jesus? God only knows who wrote those words and how they were translated. But if you're going to take anything from what Jesus supposedly said, I'd go with these types of things: have compassion, don't judge, we are all children of light, let go, don't be afraid, love one another....

"And the other stuff that the Church came up with? Original sin? If you don't get baptized you'll go to limbo? It's all crazy. To me, Jesus is not so important. Christ is. And Jesus never even knew he was Christ. Christo is from the Greeks. That came after Jesus. It means chosen one or sacred one. And in that respect, everyone is Christ. Now *that* is powerful."

I wasn't sure what Richard meant. I was still trying to figure out a lot of what he was saying, and I was definitely hoping that I'd have time to try. Many people had predicted that Richard would be dead by July, and here it was, July 1. Richard was still very much alive and, on most days, chattering up a storm.

## Death

Despite what he said about St. Francis, I felt that there was still much about the saint that was very appealing to Richard. Richard had, after all, spent his life living and working with the poor, although he told me that his vow of poverty didn't mean living in destitution. "It means not clinging," he said. "Non-attachment. Not holding on." This philosophy didn't just apply to material things. It could apply to anything – people, places, grudges, disappointments, and eventually, even life itself.

Richard had decided that his death was not going to be a mournful event. He joked about it and celebrated it. He had ordered a cardboard box from a crematorium, the kind they use to haul bodies away in. This box would become his coffin. When his hands were still working, he had painted it with colorful stripes and had written little phrases on it such as "I *told* you I was sick," "All's well that ends well," "Less is more," "When the going gets tough, the tough get *gone!*" and "I love happy endings." Across the top of the box were the footprints of a coyote, an animal that represents "folly" or "the trickster" in Native American symbolism.

"Death is good," he would tell me. "Of course, I'm not talking about some terrible, tragic deaths, especially with the very young, but in the end, we're all dying, you know. When are you going to start working on *your* cardboard box?"

When I asked him how he was enduring his slow, but steady decline – his inability to walk or do so many things – he replied, "I'm as happy as a pig in shit."

"You're joking, Richard."

"No, really. As far as walking... I've walked enough. I've been walking for 70 years. I'm not in pain. I have a nice place to live and people to care for me. And I'm not old. I won't live to be a really old man, so in many ways, I'm quite blessed. Also, I get to prepare for my death. Many people don't have that luxury."

Richard said that if you check out the obituaries you will read things like, "So-and-so finally passed away after a valiant struggle against cancer or some other disease." Nobody writes, "So-and-so died after befriending leukemia, which encouraged her to do something different with her life."

"Me," said Richard. "I've decided to look on ALS as my friend."

"Your friend?"

"Yes, it's my friend, because it's encouraging me to go further. It's helping me experience people, places and things that I wouldn't have encountered if I didn't have ALS."

"A friend that kills you?"

"That's one way of looking at it, but maybe the killing leads to something different. Life is full of change. And wouldn't it be boring if it wasn't?" Richard liked to paraphrase a quote from John Henry Newman, who said that life is change and to change often is to live well.

"Change is the one thing we can count on," Richard explained, "so why not look on all these surprises in life as a blessing. We don't know where they'll lead us. But if we live in fear about every change that comes our way, we're really going to suffer.

"Look at Plumita," he added. "When she dies, she's just going to crawl in a corner and go to sleep. She's not going to worry about it."

## 2003: Before and Beyond

My brother Jay died in 2003 from the repercussions of AIDS. Jay died on a particular date and time, but his death really existed before that moment and it endures even now.

Jay and I were extremely close. The fact that we were both gay certainly added to the reasons why. We had a lot to talk about, and Jay loved to talk. Jay's openness and emotional vulnerability were his downfall in the rural area where we grew up. And even as a child, he was identifiable as queer.

I don't need to paint the whole picture of what my brother went through. For one thing, it's too painful, and for another, it's too common.

How many gay kids have been viciously bullied and abused? How many are still being tormented? That was Jay's story too. The damage that does to a young person's developing psyche is horrendous, and Jay never recovered.

He became very self-destructive. He got into drugs and was in and out of treatment centers and homeless shelters for years. I tried desperately to rescue him. When he was well enough, we shared what we always loved about each other. We laughed, talked, and even argued the way siblings do. And I would try to save him from what I knew he was trying so hard to escape – an overwhelming self-hatred that he could never rise above.

Although he died in 2003, I continue to deal with his death. He still lives inside me, but he still dies inside me too.

I talked to Richard about Jay. Richard never told me what to do with the pain. He never told me to do anything. He just listened. He listened better than most people I know. And Richard set an example of how to deal with death, because he too lost a brother.

His brother Marty's death was the seed that grew into Marty's Place. Richard planted it and then he moved on. He moved forward into the sunlight.

"The sunlight is everything," he often told me. "Without the sun, we'd all perish. Sometimes I think we're parts of the sun, pieces of light that shoot out, then dissipate and dissolve. But we don't go away. We just exist again in another form, like everything in nature. That's why it's futile to get caught up in our egos. Ego is the false illusion that we're separate from everything else."

That was as close as Richard would get to speculating what would happen to any of us after we died. He didn't believe in heaven and hell. He didn't believe in reincarnation.

"I don't believe in anything," he said, "because I don't know. Who really knows what happens after we die? But if you look at who we are on a molecular level, we're very much like particles of light."

Richard loved the sun. That was probably one reason he survived so well and long in the Arizona desert. When he started a foundation to fund Marty's Place, he called it Aurora Dawn. He came up with the name while he was out walking one morning at sunrise. He saw the colors and light, and the words Aurora Dawn came to him.

When Richard told me this story, I visualized how he was able to carry on after his brother's death. The sunrise he described, seemed to symbolize letting go of darkness, and stepping into a new day. I thought about my own brother and wondered if I'd ever be able to do the same.

In the meantime, it amazed me how I had stumbled into the lives of so many gay men who I also came to call brothers. Richard was one. The guys connected with Marty's place were others. Then there were the men in my Secular Franciscan group. Somehow, all of our lives began to weave together.

It wasn't by design that Luz and I were the only women in the Franciscan group. Neither of us would have minded having extra women around, but since San Francisco is so populated by gay men, that was just the way it turned out. In time, I did grow to know many of the women who were associated with Marty's Place.

The shelter had a board of directors which included women, and it also had women volunteers. One of the most prominent was Marge Yeager (also known as Bootsie), Richard's oldest sister. She lived in southern California with her husband Jim, and they frequently visited San Francisco.

None of these new acquaintances would ever replace my own brother. No one ever could. But after my personal loss, I suddenly found myself falling into this loose, but securely fastened, network of support. And as many people do when faced with the death of a loved one, I accelerated my search for some kind of spirituality.

## July 3, 2009

When I walked into Marty's Place, Max greeted me at the door. He looked like he'd been crying. Max was part of our Circle of Care, and one of the homeless men who, years earlier, Richard had taken in. Max was tall, muscular, and prematurely gray. He had come to the US in the 80s from Nicaragua, after being imprisoned and tortured in that country's war. When Richard found him in 1993, he was living on the street with AIDS and was strung out on crack. Now, due to a stable home and many years of support, he was clean and sober.

In addition to caring for Richard, Max had taken on the role of the main housekeeper at Marty's Place. He had a flare for drama and busyness, and was frequently dusting, vacuuming or complaining that people around the house were making too much of a mess.

On this day, Max had an especially dramatic tale to tell. "It's just horrible to watch someone suffocate," he said. He told me that despite the BiPAP machine that Richard wore at night, he was still having problems breathing.

A BiPAP is a device that forces air into a person's lungs. The machine is connected to a mask, which typically fits around a patient's nose. A BiPAP can prolong the lives of people with ALS, as it improves gas exchange and reduces the work of breathing. Unlike a respirator, however, it will not breathe for patients or keep them alive indefinitely. Max at times had to push on Richard's abdomen to help him exhale because Richard's diaphragm muscles were failing.

As Max and I spoke, I noticed a sign posted on the wall which been written by a volunteer. "Richard loves visitors, but please limit your visits to only one hour and leave by 4:00 every day. Richard needs his rest."

After talking to Max, I ventured downstairs. Afraid of what I might find, I opened the door to Richard's room and peered inside. Richard was sitting up in bed smiling.

"Susanna!" He said. "Come in!"

"I heard you had trouble breathing last night," I told him.

"Yes, I had a bit of a spell."

"Max said it was very bad. He was crying."

"Max is a drama queen."

"It must be terrifying when you can't breathe."

"It's not fun."

I must have appeared worried, because Richard said again, "It wasn't as terrible as Max probably described. Sometimes things look worse from the outside if you're observing. If you're the one actually experiencing something, it may not be as bad as it looks."

I thought about his words and then commented, "I see that the volunteers are trying to limit your visits in the afternoon."

He scoffed. "Are people putting up signs again? I'm not a child who needs to be told what to do. I'll see whoever I want, whenever I want."

Richard took the same cavalier attitude toward his hospice nurse's instructions that he take morphine. The nurse had explained that if Richard took the morphine on a regular basis, it would prevent his episodes of severe breathlessness.

"That's all I need, to be doped up on morphine," Richard had protested. "And every time I take those drugs, Mrs. Murphy never calls." Richard was referring to the fact that morphine made him constipated. His code name for a bowel movement was "Mrs. Murphy." So whenever he needed to be transferred to the commode, he'd say to his caregivers, "Mrs. Murphy is calling!"

I had brought Richard a cup of coffee, even though his doctor disapproved. Apparently, coffee is not good for ALS. "What's it going to do?" Richard wondered. "Kill me?"

In some ways I envied him. Having a terminal illness must take away a lot of worry in life. Worry about eating the wrong thing, worry about the state of the world or worry about getting old....

As we sipped our drinks, I took out my notebook. I asked Richard if we could start at the very beginning.

PART II

# DOCUMENTING A LIFE

"Where there is great love, there are always miracles."[2]
– Willa Cather

## 1938-1963

Richard was born in 1938 and grew up on the outskirts of Helena, Montana. His family lived in the Sixth Ward, which was a poor section of town inhabited by a lot of Irish and Native Americans. His father owned a small tavern and raised chickens, and his mother, a housewife, died of cancer at 53.

Richard's Catholic upbringing, which included attending parochial schools all the way through college, undoubtedly started him on his spiritual path. He was very fond of several of his nun teachers and he was a rather pious young man. Later, he talked about those days jokingly, making fun of himself and his piety.

Bootsie told me that, in some ways, Richard took after his father. George Purcell had only an eighth grade education, but he became a valued psychologist to the many customers who visited his bar. "He was a great listener," said Bootsie, "and he had a wonderful, dry sense of humor." She didn't doubt that Richard inherited some of these same traits and used them as a priest.

I managed to interview several people who had known Richard at various points in his life. One of them was Tom Madden, who grew up with Richard. Madden emailed me this description of his lifelong friend: "I remember well the sterling personal qualities so evident in Dick's younger years... especially his lively imagination, his wonderful sense of humor, his love of verbal play and his warm personal friendship. He became a smart, witty man with striking personal charisma – qualities that were very evident in his childhood...."

After Richard graduated from high school, he spent a year at the College of Great Falls, which was run by the Sisters of Providence. Richard's greatest childhood love, besides religion, was art. Bootsie claimed that as a boy, Richard was always drawing or working on some art project. At Great Falls, he studied under Sister Mary Trinitas Morin, a renowned artist. A film was made about her, and Richard can be seen in a shot. He appears as a nerdy-looking young man in glasses and a striped shirt. The film describes Sister Trinita's habit of collecting odd bits of trash and then transforming them into art, a trait that Richard himself would eventually be known for.

After a year at Great Falls, Richard enrolled in Carroll College, in Helena, where he majored in philosophy. Following graduation, he took a train to Los Angeles with two friends, who were brother and sister twins. The twins' family parish was run by the Franciscans, and it was there that Richard got the idea that he might want to be a Franciscan priest.

Richard spoke to the church's pastor, who directed him to go speak with Father David Temple, the head of St. Barbara's Province. Temple resided at the Old Mission in Santa Barbara, so Richard hitchhiked up to the coastal city.

Richard described his meeting with Temple, in which the old priest talked to Richard through his dog. He led Richard into his study, and then, speaking to his dog, began the conversation with, "Well... what do you think this young man wants? Why did he come here?"

I questioned Richard myself about why he had decided to become a friar. He never gave me a straight answer, and I realized there probably wasn't one. Undoubtedly, at the time he met Temple, he was still in his "pious" period. He also mentioned that even though he had not admitted to himself that he was gay, he had no interest in dating women. He was getting tired of people asking him whether he was going to marry or if he had a girlfriend. Then there was the draft. Now that college was over, he didn't want to be inducted into the army.

I asked him why he chose the Franciscans, and he replied with his typical elusiveness and gay humor, “I liked the dress.”

Before deciding to enter the seminary, he took a Greyhound bus back home. He lived with his parents and worked. He bought a yellow 1947 Plymouth which he decorated with leopard skin seat covers and dubbed “Eartha,” after his favorite singer, Eartha Kitt. Richard still had no solid plans. One day, while he was still living at home, his mother asked, “Well, how are you going to waste your time this year?”

Suddenly and unexpectedly, he heard himself say “I'm going to become a Franciscan priest.”

His mother looked at him and then called to her husband, who was reading the paper in the next room. “Did you hear that, George? Dick says he wants to be a priest.”

“Uh-huh,” said George, still reading the newspaper.

Richard's parents didn't take this initial pronouncement too seriously. Later, they would come to be very proud of their son the priest, but they also knew Richard the young man along with all of his imperfections. Richard claimed that they weren't initially convinced that this priesthood deal would work out.

Tom Madden described Richard's desire to become a priest as more absolute. “I recall Richard's strong sense of vocation in his college years,” Madden said. “There was no doubt in his mind that God had destined him to be a Franciscan. He was filled with joy as he prepared to join the order. Such confident piety and joy were like a beacon to many of his friends, who, like me, were at that time still struggling with our own future paths.”

Richard began his education as a new postulant at the Old Mission San Luis Rey near San Diego. He was one of the oldest in the class, since most of the students entered straight out of high school. Richard already had a bachelor's degree, but he was required to stay at San Luis Rey for two years. The friars wanted to observe him and ascertain whether he was suited to this calling.

“I liked the life,” Richard recalled, “even though it was regimented and we did heavy work on a farm. I guess I enjoyed the discipline and the routine. I didn't learn anything, but then I never learned much in any class in school. I was always a C student. I actually hated school, and can you imagine studying theology? A friend once asked me what I studied in college and I told him theology. He really hit the nail on the head when he wondered, 'How can you get a degree in something that doesn't exist?'"

One person who stood out in Richard's recollections from that time was the friary's magister, Benedict McCormick. McCormick was a crusty old friar who had been in the army, and he inflicted a boot-camp like discipline onto the young men. In describing those days, Richard imitated McCormick's gruff voice. *"Now listen up, you hamburgers!"*

Richard said the postulants' final task each night was to listen to a "ferverino," or lecture, by McCormick. "The old man would read us the riot act about stupid little things like how much toilet paper we were wasting. He'd give us this big sermon on how we were supposed to wipe our ass." Richard mimicked *"What's the matter with you hamburgers? Were you raised up at Georgia Pacific Paper Company?!"*

Richard claimed that many of the postulants were afraid of McCormick, but Richard easily saw through the magister's rough exterior. "I loved him," he said.

One day McCormick asked Richard if he liked to read books. Up to that point, Richard had never read for pleasure. He'd read books only for school assignments. When he explained this to McCormick, the older man told him, "Well, you're going to start reading for pleasure now." He gave Richard a long list of books to read, which included such authors as Samuel Beckett, Dostoevsky, Tolstoy and Flannery O'Connor. Richard would devour these works, and then he'd be called into McCormick's office to discuss them in depth.

Richard found he loved reading much more than some of the other directives he was given as a postulant. One of them was to play sports, an activity which he abhorred. He hated it so much that he and another friend used to hide during exercise time whenever McCormick was taking a nap.

"We'd hide out in this shack behind the baseball field," said Richard. "One time McCormick woke up and caught us. He ordered us to go play ball."

Richard reluctantly went out and picked up a bat. As he told the story, he pantomimed swinging it with a limp wrist. "Can you see me swinging a bat?" he asked. "But I hit the damned ball! I ran to first base and when I slid to a stop I ripped open all kinds of tendons and ligaments in my leg. I couldn't walk for eight weeks." He grinned, "Then I really got a chance to read."

Of about 60 original postulants in Richard's class, only 25 survived and went on to the next level. Richard was one of them. He entered his novitiate at Mission San Miguel near Paso Robles. He got his new habit, and his parents and three of his siblings came out on a train for the ceremony. During the event, Richard was given a new name: Martin de Porres.

Richard's family stayed with the other novitiates' relatives in an old army barracks across from the Mission. The barracks were incredibly hot and uncomfortable, and Richard was allowed to meet with his parents and siblings only before the service. Afterwards, the families went back to the barracks. There they were fed tuna fish sandwiches while the priests and novitiates celebrated inside the Mission on lobster and steak.

That was Richard's first glimpse into the divisions between the religious and the laity. "This was before Vatican II," he said. "There was this incredible inequality that was built into the Church. You don't see such strict divisions anymore, but back then it was so much about rules and laws and so little about spirit. The friars who were caught up in this system were good people, but I started to get a sense that something wasn't right with the institution itself." Richard looked sad as he related the story. "I will never forget how my family had made such a long trip, only to be treated that way."

Despite this unfortunate experience, Richard still didn't question his decision to become a friar, and he enjoyed his year in the novitiate. When asked what he did at Mission San Miguel, Richard gave the following account of his daily routine:

Awake at 5:00 a.m.
Chanting followed by meditation and liturgy
Breakfast in silence
Clean cell
Classes
Prayer
Lunch in silence

Chanting
Prayer
Work in garden
Shower
Study
Supper in silence
Prayer

"We were living in a monastic tradition," Richard explained. "We were living like monks. This wasn't what St. Francis had in mind, but this was what was imposed on us."

I suggested that this sounded like a very intense initiation into self-discipline and meditation. Richard shrugged, "I did it because that's what we had to do. Sometimes, if we were tired enough during prayers or chanting, we'd just sit there and fall asleep. It wasn't unusual to hear some of the guys snoring."

He remembered one sleep-deprived novice shuffling into chapel one day after leaving the bathroom. "He walked down the aisle and we saw that the back of his robe was hoisted up and stuck in his underwear. The Guardian, or head priest, saw this, and barked out, right there in the middle of the prayers 'For God's sake, cover up yer ass!'"

I asked Richard about any sexual activity during his years at either of these missions. He claimed he was completely oblivious to anyone having sex. As far as he knew, "We were as pure as the driven snow."

"Was there any discussion about sex from your superiors?"

"Yeah, but now looking back, it seemed ludicrous and completely useless. They'd say things like don't eat a banana before you go to bed."

I frowned, indicating that I didn't understand.

"We didn't understand what it meant either," said Richard. "It probably meant that eating a banana might give you an erection. That's how vague and ridiculous our sex education was."

"Were any of your fellow friars gay?" I wondered.

Richard laughed. "Most likely three-fourths of them. And what was crazy, is that on some level, we probably all knew. But nobody talked about it."

## 1964-1978

In 1964 Richard moved to Old Mission Santa Barbara, where he studied for his master's degree. This was right after the Second Vatican Council, when things changed radically in the Church.

"The changes were good," Richard said. "I got my old name back, and nuns didn't have to wear habits anymore. And although it was against the rules, I grew a mustache and beard. I wasn't supposed to, but nobody stopped me. And then other seminarians started doing the same."

Tim McDaniel, who was a student with Richard at Santa Barbara, claimed that Richard was always a little out of step with the Church hierarchy. "Not in a way where he caused any real trouble," said Tim, "but Richard had a way of pushing the envelope."

For example, it was customary in Santa Barbara for some of the wealthier Catholics to invite Franciscans to their houses for meals and entertainment. Having a priest, or someone studying to be a priest in their home, was a sign of status. The private donations that these visits generated could also prove advantageous for the Church. But according to Tim, Richard avoided these types of relationships at all costs. When he was off duty, Richard hung out with people on the lower socioeconomic end of the city, mostly Mexicans and blacks.

One Thanksgiving, Richard asked Tim if he wanted to join him at somebody's house for dinner. Tim said yes, and suggested that they bring a nice bottle of wine.

"No," said Richard. "I'll show you what they like to drink."

Richard went into a liquor store and came out with the cheapest white port that Tim had ever seen. "We went into these black people's house down on skid row," Tim said, "and they were so happy to see that bottle." Tim remembered that the matriarch of the family kept a padlock on her refrigerator door so nobody would steal anything.

"That was Henrietta," said Richard, when I repeated the story. "Her daughter was Ruby, and Ruby was a prostitute."

Richard invited Ruby and her boyfriend Leroy to his ordination, which took place in Helena. Neither of them were Catholic, nor did they know what an ordination was. And they didn't have any money to make the trip. So Richard lifted a bunch of old pipes from a church construction site and sold them to a junk dealer. He used the money to buy Ruby and Leroy Greyhound bus tickets to Montana.

When Richard walked down the aisle for his ordination, with the bishop and other dignitaries present, and the church filled with his all-white relatives, there sat Ruby and Leroy. They saw Richard, smiled, waved wildly, and called out, "Richard, we made it!"

"For my parents, it was a bit tense," Richard admitted. "My parents always said they had nothing against black people, but then they had never met any. There weren't many blacks in Montana. But it worked out alright. Everybody had a good time. Ruby and Leroy were wonderful. My family ended up loving them as much as I did."

Richard's ordination was on June 5, 1968, the day that Bobby Kennedy was assassinated. Richard was ordained by Bishop Raymond Hunthausen, who eventually became the Archbishop of Seattle. Hunthausen subsequently butted heads with Rome for, among other things, his support of homosexuals. He also withheld his income tax to protest the stockpiling of nuclear weapons. His actions angered the Reagan administration and many conservative Catholics.

Richard had written a letter to Hunthausen when the older man was confronting these conflicts and widespread criticism. Richard offered his support and relayed his memories of his own ordination. He said that he didn't know if he believed in mystical phenomena, but when Hunthausen laid his hands on Richard that day to ordain him, Richard felt an incredible energy. "I felt this unbelievable force," he said. "It was moving through Hunthausen and into me – this surge of inspiration and power.

"I feel that what happened between Hunthausen and me on that day gave me courage to stand up in my career and speak the truth. He was someone I truly admired and still try to emulate."

Richard's first job was as an assistant pastor in a skid row parish in Stockton, California. He was also a chaplain for San Joaquin General Hospital and the county jail. "I hated getting phone calls in the middle of the night," he remembered. "My heart would start pounding when the phone rang, because I'd often be called in after some terrible accident or even a murder. I'd have to go down to the hospital and deal with the survivors or dead bodies."

"What do you say to someone in that situation?" I asked.

"There's not much you can say. And people usually don't remember what you say anyway. They remember who you are, though. They remember how you respond to them."

This led us into a discussion of the other functions of a parish priest. I asked him about the sacraments. I was particularly curious about confession. "What was it like to hear people's confessions?"

"A lot of it is about sex," he told me. "You wouldn't believe the guilt people expressed, at least back then, about sex. Especially white people. Even the old grannies would carry around all this guilt about something sexual they had once done. Native Americans never mentioned sex. The white people would always slip it in real cautiously. They'd try to hide it between two slices of bread. 'I cursed. I ate meat on Friday'...and then wham! '*I touched myself, Father.*'

"You touched yourself?" Richard said aloud, pretending he was in the confessional. "Where? You touched your foot? Your head? '*I touched myself in an unclean place.*' "Like where? Did you pick your nose?" Richard started laughing. "Between two pieces of white bread you'd find the bologna. But the younger generation, they don't take much stock in confession. It's all changed. It's the same with baptism. Usually now, if a family wants a baby baptized, it's to please a grandmother. And it's ridiculous, really. Baptize a baby? How does a baby choose to be baptized, and for what reason? It's insane. But I'd do it because it was important to somebody's grandmother.

"And you know what irks me about some parish priests? When there's a death and the family needs a funeral Mass, and the priest says, 'I can't. It's my day off.' Can you believe it? No wonder Catholics leave the Church and go and join the Hallelujahs." He referred to some of the storefront evangelistic churches that so many of the Latinos were flocking to in our neighborhood. "No wonder those people stopped being Catholic. They'd rather go to a place where they can find community and support."

Richard was transferred to the Papago (later known as the Tohono O'odham) Indian Reservation in Covered Wells, Arizona, in 1969. There were 52 villages on the reservation and each had its own chapel. Richard was the pastor for 14 of these places.

He recalled that when he arrived, one of the older friars warned him, "Don't think you came here to change anything."

"I had no idea what he was talking about," said Richard. "I was just a pious little shit back then, and I was ready to do whatever I was told. But looking back, that friar's comment was an omen of what was to come. I *would* end up changing things and even more so, *I* would personally end up being changed. But initially I had no understanding of the type of ingrained system that I'd be going up against."

Richard had always spoken fondly of the Tohono O'odham, and he wanted his ashes buried on the Pima (Akimel O'odham) reservation in Arizona. He had worked in both of these places. I asked him why the O'odham[3] were so important to him.

"The Native Americans are a part of me," he explained. "Most of my sleeping dreams take place on those reservations. Something happened to me there. I switched gears. And I'm not saying this because I'm trying to imitate the Indians. Something about them just got into my heart and soul.

"When I went there, I didn't have my own spirituality. What I had was my parents' spirituality, or the Franciscans' or the nuns', but it wasn't mine. The Native people had a spirituality and they didn't even know it. I came to realize that inside all of us is this deep river of perennial wisdom. So many of the Native Americans had tapped into it. They never judged or shamed others like so many so-called 'spiritual' people do. The O'odahm had respect for the deeper parts of every individual. And they had no judgment around sex. To them it was no big deal."

I mentioned that among some Native American people there was homophobia.

"Yes," Richard agreed. "There was always this conflict between the invaders' religion and their own. I found that communities that had closer proximity to our own culture – those people were more wounded.

"It was the Spanish who named the Papago. In the 80s, the tribe changed their name to Tohono O'odham or Desert People. Their cousins are the Pima or Akimel O'odham – The River People. The Pima live along the Salt and Gila Rivers. It used to be a beautiful place until the invaders took the water and built the Coolidge Dam. The resulting devastation for the people there is ongoing.

"The Tohono O'odham and the Akimel O'odham are very joyful people. I'm not saying they're happy all the time, since they've had so many tragedies… but they have this deep inner joy. A writer named Leon Bloy once said that the surest sign that the spirit is alive in a person is his or her joy. With the O'odahm, one of the ways that joy manifests itself is in their humor. They just love to laugh.

"That is the big dichotomy between Western and Native American religions," Richard continued. "The humor. From the Roman Catholic perspective, the sacred is very serious. When you pray, you're supposed to have this long face. But some Indians will have a very sacred dance with a clown who farts."

One thing Richard didn't seem fond of doing was saying Mass, but he did say it whenever necessary, as it was part of his job. "I didn't like to *say* Mass," Richard clarified. "In other words, I didn't like to repeat words that someone else had written. But I loved to celebrate liturgy. I'm talking about true, creative liturgy that came from both me and the people. And especially when I celebrated it with the O'odahm. With them, it was all theatre. They had great senses of humor and I loved to make them laugh."

He'd get them laughing early on, to set the tone for the entire Mass. For example, at the start of the ceremony when Richard was to enter the church and solemnly stride toward the altar, he would sometimes trip. This would get the congregation roaring with laughter.

Once, when Richard was addressing the choir on the Pima reservation, his fly was open. A choir member yelled out, "Hey Padre, zip up your pants!"

Richard looked down at his open zipper and then, without missing a beat, said "Wow, it's a good thing I wore underwear today."

"Some of the other priest and nun missionaries didn't always appreciate my humor," said Richard. "And some of them tried to straighten the Indians out." He spoke disparagingly about a particular group of nuns who he worked with. "I felt sorry for the nuns back then," he said, "because they suffered. But the problem was, everybody else had to suffer along with them."

With this particular group of nuns, Mass was not theatre. And they wanted Richard to say it every day and in the proper "Roman" tradition in their own chapel.

"First I said no," said Richard, "but then they got their Mother Superior on my back. She called me all the way from the Mother House and read me the riot act. So I said 'Fine, but if we say Mass, we're going to bring it to the people.'" He told the nuns that every day they were going to have to pile into his pickup truck so they could go celebrate Mass in a different village.

"Well, that didn't last long. The next thing I knew they were complaining to Mother Superior again." He imitated the nuns; "*'Mother Superior doesn't want us riding in the truck because we'll get our habits dirty and Mother Superior doesn't want us out after dark.'* The nuns also didn't want to use the O'odhams' outdoor toilets because they were afraid of being bitten by a spider.

"Finally, I had enough. I was their boss, so I fired every one of them. I sent them back to where they came from. And it was sad, because I really liked those women. They were good people, but they were caught up in this terrible system with a programmed way of being. So I had to get rid of them."

After that, Richard hired some School Sisters of Notre Dame from the Dallas Province to help him out. "They were wonderful women," he said. "They respected the people. They allowed the Indians to be themselves. They wore regular clothes and became part of the community."

Richard insisted I write down their names; Dorothy Scherer and Anne Fischer. He wanted it known that that well into their 80s, these women were still in active ministry.

## 1978

Around 1978, Richard got into a big hassle on the Tohono O'odham reservation. Much of it seemed to center around a particular nun. Richard told me that there was a conflict between him and some of the other religious leaders on the reservation. Apparently, there were a lot of jealousies. He belonged to a team of people who were quite popular among the Native Americans. Some of the other missionaries didn't like that, and in this battle, Richard lost. He was accused of some transgressions and kicked off the reservation by the bishop in Tucson. I asked Richard what he had been accused of.

"Dealing drugs."

"Did you do it?"

"No. And the nun who accused me was often drunk. She made a pass at me once too."

None of this corresponded with my own image of priests and nuns. I also was aware of the fact that, during these years, Richard himself was developing a problem with alcohol. I couldn't help but wonder whether his drinking played a part in his being kicked out.

I asked Richard's sister Bootsie about his expulsion. Even though Bootsie loved her brother, I trusted her to be unbiased. She said that indeed, other religious people, including a particular nun, had spread lies about Richard. Bootsie claimed that the Native Americans on the reservation preferred to come to Richard's church and this caused a lot of resentment from those who ran other churches. She felt that some of these religious people had spread blatant lies, and that was why Richard was ousted by the bishop.

Andrew, a friar who knew Richard at that time, told me a similar story. "Like me," said Andrew, "Richard was a product of the 60s. We played with boundaries, experimenting with feelings and attitudes. We never did anything scandalous, but Richard was on the vanguard of change. The older friars were good people, but they were stuck in the past. They weren't bad, just rigid.

"This nun that Richard was having problems with... she fashioned herself as a guru among the Native Americans, but she had a lot of personal issues, including a serious drinking problem. Richard could see right through her, and she felt very threatened by this. So she projected a lot of her hostility onto him. She started stirring this pot of trouble, and once you start trouble, there's often no stopping it.

"One thing that a priest isn't supposed to do is say the Mass wrong, especially the Canon of the Mass which, occurs during the consecration of the host. I heard rumors that Richard was changing the Mass, and this act led to his downfall. This nun reported it to the bishop and the bishop was adamant that Richard leave. I don't know where that story about Richard dealing drugs came in. I'm quite certain that didn't happen, that it was something somebody made up."

Chandika Tazouz is an artist and writer who had lived with the Tohono O'odham for years. She was very familiar with the circumstances around Richard's expulsion. In fact she herself is working on a book about

Richard's time on the reservation. "After that nun started spreading lies about Richard, the bishop finally found a reason to get rid of him," said Tazouz, "but the bishop had been after Richard for a while."

"For what?" I asked.

"For loving the O'odham people too much," she replied. "For learning their language." Her explanation reflected what Bootsie had told me. The Native Americans loved Richard and had been flocking to his church. This created jealousies and a loss of control, especially by the Church hierarchy.

A newspaper article in *The Catholic Reporter* covered some of the conflict around this situation. The writer claimed that many of the O'odahm were upset due to Richard's transfer off the reservation, and the tribe wanted to be involved in any future decisions regarding their priests. The article also said that two nuns working on the reservation at the time quit in protest over what had been done to both the O'odham people and to Richard.

Andrew, Richard's friar friend, stated that Richard was devastated with his dismissal. Richard agreed, but he added, "Getting kicked out gave me the opportunity to move on and experience other things. If I hadn't been forced to go, I might still be there. Sometimes good things come from bad. But I felt especially sorry for the Indian people and for the Sisters of Notre Dame who I'd been working with. The Native Americans were very upset. They hadn't been included in any of these decisions. So after it happened, they demanded a meeting with the troublemakers and the heads of the diocese. But none of their questions or concerns were ever really dealt with."

I was still curious about whether Richard's own drinking was involved in any of this. I asked Father Andrew what he thought.

"Richard's drinking? I heard rumors, but I never personally witnessed any of it."

"Yes, Richard drank," said Chandika, "but as far as I could see, it was always under control. If he had a problem, he concealed it well. And he was so crazy and funny anyway, even without liquor. Maybe that made it hard to know if he was an alcoholic."

"I was a high bottom drunk," Richard himself explained. "I noticed that after a few drinks, I'd say something stupid. And I started hiding liquor. I just didn't want to live like that. But I don't have some terrible war stories to tell you about my drinking. And I'm living proof that an alcoholic doesn't have to hit a low bottom to find out that he or she needs help."

Richard did admit to drinking with the O'odham. He also described a night where he found himself with some O'odham friends in a border town Mexican brothel. A prostitute approached him, and Richard, who had no interest in women, protested "*Mi esposa me esta esperando en la casa.*" (I have a wife at home).

"*Al diablo con tu esposa!*" declared the hooker. (To hell with the wife).

## 1978-1980

In 1978, Richard took two years off and began to wander. He rambled through Mexico and parts of the US Southwest. He worked odd jobs to earn his keep, and since he had no vehicle, hitchhiked or rode a bus.

"We had a right to take a sabbatical" he said, "and Louie Vitale was the provincial. He gave me his blessing."

In 1979 Richard ended up in New York City. He moved into the Men's Catholic Worker House on First Street, and got to know Dorothy Day, the Catholic Worker's founder. I asked Richard what he thought of the Catholic Worker Movement.[4]

"Those people did a lot of good," he said, "but basically, many of them were pretty eccentric, including Dorothy Day. I was eccentric too. I was rigid then, just like Dorothy. Especially about poverty. I was very strict around preaching that people should live in poverty. My thinking, and what I expected of others, was black and white and judgmental. I don't think that way anymore."

Richard is mentioned in the published diary of Dorothy Day. On August 26, 1979, she wrote, "The priest who is saying Mass daily in the auditorium on 3rd St., Mary House, irritates everyone by (his) commentaries during Mass..."[5]

"That was me!" laughed Richard. "Oh, that Dorothy Day... she was a sour one!"

Richard's views of Day reflect much of what has been written about her. He felt she could be very inflexible and hard-lined, and he offered no apologies for any of his "commentaries."

Richard also said that Dorothy Day, in spite of her imperfections, ranked among the people he most admired. In fact, Marty's Place itself was based on the Catholic Worker model. Besides Day, Richard mentioned that his other personal heroes included Eartha Kitt, Mother Jones, Eleanor Roosevelt, Archbishop Hunthausen, Dom Hélder Câmara (an archbishop from Brazil), Abbe Pierre, (a priest from France), and a dear friend of his, Father Camillus Cavagnaro, who also worked with the O'odahm. "These were all wonderful spiritual teachers," he said. "And the greatest is Plumita." His dog. He called her *El Cordera de Dios.* (The Lamb of God).

It was during our discussion of the Catholic Worker that I learned about Richard's tattoo. While he was in New York City, a stranger on the street approached him with a knife. "Give me your money!" the man demanded.

"I gave him all my money, but he slashed me anyway," said Richard pointing to his tattoo. I suddenly noticed that it had a big scar through the middle of it. "It used to be a Native American sun god," Richard explained. "Now it looks like a flying saucer."

It was in New York City that Richard bottomed out on alcohol. He ended up going to Alcoholics Anonymous and got sober. Since then, he always spoke very respectfully of AA. He said AA's 12 steps, along with what he learned from the Native Americans, constituted much of his spiritual philosophy.

"What is your philosophy?" I asked. "How would you describe it?"

"In a nut shell? Three things." He said he had formulated these ideas after reading, *Shadow Dance,* a book by David Richo. These three aspects of his spirituality were unconditional love, eternal wisdom, and the ability to heal. "If you practice unconditional love, and you tap into the perpetual wisdom that is inside all of us, you will become a healer. Or at least I have."

"You are a healer," I had to admit. "You have a wonderful gift to heal others."

"Yes!" He wholeheartedly agreed. "And wouldn't it be a shame if I didn't use that gift?" He said this with neither bravado nor humility. He took no personal credit for these talents.

I asked Richard to tell me more about his experiences with AA. What did he think of the organization?

"I believe in the 12 steps," he said, "but not when they're applied slavishly. I like the idea of rigorous honesty and community support. But with plenty of organizations, including AA, there is the danger that cults can occur. There are people in any sect who fashion themselves to be gurus – who claim the right to tell others what to do. It's the same with many Native religions. It can happen in those groups as well."

## 1980-1988

Richard left the Catholic Worker in 1980. His next assignment was as a parish priest in Arizona, working with the Pima Indians along the Gila River. On the side, he participated in the Sanctuary Movement, which was a kind of Underground Railroad for refugees fleeing the US-funded wars in Central America. Richard helped house these exiles until they could continue on their journey to more permanent locations.

At one point, some of these Central Americans used his phone to make connections with another safe house. "I didn't realize," said Richard, "that the other house's phone was being tapped by the FBI.

"I was facilitating this retreat once in Tucson, and a man approached me. He was a Catholic who had come for the retreat, but he also worked for the federal government. He took me aside and told me the whole story. He said that the feds were onto me and that there was going to be a raid on my house. But he claimed that if I promised to stop sheltering immigrants, he'd arrange to call the whole thing off. He liked me and he was trying to protect me."

"Did you stop taking people in?" I asked.

"No. I just emptied out the house for a while to let things cool down. When the next batch of refugees came through, I told them to stop using the phone. So everything worked out."

The Franciscans lived and worked on a compound that was part of the Akila O'odham reservation. When Richard arrived, he intended stay a couple of years; after that, the Church planned to return the property back to the Native Americans.

"The Franciscans had had a mission in this remote area," said Richard, "but it was time to pull out. That's the way it should be, if you have a mission. You plant a seed and then you move on. But these Franciscans had overextended their welcome. My agreement in going there was that I'd give it so many years, and then I'd leave. We needed to turn the village churches back to the people." Richard felt that if the Akila O'odham still wanted some type of religious community, they would need to run it themselves. "So I got a committee together and asked, 'what do you want to do?'

"The Pima didn't know what they wanted. After all, for over 500 years, the Catholic Church had been telling them what they were supposed to do. At first, they didn't have any expectations, but after a while, they started to come up with all these ideas. They designed a ceremony that was based on the Mass, but it was their ceremony. There was a lot of Native stuff in it... celebrating the wildflowers when they were in bloom, things like that. And you know who really got into it? The people who had never been involved in religion before, the disenfranchised individuals who used to hang out on bar stools on the edge of the reservation. Those folks became very involved.

"Several of the pillars of the Church, the big shots, didn't like this. There was a lot of controversy and hard feelings, but eventually the people won out. It was a very successful project. Some aspects of it are still going on today."

Richard had to go to the bishop before he could get approval for his plan. The bishop listened to Richard, then cautiously ventured, "I suppose it will be alright. I just hope that the people realize that without a priest, what they're doing isn't Mass."

"Oh goodness no," Richard assured him. "Of course they know it isn't Mass."

"That's good," the bishop nodded.

"They don't call it Mass," said Richard. "They call it Mishmat."

"Well then," said the bishop. "As long as they don't call it Mass, I guess it will be okay."

"What did they call it?" I asked Richard as I pulled out my notebook.

"Mishmat," he said, and then he spelled the Pima word. "M-I-S-H-M-A-T."

"What does it mean?" I asked.

"Mass."

Members of the Pima, as well as the Tohono O'odham, stayed in touch with Richard throughout his life. I met several of them who routinely made the pilgrimage from Arizona to San Francisco to visit him at Marty's Place. They continued to consider Richard a spiritual teacher, even though many of them didn't even know him when he lived on the reservations. Some weren't even born yet. It didn't matter. His reputation within the tribes lived on.

Richard told me a final story about his time with the Akila O'odham. He said he was once performing a baptism there and he was holding a candle as part of the ceremony. The mother of the baby approached him, and Richard opened his arms to give her a hug. During the embrace, the candle set the woman's hair on fire.

"She had one of those bouffant hairdos that was covered with hair spray," Richard said. "The fire started quickly, and suddenly I was pounding on the poor woman's head. I managed to put the fire out before she was burned, and I never heard a peep out of her. Not during the fire, or after. The incident was never mentioned, either by her or anyone else present.

"That's the way the Indians are," he concluded. "To say something would have been rude."

## 1988-1989

After leaving the Akimel O'odham, Richard took another road trip. He ended up near Fort Lauderdale, Florida, where he again did odd jobs, including filleting fish. During this time he saw a sign that advertised lodging in exchange for working as a property manager. The property included a group of cabins that were falling apart, mostly due to an invading army of banyan tree roots. Richard took the job, which involved repairing the cabins and collecting rent. The tenants were Haitian refugees.

"They were wonderful people," he said. "I was struck by the injustice of how the Haitians were treated, especially compared to Cuban refugees. Cubans were frequently welcomed and allowed to apply for green cards within a year. Haitians were often detained and then expediently deported, and their struggles were compounded by the color of their skin."

Richard started to get to know the Haitians, but his brief time with them was interrupted. In June of 1989 he had to leave when he heard that his brother Marty was dying of AIDS in San Francisco.

By many accounts, Marty Purcell was a competent and compassionate ICU nurse. Bootsie told me that Marty was very easy to talk to. "It was like I had a second sister," she said. "But Marty was also a troubled young man. Our mother died when he was still quite young – and it wasn't easy for him. Then there was the fact that he was gay."

He was one of the thousands of gay men who had fled homophobic regions to seek refuge in San Francisco during the 80s. And like so many of them, Marty would succumb to AIDS.

In 1986, Marty's lover Kit had died of AIDS, and Marty didn't know what to do with the ashes. Richard was living with the Pimas at that time, and he suggested to his brother, "Why don't you bring Kit's ashes out to the reservation? The desert is a sacred place. We'll leave him there."

The HIV virus was already playing havoc with Marty's own body as he traveled to Arizona. The two brothers spent some time together and one day they visited an old Pima woman. They talked to her about Kit's ashes.

"Where will you put them?" she asked.

"We're going to scatter them in the desert," Richard replied.

"You can't do that," the woman said. "Who's going to feed him? Who will bring him his things?"

Richard realized that she was talking about the Native American and Mexican custom of visiting graves. On the Day of the Dead especially, people come to graveyards with food and gifts for those who have left this world.

The old woman then immediately said that Kit could have her grave site, the place where she was supposed to be buried – even though she had never met Kit or Marty.

"The Pimas are known for their hospitality," Richard explained.

In the years to come, the ashes of Marty and other men who died at Marty's Place would end up at this site. The site would also be close to Richard's own final resting place.

## 1989

By 1989, Marty had been in and out of the hospital with complications related to AIDS. Due to his inability to work and his medical costs, Marty became homeless. So Richard secured the financial assistance of their sister Bootsie, and found a one-bedroom apartment where the two brothers could live. It was located on Hartford Street in San Francisco's Castro District, and that was where Marty died.

Richard was never one to be sentimental. He was sympathetic and compassionate with people, but he could also be very matter-of-fact when he discussed tragedies – especially his own. Regarding his mother's premature death from cancer, his sister dying from lupus, his own diagnosis of ALS... Richard admitted that he was seldom one to cry. But Richard did cry after Marty died. A floodgate of grief opened up, and he couldn't stop crying.

"Marty's death broke Richard's heart," Bootsie confided to me.

Richard felt lost for a while. He was new to the city, where he didn't know many people, and now his brother was gone. At Marty's memorial, several friends brought bottles of hard liquor and wine. The unfinished bottles sat on Richard's kitchen table for days after the funeral, and one night Richard looked at them and decided to have a drink. Even though he had been sober for several years by then, he poured himself a shot.

Suddenly the phone rang. It was the husband of Marty's hospice nurse. "I'd never met the guy," said Richard, "but his wife had told me about him. She said he was in Alcoholics Anonymous. He introduced himself over the phone and said he needed a speaker for an AA meeting that night. Could I help?

"I said no. It was too late and it was raining.

'Was it ever too late to drink?' the guy asked me. 'Was it ever too late to go to a bar?'

"I don't have a ride," Richard argued, looking at the tequila in his glass.

"I'll give you a ride," said the man. "I'll be right there."

"He showed up on his motorcycle and off we went," Richard remembered. "That meeting became my favorite AA group in the years to come. And I got rid of all that liquor in the kitchen. I dumped it down the sink."

## 1989-1993

Richard started Marty's Place soon after Marty passed away. The homeless shelter was born in that same Hartford Street apartment where the two brothers had lived. The rent was $650 a month, and again Richard relied on the generosity of Bootsie until he could secure other funding.

"I had no other money on which to survive," he said, "so I did what I could. I collected aluminum cans and donations...whatever."

I asked him why he decided to invite homeless men with AIDS to live with him in that little apartment.

"I just saw a need. This was the time of the AIDS plague. People were suffering all around me. I could have gone back to Florida or New York. I guess I came to believe that people should bloom where they're planted. Joe Chinnici was the provincial back then, and he told me to relax. He didn't give me an assignment, but I saw there was work to do here, so I stayed.

"How many people were living in that apartment?" I asked.

"Three or four at a time. As the years went by, so many came and died. Little Pete was the first one. He was a Mexican-American from East Los Angeles.

Richard showed me a photo of himself with Little Pete. In it, Richard is wearing a woman's bathing suit, stiletto heels and a wig. "That was taken on Halloween," he said. "It's significant because before that night, I had never dressed up in drag. I'd always been terrified of looking too feminine. And I used to be very judgmental of feminine men. Maybe it was my own internalized homophobia, but those kinds of men always irritated me.

"Then one day I was walking through the Castro and I read the back of somebody's t-shirt. It said 'Unleash the Queen.' I liked that. So I dressed up in that bathing suit and went out and had a blast. It was very liberating. I don't care anymore if people think I'm feminine. It doesn't bother me in other men either. It was a great experience and I'd highly recommend it."

## 1993-2009

Richard loved to tell the story of how he found an old Victorian house in the Mission for Marty's Place.

"In 1993 I was introduced to a realtor who told me about this house. It was owned by a couple of lawyers from Berkeley. The house was vacant and selling for $345,000. I offered them $280,000, and they held firm at $290,000. I said 'Great, I'll buy it.' 'Okay,' they said, 'So how much do you want to put down?' I told them 'I have $650.' They looked at me like I was crazy.

"'Listen,' I continued. 'I'll come up with $29,000 and then the guys and I will move in. Nobody is living in the house now and we'll keep an eye on it for you. Then we'll take over the mortgage.'

"I had no idea how I came up with that number, $29,000. It just came into my head. I also didn't know where I was going to come up with that amount. The couple looked at me like I was nuts. Then they went into the kitchen to talk privately, and when they came out they said, 'We like what we hear. We want to be part of your plan.'

"So that was it. I realized I had to start hustling for some money. I hit up all the rich parishes in San Francisco. Every one of them told me no. Finally I got the mortgage money from Louie Vitale and St. Boniface – one of the poorest churches in the diocese. They paid the mortgage for 12 months. The $29,000 came from an anonymous foundation. They gave me $30,000. So I put down $29,000 and I had $1000 left over!

"I knew I had to get the place incorporated to keep the funding ongoing. That's how Aurora Dawn was born. I didn't use the name Marty's Place because I also wanted the foundation to serve women.[6] I needed a 501(c) 3 nonprofit status, so I put together a board of directors and got a lawyer. The lawyer, who worked for us pro bono, had a sort of conversion experience during the process. He said after spending time with us, he didn't want to waste his life being a lawyer anymore. So he quit the bar and became a librarian."[7]

I asked Richard about some of the specific experiences he had at Marty's Place. I had worked for years as a nurse, and I knew that AIDS patients presented some extreme challenges. I was particularly curious about how he dealt with all the chemically dependent clients who ended up in the house. It was substance abuse, combined with AIDS, that made some of these guys homeless.

"Before we had any decent AIDS drugs," said Richard, "the addicts and alcoholics would just die. Then they started to survive, and I had to deal with chemical dependency as well as AIDS."

Richard said that at first he took a hard-line approach to drinking and drugging. "It was all or nothing. Either they stayed clean or I booted them out. But in time I recognized that this wasn't realistic. Eventually, if someone relapsed, but seemed serious about trying to stay clean – if they were actively involved in something like AA or counseling and they weren't disrupting the household – I'd let them stay."

He admitted that at times it was hard to deal with addicts, especially since his personality was rather easygoing and he had trouble setting boundaries with people.

"But I've always had this philosophy of opening my home to strangers," he said. "I figured if somebody turned up on my doorstep, it was for a reason. I also feel that everybody is damaged on some level. Even if it's just living in fear.

"Everybody is addicted. We're all addicted to this horrible culture. The crappy, lying educational system, the healthcare system which is based on profit and giving out too many drugs... a legal system, so much of which is built around the prison industry, the military industrial complex which we believe is saving our asses... and addicted to religion, which has no connection to the divine.

"If somebody showed up at my door, I often found that he was an angel in disguise who had come to bless me. Some of these men were wrapped in barbed wire or broken glass – but coming from this culture, how could they not be damaged? And then they got planted in this house, just like an injured bird or a withered plant that needed water and sunlight. They found a lovely place to flourish and they were given a lot of love and support. I watched these men blossom into beautiful flowers. That is an extremely gratifying experience. Sure, I had to throw out a few, but only about 8 out of 80. The rest became healthier members of society until they died in peace. And as you can see, some are still around and caring for me."

The phone suddenly rang in another part of the house, not the extension at Richard's bedside. "Should I answer that?" I asked.

"No, we never answer that phone," he said.

"Why do you pay for a phone line if you don't use it?"

"I'm not sure. I guess it's an official phone for the foundation. We still get calls – people looking for a place for men with AIDS." He shook his head sadly. "There's still such a need. There's always been a long waiting list of men wanting to get in here."

"How did you screen the clients?"

"It basically came down to whoever showed up at the door. That's one reason I so seldom answer the phone. I wouldn't know how to screen people... who to turn away and who to take in. So I figured, if somebody showed up at the door, it was for a reason. If we had a bed, we'd let them in.

"One time," he continued, "I looked out the window and saw an ambulance parked in front of the house. I opened the door and here were these 'moon men,' ambulance drivers dressed up the way people used to dress when they were touching someone with AIDS. They were wearing masks, gloves, gowns... they told me, 'We've got your patient.'

"I wasn't expecting any patient. It turned out that a local hospital had heard about Marty's Place and sent this guy over, without even clearing it with me."

"A dump?" I asked, referring to the medical slang for that type of transaction.

"Yes, it was a dump. And the patient was very sick. His name was Clarence. He was a black transgender – probably a hooker because he looked like he'd had a rough life. Like he'd been living on the street. And he was totally out of it. He was in diapers. He had bedsores. He was just filthy when they brought him in.

"We didn't have any extra beds so they laid him out on the couch. A lot of people told me I should send him back where he came from, but I couldn't, because he had ended up on my doorstep and I felt it was for a reason. The ambulance drivers gave me some paperwork on him but it was very limited, mostly just his name and birth date – no next of kin. And Clarence sure couldn't give me any information. He was too far gone.

"We cleaned him up and eventually got him a room. We took good care of him, and he lasted seven weeks. One day I was bathing him and one of the guys stuck his head in the door and said he was going to Walgreens. 'Do you want anything at Walgreens?' he asked.

"'No,' I told him. Then I addressed Clarence. I always spoke to Clarence out of respect when I was with him, even though I didn't know if he could hear me. 'Do you want something at Walgreens, Clarence?' I asked. And then, to our utter amazement, he said 'Yes. Nail polish.' Just like that. Clear as day. So I asked him 'What color?' He said 'Orange.' That was the first and last time we ever heard him speak.

"We got him some orange nail polish and gave him a nice manicure. Then for the rest of his life, he was always holding out his hands, staring at his beautiful nails, admiring them.

"Once I was checking in this new client. He was this extremely handsome guy named David. I was showing him around, and as we stepped past Clarence's room, I led David inside. 'This is Clarence,' I said. 'Clarence, this is David.' David bowed, took Clarence's hand, and graciously kissed it. 'Pleased to meet you,' he said and added, 'My, you have such beautiful nails!' Of course Clarence didn't say anything.

"Then I showed David his room down the hall. As David unpacked, I walked back past Clarence's open door. I looked inside and he was dead. Just like that. Clarence went that quickly. That quietly."

## 2009

Even after Richard could no longer walk, he still managed to get out of the house and go places. Friends or family would take him out to dinner and he went to several events involving the friars. He also continued to lead our Days of Dialogue at San Damiano. And as long as we could get him in and out of the shelter's van, we would take him to visit Luz.

By 2008, due to her back and hip problems, Luz had lost her ability to walk. Because it would be too difficult for her daughters to care for her, Luz gave up her apartment and moved permanently into Laguna Honda Hospital.

Laguna Honda was a monstrosity of a building that served as a nursing home for the city's indigent. Walking through it could be pretty depressing. Many of the severely disabled people who crawled around the place in their wheelchairs had been there for years. Many too, had no outside contacts. Some would beg for spare change as visitors walked by.

The building was in the process of being rebuilt, and Luz still lived in the old section in one of the hospital's wards. These were the kind of large, open rooms you'd see in photos of hospitals around the time of World War I. Beds were lined up in rows, with only curtains providing a little privacy. Luz had been in pain for a long time, but by 2009 she was stabilized and kept comfortable with an occasional Vicodin.

Despite her crowded living conditions, Luz surprised us by saying she loved her home. "I'm with the poor," she said. "This is where a Franciscan finds happiness."

She had befriended the many abandoned disabled people that surrounded her, and as the months and then the years wore on, we could see that Luz had become a bit of a celebrity on her ward. The nurses adored her. At our Secular Franciscan meetings, we joked that she should start a secular chapter at Laguna Honda... because she seemed to be having such a profound effect there on the patients and staff.

When I was sitting beside her, my perspective of the hospital shifted. A place that had once saddened me now took on a beautiful rhythm of order and peace.

When Richard visited Luz, they would talk of many things. They spoke of their families, people they both knew, and the things they had done. "This is retirement, isn't it?" Richard said one day. "The two of us can rest now. No work, no worries...."

Luz nodded. She did seem to be enjoying her retirement.

They talked about death too. Neither of them feared it. Luz's myeloma was in remission, but like any of us, she didn't know when death would come knocking.

"People worry about where they'll go after they die," said Richard. "But 'place' has to do with the ego. That's why Western cultures need heaven and hell. In truth, I believe we are already part of wherever we will be. We are already part of the divine."

Richard and Luz were close in age. They talked about what it was like to reach their 70s. "It keeps getting better," said Richard, "and this last year has been the best!"

"Yes, yes, it's true!" Luz exclaimed.

"The best?" I wondered. "With both of you trapped in wheelchairs? Unable to care for yourselves?"

"For me," reasoned Richard, "it's been a chance to let *being* supersede *doing*. And the end result is so much peace and joy."

Luz nodded. She felt the same way.

In time, Richard was no longer able visit Luz, but they still talked on the phone. I continued to see her whenever possible. She slept a lot, but when she was awake, she was totally alert and present. And she would always greet me with that same lovely smile. As we'd chat and watch the activities of the ward, Luz seemed to be basking in front of a warm fire.

"Maybe it's the Vicodin," I suggested to Richard when I was referring to her behavior one day.

"No," he disagreed. "That's Luz."

PART III

# SAYING GOODBYE

"The presence of a person who has stillness and contentment of heart engenders trust. They can sift from the chaff and talk and select what has weight and worth. Sometimes the dignity of their composure can bring the company of those present to a finer level of attention and worthiness."[8]
– John O'Donohue

## August 26, 2009

We were hanging out on the patio at Marty's Place. It was late summer and the garden was alive with flowers and foliage. A former client named Zach was trimming branches and watering plants. I had heard that Zach was an alcoholic and would occasionally go on benders. I had been advised not to give him any money or he'd drink it up. Another visitor liked crystal meth, and I was instructed not to give him money either. It amazed me, that despite their problems, these guys continued to show up completely sober to help out around the house. That's how much they enjoyed being near Richard.

As Zach worked, Richard and I chatted about art. Richard said that he regretted he hadn't created more art. I had seen a few of his creations. One was the paper mache mask of a coyote, another was a beautiful piece of pottery.

I had also talked to Susan Cervantes, the founder of The Precita Eyes Mural Arts Center. The center was well known in San Francisco for bringing beautiful murals to the city. Richard had volunteered for Precita Eyes, worked on several murals, and for a while served on the organization's board of directors. One project he helped paint was the AIDS mural on the corner of Market and 16th Street. At the time of this writing, it is one of the only surviving murals about AIDS in San Francisco.

"It was a huge project in collaboration with over 16 artists affected by AIDS," Susan told me. "I remember Richard getting on top of the scaffold, which was over three tiers high and 85 feet long. He was determined to paint in the Rainbow Flag and an AIDS quilt with the names of people who had passed away." Susan also lauded Richard as an excellent calligrapher who had done much of the lettering on the mural.

In spite of all this, Richard still believed he hadn't created enough art in his life. And now his hands and fingers were failing.

"You've produced a lot of art," I insisted. "And art isn't always visual. I mean, look what you've accomplished with Marty's Place. This household is truly a work of art."

Richard had to agree. "And in creating any kind of art," he added, "you can't wait around for the spirit to move you. You just have to start doing it."

"You sure did that with Marty's Place! You had no idea what would become of it or what problems you'd encounter, you just went ahead and did it."

"Exactly. And when we try something and make a mistake, we just get back up and keep trying. It's like a child learning to walk. If he or she falls down, it doesn't mean the child will still be crawling around at thirty. Can you imagine? People crawling up and down Mission Street... hundreds of them, who gave up after they fell down?"

That image really got us both laughing.

## Juan

After Richard was diagnosed with ALS, the residents of Marty's Place began to look for other places to live. Juan, a short and stocky man from Mexico, was the last to leave, but even after he moved, he still returned to Marty's Place almost every day.

Juan had studied to be a priest for a while in Mexico. He said he had to leave the seminary "*Después de estar infectado.*" (After I was infected). Juan was usually the person who gave Richard his bath. With his broad shoulders, Juan could easily lift Richard onto the lawn chair that we placed in the shower. And since Juan was always so even-tempered and sensitive, Richard trusted him the most with this intimate task.

Juan was studying English and I was learning Spanish, so we helped one another with our language skills. Slowly, I got to know his story.

While living in Mexico, Juan had had several homophobic encounters with the police. They arrested him and subjected him to some atrocities, all because they perceived that he was gay. One night they beat him up and dumped him into a quarry, leaving him for dead. Juan somehow swam to safety. In recounting this and other episodes, he told me, "If I hadn't left Mexico, I would no longer be alive." Juan still suffered from severe flashbacks surrounding this abuse.

Once on the California side of the border, Juan's troubles weren't over. Through a lethal combination of AIDS and tuberculosis, he almost died in a San Diego hospital.

"I was so alone," he said. "I remember knowing I was dying, and yet having nobody around who cared about me. I looked to a hospital janitor as someone to talk to." Fortunately, Juan recovered, and through connections with people he had known from his Mexican seminary, he contacted Richard. Richard invited him to live at Marty's Place.

After Richard got ALS, Juan moved to a tiny hotel room in San Francisco's Tenderloin District. The place was noisy, and riddled with drugs and violence. I asked Juan if he had any friends there. He said no, and that he was frightened of the residents.

Juan was allowed to stay in the US temporarily because of conditions related to his illness. He received General Assistance (GA), but it wasn't enough to live on. So he ate and did his laundry at Marty's Place, and wore Richard's old clothes.

Juan talked about the homophobia in Mexico. In his opinion, Mexicans were, in general, much more hospitable than North Americans, but many Mexicans were very homophobic. "*Ellos le mataran.*" (They will kill you).

"Are things getting better there?" I asked.

"*Teóricamente pero no en la practica.*" (In theory, but not practice).

Eventually, with Richard's help, Juan sought and won asylum based on his sexual orientation and HIV status. Richard helped at least one other Latino man at Marty's Place do the same. These were real victories, since asylum based on sexual orientation was extremely hard to acquire.

Historically, sexual orientation used to be a factor that specifically forbade people from coming to this country. The Nationality Acts of 1917 and 1952 used terms like "mentally defective" and "psychopathic personalities" which the INS applied to gays. Asylum based on sexual orientation was first initiated in 1994 and was spearheaded by the then attorney general, Janet Reno. Winning asylum around this issue, however, has never been easy. Only about 62 percent of these applications have been successful.[9,10]

Juan felt that stigma, lack of education on sexuality, and the Catholic Church, contributed to violence against gays in Mexico.

I suggested that these conditions were not limited to Latin America. They could be found everywhere, including in the United States.

"*Si,*" he nodded, but he was still grateful to be here, and extremely excited to be granted asylum. Yet both of us realized Juan's life in this country would continue to be an ongoing struggle. He had AIDS, no family, and the small income he received could hardly sustain him. I wondered what would happen to him after Richard died. Marty's Place had been a great resource for him and for so many other men.

I thought about all this one night as I drove Juan back to the Tenderloin. We had spent the evening talking in Spanish, and I was exhausted. It had been tiring for me, struggling with a new language all evening. As Juan tried so hard to learn English, I got a glimpse into what he was dealing with every single day.

## Max

One day Max and I were standing in front of the mantel in the living room of Marty's Place. We looked at the pictures of men who had died in the house. "I knew all of these men," Max told me. "Richard and I cared for them. Richard worked so hard, from six in the morning until after midnight. He's a saint, you know." Then Max told me about the men in the photographs. Some he liked and some he didn't. "That one was a junkie and ripped us off. Those two were lovers. That one was *loco*."

"Was this always such a loving household?" I asked Max. "Like I feel it is today. I feel so peaceful and good whenever I visit this place."

Max twisted his face. He didn't seem to think so. "There were problems," he admitted. "Just like there are problems now. But Richard kept everything under control. And Richard set the tone, so things worked out."

"Richard is my father," Max said suddenly. He had told me this before and so had some of the other men. They saw Richard as the father they never had.

Max then described own father, who'd called Max *basura* (garbage), because he could see that his son was gay. "He thought he could change me by making me into a boxer," said Max. "Whenever he saw me, he would box me in the shoulders to toughen me up. He used to tell the neighborhood kids to fight me, and if I lost, he would beat me up himself. When my father died, I was in some ways relieved. My suffering was over."

Then one day, through the help of a spiritual medium, Max visited his father again. Max's eyes were wide and his voice was breathless as he told me the story. The medium invited Max to join him in the darkness just before dawn. He said that this was the best time to connect with the spirit world. Then he led Max to a room where his father's ghost appeared. "*¡Vi a mi padre!*" Max said. "I felt chills up and down my spine and the hair stood up on my arms. My father embraced me and said '*¡Perdóname hijo mio! ¡Perdóname!*' I told my father, 'I have already forgiven you.' We held each other in our arms, then just as the sun rose and lit up the room, my father vanished. I was standing there embracing myself. "

I listened quietly and then gently asked, "Max, was this a dream?"

"No! This was real! And I think I am psychic. Things happen to me. Like three days before the Managuan earthquake, I dreamt the whole thing. I saw it so vividly, everything that happened, and three days later, it did happen!"

Max then talked about the war, and the period when he was imprisoned and tortured. I stared at him, and couldn't believe what this man had lived through. And I wondered, was he truly psychic, or, perhaps due to so much trauma, had he slipped off some psychological edge?

Then he told me about his mother, Raquel, who might have also had a clairvoyant streak. Max said that as a boy in Nicaragua, he had terrible asthma. His mother had a dream that he should take "*una píldora de Rosada*" which was made in England. Max took the pill and he was cured.

Raquel met Richard only one time, when he had traveled with Max to Nicaragua. Yet Raquel came to love Richard so much that she often fasted for him for several days while she prayed. Max believed that one reason Richard had survived so long and well was because of Raquel's fasting and praying.

Max was supporting his mother financially. He had given her money ever since he turned ten. "Ever since my father left," he said. "The only times I couldn't send money was when I was addicted to drugs."

Max adored his mother and said that his father's family completely rejected her after his parents' separation. "My father was light skinned and my mother is Meztiza. She was such a beautiful young woman, gorgeous like a model. When she walked through the streets, all the men's heads turned, their eyes following her as she moved along. She stopped traffic. They called her *La Venus de Bronce.*" (The Bronze Venus).

Max imitated his mother walking. As he told me this story, he strode proudly across the kitchen floor with his head held high, as if balancing a book.

## Modesty

Eventually, Richard was no longer able to help us when we lifted him from his bed or wheelchair. He became dead weight, and despite the range of motion exercises we put him through every day, his limbs began to contract. He developed foot drop, and told us he felt like Bette Midler, in the film when she plays a mermaid. He said his lower extremities felt like a mermaid's tail.

He became more and more difficult to dress, so the men eventually omitted his underwear. They ripped the elastic waistbands out of his sweat pants, so the pants would be easier to put on. This became a problem, because when the men moved Richard, his pants often fell off. To further simplify things, when Richard was in bed, he wore nothing at all. Richard surrendered to all of these indignities with grace and humor.

In watching all this, I was reminded of Richard's interpretation of the word modesty. "It means not calling undue attention to yourself," he had told me. "In that sense, even dressing like a nun can be immodest."

One morning Juan was getting Richard ready for a bath, and I accidentally walked past the open door. As a nurse, I was used to seeing naked men, but I initially tried to respect Richard's privacy and leave his more intimate care to the men. Yet as I inadvertently glanced through the door, there sat Richard. I hurried past, pretending that I saw nothing.

Instead of pretending himself that the incident didn't happen, Richard called out to me. "*Hola Susanna*! Have you seen the gladiolas?" He was referring to the fresh flowers that someone had picked from the garden. They were sitting across from him in a vase on the sink.

## San Damiano

The San Damiano Retreat Center in Danville is less than an hour's drive out of San Francisco, yet whenever I drive up there, I feel like I'm entering another world. The intensity and fast pace of the city falls away as I climb the mountain road which borders a state park. As I arrive on the Franciscan's property, I'm greeted by a gentle forest of live oak and bay laurel, and sometimes a passing deer.

The center itself, with its bright white Spanish architecture, sits peacefully on the top of a hill, looking out over panoramic view.

I've visited this place many times through the years, and have so grown to love its beautiful gardens and winding trails. I especially enjoyed going up to San Damiano with Richard. Every three months, we'd drive up there for our Day of Dialogue retreats for LGBT Catholics and their families and friends.

On Sunday, August 30, 2009, I drove to the center for what I believed would be Richard's last Day of Dialogue. Richard and Ben, one of the men from Marty's Place, accompanied me in the Marty's Place van. As we drove, I prepared myself emotionally for the fact that Richard's leadership in these Talking Circles might be coming to an end.

Richard was preparing too. He knew someone would have to take over as a moderator of the discussion after he died. He suggested a few regulars in our group, including Ted and Helen Johnson, a straight couple who had lost a son to AIDS. Richard had a pet name for Helen and Ted. He called them "Ma and Pa Kettle."

I had emailed the Johnsons this information, but they never replied. On this particular Sunday, when Richard and I cornered them during the break, we got the same blank response. They didn't say yes or no. They said nothing. Finally Helen told us that when she was speaking to some members of the group about who was going to take Richard's place, one gay man said that he felt that only a gay person should be appointed.

Richard said to the two of them, "You're not gay, but you are queer." We all laughed, but then he insisted, "You are queer in the fact that you live against the grain. You have spoken out against homophobia, and you yourselves as the parents of a gay son, have faced prejudice."

Helen and Ted remained silent. I assumed they were trying to decide what to do, and I also knew they were both busy with other commitments. When the group reconvened, Richard suggested that perhaps Ted and Helen could take over his work.

An older gay man named Neil spoke up. He was the same man who had told Ted and Helen that only a gay person could lead the Days of Dialogue. "I believe," he said, "that a gay religious person should take over the position. A priest, a nun, or a brother."

"And I think you're out of your gourd," Richard responded. He explained that, first of all, there were no religious people available to take on the task, and second, even if there were, very few would be gay or admit they were gay. Third, Richard emphasized, just because someone held the title of nun, priest or brother, didn't mean that person was qualified to lead this or any group.

Neil was an endearing fellow who'd been through a lot in his life, including hiding his sexuality for decades. He had been married to a woman for 25 years, and finally, after he realized he could no longer live a lie, came out. He shared a lot of good insights during our discussions, and was always present at every gathering. However, his tone on this day was pedantic. And despite Richard's words to the contrary, Neil continued to insist that only a priest, brother or nun was capable of taking over our group.

Richard carried this disagreement just so far before he dropped it altogether. He seldom argued, in fact, he could be almost passive to a fault. When conflicts came up, he had a tendency to change the subject, which was what he did in this situation. He quit arguing with Neil, and started our discussion by giving us one of his "sermonettes."

Richard talked about "secrets." He said it wasn't our homosexuality that was ailing us, but the fact that we had to cover it up. He told a story about himself. He said that when he was a younger man and working with the Tohono O'odham, a woman asked him, "Richard, why are you so standoffish?"

He realized what she meant. He said that as a gay man he had to cover up many of his mannerisms for fear of being found out. He worried that the tone of his voice or the way he walked might identify him as queer. He tried to bottle all this up, so he came off as being uptight and guarded. In the end, this wasn't who he wanted to be. He wanted to be open. He wanted to get to know people and have them know him.

Richard mentioned Abbe Pierre, the French priest who he so admired. Pierre said that as the followers of Jesus, we had two tasks: to say what has not been said and to do what has not been done. In other words, to speak and live the truth.

Richard spoke of the Pimas who had been visiting his house over the weekend. He said that he had never come out to any of the Native Americans when he lived on the reservations. He wouldn't have lied if they had asked him about his sexual orientation, but as their pastor, he didn't feel it was appropriate to bring it up.

"In some ways, the Indians are very conservative," he said. "Living in rural Arizona is not like living in San Francisco. Basically, I've seldom heard the Native Americans even talk about homosexuality.

"But since they were visiting my house, I felt I needed to bring it up. After all, I've been working all these years with mostly gay men with AIDS, and I was leaving today to come to this workshop. So I did speak openly about gays and lesbians throughout the weekend. At one point, an older woman broke down and started crying. It was very unlike her to show that kind of emotion. She said 'Father Richard, thank you, thank you, thank you!'

"It turned out," Richard explained, "that this woman had a transgender child. She was so grateful that I broke the silence and said something that she herself was afraid to talk about. The other Pima responded very lovingly toward her. They assured her that they had no problem with her son's gender. And it made me feel good that I was able to bring her this comfort, just by saying what in polite company is not said."

Richard then mentioned Ted Kennedy, who had just passed away. He spoke of all the opposition the senator had faced, just because he had the guts to fight for the rights of the little people who had no power. "The poor people, the gay people... " said Richard, "that is why he was so loved, and will be remembered." Then Richard repeated a phrase he had often expressed, "If you want to follow Jesus, you'd better look good on wood." In other words, if you speak the truth, expect to be attacked and criticized.

Later, discussing ALS and dying, Richard said "You can view things positively or negatively. But if you're negative, you'll pay the price because people will run from you." At that moment, Ben pulled Richard up in his chair. Richard's body had been sliding down as he spoke. "I'm surrounded by angels," Richard said, referring to Ben. "I have ten unpaid caregivers, night and day. You attract people if you're attractive, and positive is attractive. Negative is unattractive. It's very easy, really. All that is, is. And that is my only prayer. My prayer in life is so simplified.

"I used to pray the rosary and do this and that. I used to read all these prayers in prayer books. But it's been so simple the last few years. Now my prayer in life is 'Thank You.' That's all. 'I am fully grateful for this day. I am fully grateful for my home. I am fully grateful for Plumita and for all the people I love.' There doesn't have to be any breast beating...'Oh, I'm so sorry' and all that crap. Just an openness to life. It's very doable.

"It's the same with death. There is no such thing as death; only a change into another way of living. Just because this 'container' dies," Richard said, pointing to his body, "doesn't mean much in the whole scheme of things.

"After I got my diagnosis, a friend asked me, 'Are you going to heaven or hell or purgatory?' I told her 'None of the above.' She said, 'Well, I thought you were a Franciscan?' I said, 'I thought I was too.' 'Well, what's going to happen?' I told her, 'I don't give a shit.' It's the least of my worries, and I don't have any others, so there are no worries. I told her, 'Maybe I'll be a twinkling star out in the universe, because that's where I came from.' I don't have to know I'm Richard, for God's sake, after I'm ashes.

"You know there is a God," he continued, "but it isn't the God we know. My definition of God is the Dazzling Darkness. Well, you can't have Dazzling Darkness. If it's dazzling, it's light, and if it's darkness, it's not dazzling. It's like in the Old Testament when they ask God 'Who are you?' And God says, 'I am who am.' In other words, mind your own goddamned business. Stop asking questions. So for us to try and understand who is God, and if God is giving us this or that – it's just ego-babble. So I say, 'Just let go.' I just think that we're here to be – well... queer. In other words, to just be ourselves."

Richard's head drooped and his glasses began to slide down his nose. Ben reached over to adjust them. "It's in giving that we receive," Richard continued. "That's why I'm surrounded by angels. And the men who died at Marty's Place are surrounding me still. They are also present, because in the end, it's all about spirit."

We sat quietly, staring at Richard and contemplating his words. Suddenly the silence was broken. "You misquoted the Old Testament," Neil commented. "It's not 'I am who am,' it's 'I will be who I will be'."

Richard looked at him. "Same thing," he said. "And it still means, mind your own business."

## September 10, 2009

Richard's caregivers had gathered to meet with Lee Guion, the respiratory therapist. She showed us how to use a new machine called an in-Exsufflator. The machine is designed to deliver a volume of air into a patient's lungs and then quickly reverse the air flow to pull out secretions. We hoped that it would prevent those episodes when Richard choked on his own phlegm. He didn't have the strength to cough very hard anymore, so on occasion, mucus got caught in his trachea and he'd almost strangle.

"The first time it occurred," Richard said, "was at four in the morning. I couldn't breathe, and then miraculously, Max peeked in the door. I was gasping and pointing at my throat." Max pounded on his chest and did some quick Heimlich-like maneuvers on Richard's abdomen. It was a miracle that Max appeared just at that moment. Since then, Max rarely dozed during the night, and had begun sleeping on the floor just outside of Richard's room.

"Richard has choked on other occasions," said Lee. "We want to prevent this."

I surveyed the faces in the room. All of us were hanging on the edge of a frightening reality that we were just buying time. We knew that eventually there would be nothing we could do to preserve and maintain that precious commodity: Richard's breath.

ALS is a disease that affects the neurons that control voluntary muscles. So the disease wasn't harming Richard's lungs, it was killing off the mechanisms that operated his diaphragm.

Lee pointed to Richard's chest and his rapid respirations. "Do you see how he's using his shoulders to breathe? The rest of us use our diaphragms. The way Richard breathes is exhausting. I think that in addition to using the in-Exsufflator, he needs to be on the BiPAP longer during the day."

We were crowded into Richard's little room. Some of us were on the bed or floor or leaning against the wall. Richard was in his electric wheelchair. I marveled at the diversity of our motley group.

Those present included Juan, Max and some other Latino guys. They included Julio from Brazil, Alejo from Uruguay, Raul from Columbia and Rogelio – who was part Mexican and part Yuma Indian – from Arizona. Also present were Tree and Angela, a white married couple who had been volunteering at Marty's Place for years. Angela was a registered nurse who oversaw much of Richard's care (Richard also had a visiting hospice nurse who was paid for by his Kaiser insurance). Tree was a local legend from around the Mission. Wearing faded jeans, a flannel shirt, long hair and a beard, he was a hold-out from the 60s. He told me that he hadn't held a real job since the Vietnam War. He quit working then because he didn't want his taxes to support the killing.

I wasn't sure how Tree had survived before he married Angela. He did say he'd lived on a commune for many years. Now he was devoted to a full time endeavor – helping provide free produce to the needy in San Francisco. He oversaw a variety of urban gardens and he harvested fruit trees that people didn't use. He gave all the food away.

When I first met Tree, I assumed he was doing this work for spiritual purposes, and in a way he was – but not the kind of spirituality I imagined. Tree said he wasn't religious, he just believed that people should follow their passions. His passion was gardening.

In some ways, Tree's work reminded me of what Richard himself had accomplished. Richard couldn't cure AIDS, and he couldn't end San Francisco's terrible problem with homelessness. Yet he did cultivate an abundance of joy and comfort in situations that many people had perceived as hopeless.

Likewise, midst the concrete of the inner city, where people were purportedly going hungry, Tree was growing so much food, he couldn't even give it all away.

## The BiPAP and other Bedside Characters

When I first started working evening shifts at Marty's Place, Angela demonstrated how to prepare Richard for bed. This included learning the animated names that Richard gave to inanimate objects. He not only gave people nicknames, he habitually assigned monikers to things. And when he gave these names to his medical devices, it somehow made them more friendly and less clinical.

When his arms still worked, Richard moved his legs with shoestrings that we tied to his feet. He bent his legs by pulling the strings, then straightened them out with a cane. He called the cane "Tiny Tim." And indeed, it looked just like the short little crutch that Tiny Tim uses in some of the films of Dickens's *Christmas Carol*. Richard called the main

BiPAP mask that he wore during the day "Miss Piggy" because of the snout-like device that fit under his nostrils. He had another mask that covered just his nose and left his mouth free for eating. This one he called Tortuga (turtle). His nighttime BiPAP covered his entire face and reminded me of a deep sea diver's helmet. Richard dubbed it "Darth Vader."

When Angela put Darth Vader on Richard, it quickly fogged up and started its hissing rhythm. Richard tried to communicate with muffled sounds, as if he were underwater. It pained me to see him like this, and he would be stuck inside this contraption for the night's duration.

At breakfast, I asked him, "Richard, are you suffering?" I couldn't imagine wearing that mask and not being able to move all night.

"It's not as bad as it looks," he assured me. "It's amazing what you can get used to."

I wasn't sure if I believed him, but I did know one thing... he was getting excellent care. The previous night, as I watched Angela go through the details of his bedtime routine, I decided that I had seldom seen a patient get such thorough attention. Angela did a great job in overseeing Richard's nursing needs. She also served as an instructor, teaching nursing skills to the other members of the Circle of Care team. They were all enthusiastic learners, and their labor of love was clearly one big reason that Richard survived so long and well.

## Homosexuality

I asked Richard when he first realized he was gay, and he gave me an answer that I have heard repeatedly from other gay people – "since I was a child." Richard went on to clarify that as a child he didn't know that he was specifically gay, but he knew he was different when it came to his sexual orientation. As an adult, he became increasingly aware of this reality, and eventually identified as a homosexual, but for years kept the information to himself.

After he got sober, he realized he needed to talk to somebody about his sexuality. He told a therapist, and the therapist suggested that he come out to someone in his family. Richard was mortified by the thought, but decided that he could at least tell his younger brother Marty, who was openly gay.

Richard was living with the Pimas then. He called Marty and said he had something to tell him. He added that it was so serious that he couldn't tell him over the phone. He drove all the way to San Francisco to talk to Marty in person.

After he got to San Francisco, he talked about everything except his homosexuality. He didn't know how to bring it up.

Finally, Marty asked him, "What did you come here to tell me?"

Richard hemmed and hawed, then eventually said, "I'm... *gay*."

Marty was silent for a moment, then wondered aloud, "Richard, don't you have anything else to tell me, maybe something that we haven't all known for years?"

## Sex

Richard never claimed to have lived a priest's life of celibacy, but he said that the details of his sex life weren't important. "What is important," he emphasized, "is that I've always been faithful to my Franciscan vow of chastity. Chastity means keeping my heart pure and good. When they say Mary was chaste, they meant she had a pure heart. It didn't mean she was a virgin.

"Being chaste means not using people, not intentionally hurting people, not lying. In that way, I've kept my vow of chastity. I've been a good Franciscan."

Richard said that sexuality isn't something that can be kept in a box. "We don't want to disrespect , dismiss, or neglect our sexuality, because it's part of who we are."

During our Talking Circles at San Damiano, Richard told us that being a Christian means learning to love. "And how can one know how to love, if one is not loved? A very important way that adults learn to love is by having an intimate relationship – having a close partnership with someone who really cares about them."

Richard then told me how he had followed another Franciscan vow: obedience. "Regarding sex and so many other things," he said, "I've always been obedient to my own conscience."

## Animals

Animals had always been a big part of Richard's life, although he told me that he hadn't always really appreciated them. He had always enjoyed them and had never been cruel to them, "but it took me a while to understand that they're just as gifted and important as we are. In many ways they're better than us. They have senses and intuitions that we've lost."

Richard would begin the Talking Circles at San Damiano by reading from a book called *How the Wild Thing Pray* by William Cleary. Cleary quotes Job 12:7: "Ask the animals and they shall be your teachers; become a disciple of the birds and they shall instruct you."[11]

Richard said we should always give thanks for "the four-legged ones," a term he learned from the Native Americans. He had animals on the reservations, including a pig named Lulce.

"I fed Lulce the surplus food that we got for free," said Richard. "Big bars of cheese, peanut butter, Karo syrup and even canned pork, so she sometimes ate her cousins. She was huge. She used to just wander around the village freely and one day she came into church during Mass. She waddled right up the center aisle and tugged at the tablecloth on the altar. Everything fell off. The candles, the missal, everything.

"I told the congregation, 'We have to catch her,' so we all started chasing her around the church."

Somebody gave Richard a coyote puppy once. "I didn't want to keep him," he said, "because it isn't good to keep wild animals. Besides, some of the O'odahm were afraid of coyotes. Like buzzards, coyotes are considered power animals that can make you sick. But in the end, I did keep the coyote. I raised him like a dog and named him Groody."

Richard also had a rattlesnake that spent the winters in his cabin. "It was a sidewinder, and they can live up to 30 years. Every winter that same snake would crawl into my house. He'd curl up in this little space between the wood stove and the bookcase. He wasn't hurting anybody. He just wanted to stay warm."

To me, Richard's love of animals was most evident in the sweet relationship he had with his little dog Plumita. She was a white terrier mix, and had ended up at Marty's Place in the same manner as its other inhabitants – she showed up at the door. When she was a puppy, Richard found her crying and alone on the back patio. He took her in, then started looking for her owner. Her owner, it turned out, was a neighbor.

Richard told him, "I found your puppy."

"You can keep her," the man replied.

"Why?" Richard asked.

"Because I threw her away."

"He threw her away in the dead of winter!" Richard exclaimed. "Can you believe it? She was an orphan." And like so many other orphans, she came to call Marty's Place home.

Richard adored that dog, and the feeling was mutual.

Max told me a story about one of the rare times he saw Richard get really mad. One of the guys in the house had baked some hash brownies. After eating the brownies, he put the pan on the floor for Plumita to lick.

Max imitated a stoned dog with his eyes rolled back and his tongue hanging out of the side of his mouth. "We thought Plumita was going to die," said Max, "And I've never seen Richard so angry in my life."

Richard's and Plumita's relationship had become so symbiotic that as Richard's hands grew swollen and deformed, Plumita began to lick the parts that hurt.

"Look at Plumita," he said one day when she was licking. "She does the same to this area on my shoulder that hurts. The exact spot. Isn't it amazing?"

"How does it feel?" I asked.

"It feels good. It feels like a gentle massage."

One night Richard had a dream where Plumita talked. She looked up at him and said "Boo-Boo's been a bad boy."

"What?" asked Richard in his dream.

"Boo-Boo's been a bad boy," Plumita repeated.

Richard had a friend whose dog was named Boo-Boo. Richard called this friend the next day to see how his dog was doing. The dog was doing fine and, according to the owner, Boo-Boo had not been bad.

"You know," Richard told me, after sharing this story, "some American Indians claim that if a dog talks to you, it means you're going to turn into stone."

I remained quiet, but Richard spoke what I was thinking. "I am turning into stone," he said.

## October 20, 2009

I asked Richard about the Pope's new pronouncement, welcoming disenfranchised Anglican priests into the Catholic fold. As one of my Anglican friends told me, "We've gratefully gotten rid of a bunch of sexists and homophobes, and now your Pope wants to take them in."

"That man," sighed Richard, referring to Pope Benedict. "If he keeps at it, he'll alienate both Roman and Anglican Catholics, and all we'll be left with is a bunch of right wing malcontents. He's already invited in that whole St. Pius X crowd."

"Who?"

"The Society of St. Pius X. It was founded by a character named Archbishop Marcel Lefebvre. He was a traditionalist and against the changes that came with Vatican II. That society still wants to say Mass in Latin and turn their asses to the people. Benedict XVI revoked the excommunication of some of their bishops, including one who claimed that there was no such thing as a Holocaust. Talk about really messing up relations between the Catholics and the Jews!"

Richard shook his head then added, "But the Pope has said a few things I agree with. He's spoken out against the death penalty and the wars in Iraq and Afghanistan. It's funny how conservative Catholics don't bring up those kinds of things when they're talking about the Pope."

I had been reading *Practicing Catholic* by James Carroll, and I found our discussion a good segue into this book. Carroll is Irish American and a former Paulist priest. He was of Richard's generation, and like Richard, highly influenced by Vatican II.

Carroll is uncompromising in his criticism of the Catholic Church, especially of Pope Benedict XVI. He summarizes the influences that Pope Benedict (formerly Cardinal Joseph Ratzinger) has had on the Church. Ratzinger halted the use of gender inclusive language in Mass; declared liberation theology as "heresy;" condemned the term "martyr" for the assassinated Salvadoran Archbishop Oscar Romero; recognized the CIA-backed military coup that overthrew Jean-Bertrand Aristide of Haiti (a former priest); claimed that the exclusion of women as priests is an infallible Church teaching; and for a while condemned the use of condoms, even for married couples when one was infected by AIDS.

In his response to the priest sex scandals, Benedict forbade admission to the priesthood any man who had "homosexual tendencies." Carroll, who is straight, acknowledges that for centuries, Catholic orders have accepted gay men and women, so long as they observed the rule of celibacy. Benedict downplayed other factors that might have contributed to the sexual abuse of children by clerics. And he never acknowledged that there is no link between pedophilia and homosexuality.

When asked whether he knew any gay people, Benedict replied, "Yes, in Berlin. They were demonstrating against the Pope."[12]

Carroll himself is still a practicing Catholic, although leery of the wave of conservative fundamentalism that seems to be taking over the Church. He adds that it's good and right that people constantly question the Church, and that they not abandon the religion just because they ask questions.

Richard agreed that it was good to question Catholicism, and he also emphasized that he couldn't measure his own reality by whatever the Church was doing. "My own life goes on," he said, "in spite of what the people in Rome believe. I really don't waste any time worrying about them. I've got more important things to think about."

## San Damiano, October 25, 2009

Ben, Richard and I climbed the mountain up to San Damiano. When we arrived, we saw new faces in our circle, as well as old friends. The group included Ted and Helen Johnson (Ma and Pa Kettle), Jerry from my Secular Franciscan group, and a Filipina lesbian named Elizabeth. Neil, the older gay man who only wanted a "gay religious" person to take over the group after Richard left, was there too.

Richard again explained to everyone that he was dying.

"Who will take your place?" Neil wanted to know.

Richard looked up at him wearily. "I don't know," Richard mumbled. It appeared as if Richard didn't want to revisit this discussion about who would take his place. And I suddenly wondered whether the group would even continue after Richard left.

I knew that Richard had faced criticism about the Days of Dialogue from conservative Catholics. He'd ignored this criticism and refused to stop the group. I wondered whether any future leaders would be courageous enough to do the same.

I worried about what would happen if the group didn't survive, since there certainly was a need for it. For example, a new woman questioned me about the Secular Franciscans. She said that she had wanted to join a chapter, but when she called to inquire, she had been turned down. She told the man on the phone that she was drawn to the teachings of Saint Francis, and then honestly admitted that she was gay.

"You wouldn't be a good fit," the man said.

Elizabeth too had some concerns. She was the only child in a traditional Filipino Catholic home. Her parents didn't know she was gay, and were pressuring her to marry and give them grandchildren. Elizabeth didn't know what to do.

Richard spoke quietly about honoring our own truth. "We can't live by other people's truths, even if we love them. This is a difficult path, but what's the alternative?"

Richard's voice was weaker than at previous meetings, and his breath was shorter. Still, he continued to captivate his audience. I pulled out a tape recorder as he began to speak:

"All cultures and people have superstitions. A superstition is something that you think will influence your life, but it doesn't. Many religions are rooted in superstition. All tribal animal and nature-based religions are superstitious. I lived with the Papago and Pima Indians. They are Catholic, but they also have many of their own tribal practices based on superstitions.

"Sometimes Western, so-called 'educated' people make fun of indigenous beliefs. We call Native people backwards, but we have our own superstitions.

"There are many superstitions around sex and sexuality. They can be tremendously hurtful, and that's what we're fighting and have been forever fighting. But right now, the pus is really on the pimple. If we keep this idea of superstition in mind, we can become more patient and understanding, and less fearful.

"If I had known about these superstitions in high school, maybe I wouldn't have been so secretive. Maybe I wouldn't have been so afraid to be recognized for who I am.

"When I grew up, I used to study men and boys. I studied how to walk and talk and think like a man, and never let one drop of femininity come out. I wouldn't dare let a movement, word or a preference ever represent my feminine side. Now I realize that society may not need women's liberation. I think we need men's liberation. If men don't realize that they're not fully human unless they're a good part feminine, they're going to have a lot of problems.

"A lot of men believe that if you like to paint, garden, play the piano, or if you care for others, you're weak. As if women or the feminine are inferior? We have this superstition that women are bad and then we beat up on women and destroy the feminine.

"I used to work in the prison system. And I saw some male inmates there who produced remarkable works of art. They made beautiful tattoos and they'd create sculpture out of tin foil from cigarette packages. And I'd wonder at times, I bet a lot of these guys are in here for violent acts, because their wonderful creative natures had been suppressed. And then these natures came out in a destructive form. If we hold things in or are ignorant, we start to do destructive things.

"We certainly see this in religious structures. And most of the people making judgments about women and gays in the church are bloody queens! I saw this photo of the Pope the other day in a newspaper. Well, His Nibs was wearing patent leather red Pradas. On top of his white dress he had on what looked like an embroidered table cloth and a silk shawl that had ermine along the border. I swear, he must have been going through the Vatican closets from the 16th century. And he's calling us names? Get a grip, sweetheart!

"This is why we have to fight. And we don't have to do it maliciously. It just comes to a point, though, when you have to commit yourself. You have to speak up.

"I can't even go to Mass anymore because when I leave, I feel worse than when I went in. I was celebrating Mass until I got ALS, and this disease came just in time. Because I was believing one thing and doing another. I don't believe in playing games with the sacred.

"One time I was celebrating Mass at a church in San Francisco. From the pulpit, I mentioned that it would be nice if some of us, as members of this church, marched in the gay pride parade. Well, this woman stood up in the front row and went ballistic. She stood up and shouted 'That's enough! Shut up!'

"So, I shut up. I wasn't about to argue with her right there in the sanctuary. She got out of her pew and started pacing in the back of the church. The next day, I got a call from the pastor. He said, 'Hey Richard, I hear you had a little showdown at Mass last night.'

"I said, 'Yeah. A little. I'm used to it.'

"He said, 'Well, I want to see you in my office today at 2:00.'

"I said, 'Sorry, I'm busy.'

"He said, 'Then I'll see you at 10:00 on Monday.'

"I said 'I'm busy on Monday too.' I wasn't going to let him get the upper hand. I said, 'No, if you want to see me, you come to my office.' And I didn't have an office.

"He said, 'Well, we can't have you saying Mass here if you're talking like that.'

"I told him that was fine with me. Well, he was a good friend of that woman who chewed my ass off. And he was gay himself! He even had a boyfriend!

"The thing is, if church doesn't work for you, then start your own church. I mean, what is church anyway? It's people gathered together in community. It's a support system that helps keep you balanced.

"I grew up in an Irish Catholic family, so we had many superstitions. One was that repetitive prayer such as the rosary, or saying novenas, would help us. As if God was up there watching us, counting our prayers and taking notes.

"Thank goodness I grew into another plateau in my spirit life. I don't believe in superstitions anymore, but I do believe in having a caring heart."

Ben adjusted the neck brace that Richard now used to help hold his head up. Then Richard continued. He diverted a bit from his previous topic, and began to talk about prayer:

"Someone supposedly asked Jesus 'When should we pray?' He reportedly said 'Pray always.' I wondered for a long time, what did that mean? I believe he was talking about contemplative prayer.

"The way I see it, there are three types of prayer. First there is active prayer where we use words. These are prayers of petition or supplication or gratitude. Secondly, there is meditation. With meditation, we empty our minds of words or thoughts. Finally, there is contemplative prayer. When we are contemplative, we automatically recognize the divine in everyone and in everything. We become aware and mindful that everything is sacred. I think that's what Jesus was talking about."

"Contemplative prayer sounds like a tall order," I said to Richard as we drove home. "To see divinity in all things… "

He nodded. "It takes practice."

## Loving People We Don't Like

The next day I brought Richard some lunch. I exchanged Miss Piggy for his Tortuga breathing mask and stuck a napkin under his chin. Then I opened the foil around a fresh quesadilla and offered him a forkful. As he chewed, I shared something that was on my mind. "Richard, I was thinking about what you said yesterday. About seeing divinity in everyone and everything. I struggle with that. I mean, there are some really bad people out there. I don't think everyone is divine or sacred."

"Oh, yes they are," he asserted. "I learned that a long time ago. Because when they behave badly, it's not them. People are beautiful, good and holy. We are not what we do. It's like tinsel hanging on a tree. If people seem good, maybe they have tinsel or colored lights hanging on their tree. Or if they seem bad, maybe it's garbage hanging on the tree. But in either case, the tree is healthy."

I had my doubts about his answer, but I did mention something Deepak Chopra had said recently. Chopra was on a television panel discussing the recent gang rape of a 15-year-old girl in Richmond, California. A psychologist on the panel said that many young people have deficiencies in their pre-frontal cortex, the area of the brain that houses empathy. A deficit there might make people capable of cruel acts. Chopra agreed, but he added that the volume within this frontal area could change with meditation, or with parents teaching their children loving kindness.

Richard nodded. “We’re deeper than our brains,” he said.

I asked him if he had ever witnessed someone drastically change from bad to good.

“Oh yes, many times. I’ve worked with some Franciscan friars who were mean or controlling. Through changes in the church and through self-help programs, I’ve seen these men really transform themselves. Many of them are now very loving people.

“I’ve also seen it happen with drug addicts who some people believed would never get well. Look at Max. Max was a mess when he moved in here. He’d been in and out of so many treatment centers. He just could not get clean. But one day he said to me, ‘Richard, will you come with me to Nicaragua?’ He had saved up his pennies and he wanted to go back and see his family. I said sure, so we flew to Nicaragua and something happened to him there. I don’t know what it was. There was something he needed to make peace with, and he’s been sober ever since. And you see how he is now. He’s wonderful.

“In another example, we had this guy at the house who was very troubled. He got mad once and started sharpening knives. We thought he was going to kill us, so we called the police. I kicked him out, but two years later he showed up on my doorstep. He was homeless and had nowhere to go. I let him move in, but I asked him, ‘what will it take for you to change?’ He told me, ‘I need a companion.’ I said, ‘Great, then go find one.’

“He was straight, so he started dating women. At first none of them worked out, but eventually he met this woman named Barbara. They fell in love and are still together. He got some psychological help, and he’s now stabilized on his HIV meds. He’s doing fine. Yes, I think people can change if they’re given enough love and support.

“But you have to be careful,” he warned me, “You personally can’t change others. So you have to set up good boundaries, and protect yourself from any danger. You can sometimes stop people’s destructive behavior if you have enough authority; but ultimately, they are the only ones who can change themselves. We just have to learn to see beyond the horror of their outer shells. Because if we continue to hate them, that just ends up hurting us."

After he finished his lunch, Richard started talking about Brian, a man who had died at Marty's Place in the 90s. Brian was another "dump," a client that Richard had been duped into taking. "Some service agency called and lied through their teeth," said Richard. "They told me that Brian was a wonderful person. Well, as soon as I met him, I realized that he was probably a sociopath. That other AIDS agency was trying to get rid of him, so they pawned him off on me.

"I realized that this guy was big trouble, so I had an idea. I put him in a room with another troublemaker. The other man was black and Brian was white, and a real racist.

"Brian almost hit the roof when he saw his new roommate. They hated each other, but I told them they had to live together, so what could they do? They had nowhere else to go and they were dying. Eventually they both got so sick they couldn't leave even if they wanted to.

"Oh, that Brian! He had such a foul mouth! He was giving me lip one day while I was trying to take care of him. I got so irritated that I told him, 'why don't you just roll over and die!' That very afternoon, I went in to check on him and he was dead. He had even rolled over and was facing the wall." Much to my amazement, Richard started laughing. "And you know what? I don't have one ounce of regret over what I said."

"Where does this fit into your philosophy of unconditional love?" I wondered. "You just said we are supposed to love those we don't like."

"Exactly," said Richard. "And love does not mean like. Jesus said to love your enemies; he didn't mean you have to like them. We don't have to hang around and put up with their bullshit. Because we are all temples of the spirit. So if I let someone into my temple who abuses me, I'm as guilty as he is. Besides, this guy Brian was in a lot of pain. When he finally died, his suffering was over."

"How do we love people we don't like?" I asked him again. This was a question I still hadn't resolved.

"We just wish them well and pray for them. It's easy to love our friends. But to love our enemies? That's the kernel of the corn. I had to kick out some of the characters who lived here; but others... I made a conscious decision to accept them for who they were. That didn't mean I put up with their crap. But I realized that there was no way I could understand what made them who they had become. So I stopped trying to figure them out, and I made a decision to love them in spite of their faults. And most of these guys... I ended up appreciating in many ways. I found out that they weren't all bad. They had good qualities too, and some of them are now even caring for me."

## Michelle

Michelle was a tall, dark-eyed French woman in her early 40s. She had traveled extensively and spoke three languages. While in-between jobs, she had landed at Marty's Place in July of 2009.

After the last residents at Marty's Place found more permanent housing, Richard needed a live-in assistant. People were constantly coming by to help care for Richard, but Angela felt we needed a "point person" who could move into one of the empty rooms and really keep an eye on things. Since Michelle needed a place to stay, she was chosen.

Michelle was going through some changes. She had ended a long-term relationship with an older man, and although the two no longer saw themselves as a couple, they were still devoted friends. And on a recent trip to South America, Michelle had fallen for a younger guy and was considering returning to Peru to see him. While she was trying to decide what to do next, she moved into an upstairs bedroom at Marty's Place.

Michelle was extremely independent. She didn't define herself by her relationship with a man, and she refused to accept anybody else's definition of love and commitment. For instance, even though she had ended things with her former older boyfriend, he was still a serious part of her extended family. He suffered from a chronic disease and although he lived with another woman, Michelle often ran errands for him or brought him something to eat.

Michelle carried this same type of commitment toward other people she cared about, including Richard. She soon proved a very reliable member of our team, a rock we could all depend on. She was a stellar cook, and kept a steady hand on the logistics of the house by screening visitors, taking the pets to the vet, and making sure the garbage went out on the right days. She also took excellent care of Richard.

Michelle longed to return to South America, but she also had made a decision to remain in the house until Richard died. And like most of us, including Richard, Michelle expected that Richard was not long for this world. But we were mistaken. Richard wasn't going anywhere, at least not in any hurry. He kept on living, which taught us all a lesson about predicting the future. It just couldn't be done.

One afternoon, Michelle and I were sipping tea in the living room, and she asked me what had become a familiar question at Marty's Place. "How long do you think Richard will last?"

Because I was a nurse, people thought I had some inside information on this matter. But I had no idea, and didn't even want to speculate. I had already made the same mistake that everyone else had made in the beginning, when we first learned of Richard's diagnosis. All of us, including Richard, had scrambled to prepare for the end. Richard had written his obituary and designed his coffin. I had refused to enroll in classes or take extended trips, for fear that Richard was suddenly going to leave us. But he kept ticking away.

Eventually, we ended up in a suspended state, not predicting when or how the end would come. We chose instead to live for the moment. And this turned out to be a good thing, not only regarding Richard's illness, but also in terms of the rest of our lives. Living for today, without excess concern about the future, was not a bad idea.

However, as we sat there that afternoon, I guessed what was on Michelle's mind. She missed her lover and wanted to return to South America.

"Richard is sleeping a lot more lately," she noted. "He's getting weaker." I knew that she wasn't hoping that Richard would soon die; she just wondered if his excess sleeping meant anything. She was trying to plan her life, a life that because of Richard she had put on hold. She was in a difficult position – loving someone who was dying and yet having her own personal agenda to deal with. Many of us at Marty's Place were in the same situation.

I didn't know what to tell her. "If he's sleeping more, it could mean he's getting ready to go," I said, "but none of us really know. Death is always so unpredictable – and because Richard is such an unusual person, perhaps even more so."

"You got that right," she told me.

## Then Call Richard

Despite Michelle's concerns around Richard getting weaker, I visited him that afternoon and found him smiling and wide awake. "How are you?" I asked.

"Fine!" he declared.

"People are worried about you. They say that you seem weaker."

He laughed. "Everyone thinks I'm ready to croak. I can hear them whispering about me in the hallway."

His color looked good and his eyes were twinkling. He appeared as if he might be around for a while. Then we both chuckled about a sign that someone had posted on his wall. "If Richard dies, don't call 911. Call hospice." Under that, Angela had written, "Then call Angela." Under that, Jane, another caregiver, had written, "Then call Jane." Under that, Julio had written, "Then call Julio." So people were "lining up" to get their name on the list, to be one of the first to know when Richard died.

"Hurry! Get your name on the list!" Richard urged me.

"No," I shook my head. "I figure I'll find out soon enough."

"Better still," he smiled, "write, '*Then call Richard.*' When the time comes, that will really confuse them."

## Richard's 71st Birthday

Over 90 people showed up to celebrate Richard's birthday. He sat at the center of the room holding court, wearing a tiara and an embroidered white shawl.

I had by now been to a couple of Richard's birthday parties, and I knew what to expect. They were pretty wild affairs and basically, anyone Richard knew was invited. Guests included the wealthy funders of Marty's Place, the board of directors, other friars, his relatives, and the impoverished people who had been helped by Aurora Dawn. We'd all come together, and although Marty's Place had a limited budget, there was always plenty of food.

I recognized several faces. One was Paul, a black former postulant. Paul left the Franciscans before he finished his training, and now kept what he called "a healthy distance" from all that was Catholic. Still, we chatted easily about our shared Catholic backgrounds.

Paul grew up in Mississippi with a single mother who was originally Baptist. She joined the Catholic Church when she found a parish school that welcomed black children. Paul praised the nuns who had started the school, and all that they had done for economically deprived kids.

I asked him if he'd seen the film *Doubt*, which is about a black boy in a predominantly white Catholic school. The film deals with the issue of priest sexual abuse. A nun in the movie suspects a priest of sexually abusing the boy, and she reports the priest to the Church authorities.

Paul had seen it. "That film was very real," he said. "Priests have been having sex with kids for a long time. I was aware of it during high school. And when those priests would be shipped off from parish to parish, you know it must have been the nuns doing the complaining. Nobody else complained. Even a lot of parents knew about it, and said nothing. That's why it was very feasible – what happened to that kid in the movie. His mother suspected something was going on, but what were her options?"

Another friend, Greg, joined the conversation. Greg is a therapist and the leader of our secular group, as well as a former Franciscan brother. He had an additional take on the priest sex scandal. "You know 95 percent of the sexual abuse of children takes place within families," he said. "And in over 80 percent of these cases, the perpetrator is the heterosexual partner of the child's mother. It's funny how those statistics get ignored in our society. This isn't to say that child abuse hasn't been a terrible crisis with priests, and that it needs to be stopped. But it's sad that all religious men are often blanketed with blame, when only a small percentage committed these crimes. And it's terrible when pedophilia is linked with homosexuality, since most offenders are straight."

When I checked in with Richard that evening, he was chatting with Jeff, another friar. They were gossiping about some other Franciscans in the province and, at times, roaring with laughter.

Jeff, especially, bemoaned his life with other friars. Unlike Richard, he had been living "in community" with other priests. He complained about the daily annoyances of dealing with a bunch of old men's bad habits, grumpy moods, and fussiness.

"I got so fed up," he said, "that I was really reaching the end of my rope. But then I just adjusted my attitude. Now I try and accept these people for who they are, and I realize that inside all of us is the need to be loved. If I see my housemates from that angle and if I make an effort to love them, I feel better about these men."

I knew that Jeff was a good priest, and I guessed that he gave inspiring sermons. But now I saw him giving a pep talk to himself, trying to apply the principles of Jesus' teaching to his own life and to the ongoing irritations that we all have to tolerate in others.

He and Richard then proclaimed how great their brother Franciscans were. "They really are wonderful men," said Richard.

"We all love each other very much" Jeff agreed. "Men may not be as demonstrative with their love as women, but the caring and devotion are there, and you can feel it on a deep level."

## Personalities

At times, personalities clashed at Marty's Place. This didn't happen frequently, but it did occur.

Despite the numbers of people coming in and out of the house, there was only a skeleton crew that performed the day-to-day labor. People loved Richard but only a limited number of them lifted him, cooked for him, or made sure he didn't get bed sores.

Among those who did the hardest work, resentments occasionally simmered. I volunteered at Marty's Place only one day a week, so I remained on the periphery of Richard's nursing team. Because I was a bit of an outsider, I often became a sounding board for people's complaints. When I went to the house, I'd sometimes get an earful.

"So-and-so is too controlling and so-and-so has a bad attitude." "This one is messy and that one is stealing food."

Richard himself was well aware of these problems. He was adept, however, at ignoring them. He tried to love people unconditionally, to accept their faults, and whenever possible, joke about these household conflicts.

For example, there was a big hassle at Thanksgiving. A few of the workers were vegan, and they didn't want the holiday meal to include turkey.

"Oh, it was a terrible fight," Richard explained to me later. "There were feathers flying everywhere."

## Christmas

Juan loved to sing. As Christmas approached, he spent an afternoon decorating the tree and playing Christmas carols on the stereo. With his beautiful tenor voice, he sang along with the music.

As I watched him work, I warned him that he was putting up way too many ornaments. "You're only going to have to take them all down again," I said.

He didn't care. "I love Christmas!" he exclaimed, his eyes shining. Then he told me that he'd been up until two the previous night, decorating his SRO (single room occupancy) in the Tenderloin. He'd bought a tree and some lights at Goodwill.

"Who will come to visit you to enjoy the decorations?" I asked.

"*Nadie*," he laughed. Nobody. But he had a good time decorating anyway.

Everything at Marty's Place, including the furniture, dishes, books and artwork, had been left behind by previous residents. Thus, nothing really fit together, and it all reflected a wide variety of tastes and eras. A gaudy vase once belonged to an aging gay queen. A Silence = Death magnet from the early 90s still clung to the refrigerator. A Teletubby Christmas ornament was circa 1999, (the year Jerry Falwell claimed that Tinky Winky was queer).

The nativity scene or crèche that Juan unpacked was similarly mismatched. It contained an odd collection of little figurines from who knows where. Mary, Joseph and Jesus belonged in the same set, but the other characters, such as some plastic horses and angels, looked like strays. They didn't fit, much like the men themselves, who ended up at Marty's Place.

The weirdest part of the nativity scene was the dinosaurs. A plastic toy Tyrannosaurus, an Apatosaurus, and a couple Triceratops were all gazing down at Baby Jesus.

"Richard's idea," Juan informed me. Humor that only Richard could conceive.

Richard slept a lot, but when he was awake, he was remarkably busy. In fact, even when he could no longer use his hands, he still engineered a lot of the house's daily logistics. To do so, he needed the rest of us. We served as his hands, fingers and legs, but in many ways, he was still running the show. He seemed to become especially active as Christmas approached.

I wandered downstairs one day and found him dictating letters to Jane to send out with Christmas cards. As he did this, Juan stopped by to get further orders about Christmas decorations. He asked where to find extension cords, a step ladder, and more boxes of ornaments and lights. Then Michelle phoned from Trader Joes. Michelle was preparing a Christmas feast and Richard was designing the menu.

"Look at all these people at your beck and call," I told Richard. "You've got folks waiting on you hand and foot!"

"I know," he agreed. Then he started to sing, "*Whatever Lola wants, Lola gets…*"[13]

Marty's Place was packed with visitors on Christmas Eve. Before dinner, we all held hands and Richard said grace. As part of the prayer, he told us where Christmas came from.

"It comes from the pagans," he said, "and it's a celebration of Winter Solstice. The Romans and then the Christian's adopted this tradition. We light lights, but we're no different than many other cultures in the Northern Hemisphere. The Japanese have a festival of lanterns. Scandinavian countries have the Festival of St. Lucy, where people wear crowns of light on their heads. Hanukah is a festival of lights, as is Diwali, a Hindu holiday."

Richard then expressed his thanks that we were together, and his gratitude for the food we were about to share.

"Your prayer was very nice," I told him as we sat down to eat. "But short."

"There was nothing else to say," he said. "All that exists is light. That's what I think. Even sound waves are light. And Jesus said, 'We are the light of the world.' If we don't show light, the world is darkness. He also said that we are the salt of the earth. Without salt, life is tasteless."

## Owls and Oceans

Richard told me about one of the last times he saw his mother. She was in the hospital dying of cancer, and she'd probably had too much morphine. She asked Richard, "What is that big owl doing at the foot of the bed?"

"I had just returned from the reservation," he said, "and I knew what the Indians had to say about owls – that they are the harbingers of death."

"I hope you won't be seeing any owls soon," I ventured.

He shrugged. "I don't care if I die. I'm ready for it whenever it happens. And if it doesn't happen...well, that's okay too. The way I look at it, each of us is like a grain of sand on an ocean shore. The waves come in and the waves go out. They bring in new grains and they take away others. But the beating of the waves themselves is constant – eternal. That's all each of us is, no more than a grain of sand. But without us, what would the beach be? It wouldn't exist."

## Precarity

Richard liked to talk about "precarity," which was a term that Dorothy Day frequently used. "St. Francis envisioned that we were to be mendicant friars" he said. "In other words, people who went around and begged. When living like that, one lives by precarity. In other words, your life is precarious. You never know what's going to happen from one day to the next. But it doesn't have to mean destitution. You do have a safety net, but it isn't a bank account. Your safety net is your community. If one friar is too sick to beg, someone else begs for him.

"It's in line with what Jesus taught. Jesus told us to take heed from the birds. They do not sow or reap or store away in barns, and yet the heavenly Father feeds them. God also clothes the lilies of the field and yet they do not labor or spin. 'Do not worry about tomorrow,' Jesus advised, 'for tomorrow will worry about itself.' Each day has enough trouble of its own."

Richard talked about some of the problems that the Franciscans had since he entered the order. "They lost two big buildings in Malibu because of fire, and, with the sex scandals and subsequent lawsuits, the order has lost so much money... "

Richard didn't necessarily see these problems as negative. He said it forced the men in the province to live closer to authentic Franciscan principles – especially regarding precarity.

"But you need buildings to live in," I said, referring to the ones that had burnt down.

"That's true," he replied, "but we can live with the poor, within the general population. St. Francis never advocated that we live in buildings apart from everyone else. That was something Rome came up with."

## The Anawim

I commented to Richard that despite all the people who claimed to love him, just a few individuals did the bulk of the work around Marty's Place. Most of the nursing care was being done by men who had no money and their own health problems. They were risking their backs by lifting Richard, and sacrificing their sleep by getting up for him throughout the night. They were also the least likely to draw attention to themselves, to act like they were doing something special.

"It's always like that," said Richard. "It's often the ones who have the least who give the most." He referred to these individuals as "*Anawim*," a Hebrew word, which according to Richard, meant *the ragged remnant*. "These are the people who call us back to the center of our being."

"Like the Haitians?" I asked. It was impossible not to discuss Haiti, because it was late January and the country had just experienced its terrible earthquake.

"Exactly," said Richard. "I knew a lot of Haitians. I used to live with them. They are the most beautiful people. They have so much to teach us spiritually."

"What do you think about that whole Haiti disaster?" I asked. "How do you make sense of it from a spiritual point of view?"

Richard didn't have an easy answer to my question. He finally replied, "I think the bottom line is that you can't screw around with Mother Nature and not expect things to get turned upside down. You can't muck with the natural order of things. In other words, the people of Haiti have been exploited and abused for so long – sooner or later something this terrible was bound to happen. And it's not that those innocent people deserved it... but this is what goes down. For every action there is a reaction. It's like the priest sex scandals. The authorities covered it up for all those years and eventually the chickens came home to roost. Most of the friars were not involved in those incidents, but the entire province ended up paying for it."

## January 25, 2010

Michelle had made up her mind. She realized she could no longer put her life on hold and she decided to return to South America. It seemed that Richard was going to continue living indefinitely, so Michelle made the painful decision to leave. But before she did, she treated us to a goodbye dinner. As I watched her cook, I could sense her trepidation.

Throughout the evening, I saw Richard and Michelle engaged in intense conversation. Often, Michelle was wiping her eyes. As Bootsie witnessed this, she whispered to me, "After Michelle leaves, she'll probably never see Richard alive again."

When I met with Michelle myself, her mood was more upbeat. She said that she had learned from Richard that she really had to live in the moment and not worry. He had also taught her that life was change, and she repeated one of his favorite phrases, "To change often is to live well."

The next day we had a Circle of Care meeting. Our circle included Michelle, Richard, Tree, Angela, Rogelio, Max, Bootsie, Jim, Juan, Tim

McDaniel, two Kaiser Hospice social workers and me. Gary, another volunteer and former Franciscan brother, was also present.

One issue we discussed was the gap that Michelle's departure would leave in the schedule. Angela talked about hiring a paid caregiver, at least for Saturday nights. It wasn't clear how we'd get the money for this, but I trusted Angela's diligence in figuring it out.

Then we went around the room and checked in. Each person said a little about how they were feeling. Richard spoke at length. He expressed concerns about some of the communication issues in the house, stressing that we needed to speak openly with one another, instead of complaining behind people's backs. He also warned caregivers that if they were tired or resentful about the work, they needed to admit it and not schedule themselves for shifts. "Get out of the kitchen if it's too hot," he said. "Don't be afraid to say I've had enough." But he warned us to say it openly and honestly. "Don't just get mad and walk out without discussing how you feel."

Richard seemed unusually angry, and justifiably so. A few days earlier, he'd been left alone for an hour, soaked in urine. Another time, the person on duty slept through his call bell. He also accused some caregivers of smoking marijuana. "No puffing if you're here to work!" he admonished.

Angela had more encouraging things to say. She informed us that we were in the 20th month of her scheduling 24-hour nursing shifts. She also said that in her entire career, she had never seen a patient receive such excellent care. The social workers agreed. They had never seen anything like the likes of us.

When Michelle shared her thoughts, she again started to cry. She talked about leaving and said she had many conflicting feelings. She felt sad and excited and guilty. She also claimed that living in thc house had probably been the best experience of her life. Despite any of the problems at Marty's Place, it was the most cooperative situation she had ever experienced. In fact, as she was leaving, she knew that there would be others who were able and willing to take her place. That was the beauty of cooperative living, she said, and a lot of what Richard was trying to teach.

I had to agree. Our little community reminded me of the parable of the loaves and fishes. With more people around, there weren't always fewer resources. Instead, everything, including love, food and labor, had the potential to multiply.

Then Bootsie spoke. She revealed the fear she had about losing her brother, and through tears she expressed gratitude for how well we were caring for Richard. Juan also began to cry as he told us in excellent English, that he saw Richard as the father he never had.

One of the social workers brought up anticipatory grief. "Sometimes it can be more wearing than other types of grief, because we know we're losing someone, but don't know when or how."

## Big Mamma

Rumors were flying around Marty's Place. Apparently there had been a huge blow-up among some caregivers. Richard had been right in the middle of it. When I came to visit the next day, I asked Richard what happened.

"Oh, it was a big scene," he said. "There were fireworks. I haven't had so much fun and excitement since we used to get drunk in Montana."

I pried for details, and Richard filled me in. After he spoke, I considered what had happened, both with this conflict and with so many other problems in the house. When issues emerged, it wasn't that people so much resented the ongoing work. Yes, they were weary of some of it – but more than that, at times there seemed to be an undercurrent of jealousy. People loved Richard so much that they sometimes struggled to prove who could take better care of him. In many ways, the situation was rather amusing.

"There's some jealousy around here, isn't there?" I said.

"Oh yes," Richard agreed. "Everybody wants to suck on Big Mamma's tit." Then he wearily added, "But this tittie is almost done-dried out."

## February 3, 2010

All was still not well at Marty's Place. More difficulties were cropping up, and part of it had to do with a conflict between Richard and Angela.

Since Richard had run Marty's Place since its inception, he was now in an odd position. He had less control over his own body, but he still wanted to dictate a lot of the household decisions. And as the head caregiver, Angela had also taken on a leadership role. At one point, the two of them butted heads.

After they did, Angela turned in her resignation. Richard told me his side of the argument, but as with all conflicts, there were many perspectives. I didn't hear Angela's account because at the time the incident happened, I hardly knew Angela at all. So I was startled one day when she called me and asked if I wanted to take over her job. Angela, Jane and I were the only registered nurses around the house. Jane was a research RN who had known Richard for many years and had once been on the Aurora Dawn Board. She currently did the bookkeeping for Marty's Place and wasn't interested in taking on more responsibilities. So Angela called me.

I managed to say no. I simply didn't have the time.

"I don't care if Angela leaves," Richard told me. "I can run things around here. We'll get along fine without her."

The Aurora Dawn Board felt differently. They wanted Angela to stay, and this ignited more disputes and discussions in our circle.

"What a mess!" I said to Richard. The house appeared to be hanging in what Richard and Dorothy Day described as *precarity.*

"Conflict is good," Richard told me. "Sometimes, in the course of human interactions, somebody will lay a surprise on the table. A grenade."

"Oh, great," I said.

"And it will explode. And personally, as far as things around here are concerned, I'm not afraid to be the one to take the bruising. Because often, inside the fragments, if you look close enough – you can find a pearl."

As the days wore on and the conflicts continued, I asked Richard, "Where is that pearl you were talking about? I keep looking for it."

"It's growing," he answered. "It might be just a grain of sand right now, but it's growing."

## Felipe

A new resident moved into Michelle's room. Before Michelle left, she'd found a friend who was looking for a place to stay, and she invited him to meet Richard and some of the caregivers. His name was Felipe. He agreed to do some gardening and day shifts in exchange for rent, but he couldn't work any nights.

"I think some of the caregivers are upset that Felipe can't do nights," I told Richard.

"Well, what do they want?" he asked. "Do they have any alternatives? Do they have anyone else they know who can help us out right now? Michelle was doing us a favor by finding Felipe."

"Maybe we should have gotten a copy of his ID. I mean, we don't really know him. You yourself have said that people will tell you anything when they need a place to stay."

"He'll be fine," said Richard.

I wasn't so sure, although Felipe seemed nice enough and I trusted Michelle's judgment. Apparently he had a wife and kids back in Mexico, and he was up here selling Mexican artwork.

"He's straight," I mentioned. "He might not feel connected with this place because he's not gay."

"Michelle isn't gay."

"Yeah, but Michelle is a woman. Women can be a lot more nurturing than men... at least straight men. Michelle really took on the work of caring for you – just like a lot of the gay guys do. I just hope Felipe will work out."

"Of course he'll work out. Didn't you and I work out? What kind of litmus test do you have to put people through in order to prove that they deserve a place to sleep? If there are problems, we'll deal with them. But why stress out worrying about things that probably won't even happen?"

I felt a little embarrassed. And I perhaps felt like some of the Aurora Dawn Board members did when Richard suggested that Marty's Place be given away after he died.

"We can't just give this place away!" some of them had declared. "It's worth almost $2 million! What if the people who receive it don't use it the way they're supposed to?"

"That's not our problem," Richard had told them, and eventually he'd won out. Somehow he'd gotten them to see his point of view. Marty's Place had existed in a spirit of openness and giving since it began. Richard didn't feel that his death should change anything.

"Besides," Richard said to me, "I've always believed that if someone shows up on my doorstep, it's for a reason. This place might be a real blessing for Felipe. And he might be a blessing for us. We'll just have to wait and see."

## February 7, 2010

The winter rains had washed away the dust and the occasional whiffs of urine and garbage that one sometimes caught in the Mission. For the moment at least, the streets were fresh and clean. Likewise, a lot of the conflicts at Marty's Place seemed to be subsiding.

Angela had decided to stay on and the Aurora Dawn Board hired two professional caregivers to help us. The first was Annie, a friendly and kind white woman who began working Saturday night shifts. The second was Maegly, a young woman from Guatemala who helped out during the day. Angela's continued presence, along with the addition of Felipe, Annie and Maegly, definitely helped alleviate some of the Marty's Place hassles.

I stopped by the house one afternoon, and found Felipe chatting happily with Richard. Like Annie and Maegly, Felipe seemed to be integrating well into our community. He was responsible and likeable, and people enjoyed having him around. Later, Ma and Pa Kettle arrived, and Richard showed them his coffin. It was completely finished, and I noticed something new on the cover. Above the coyote footprints was a labyrinth with a picture of a little stick man.

"That is I'itoi," Richard said, using a Tohono O'odham word. "It means Earth Maker. Among the Akimel O'odham the Earth Maker is called Se:he, or the Elder Brother. The maze is his Ki, or house. The maze represents the path that each human being must take as they walk through life. At the center of the path is death. As we approach death, we reflect back on all of the wisdom we've gained, until we reach the dark center, or eternal life. We need to follow the Earth Maker as we go. He'll lead us home, but if we don't follow him, we'll get lost."

## February 28, 2010

As I fed Richard lunch, I pried again into his wellbeing. "Richard," I said, speaking as frankly as possible, "How is all this? How are you doing?"

"Fine and dandy, sugar candy," he replied. Fine and dandy, sugar candy was one of Richard's favorite lines. He had learned it from an old Franciscan, Brother Isidro Garcia. Brother Isidro would always repeat this phrase, and now Richard had taken up the habit. "I'm doing great," he added

"No, seriously," I insisted. "I want to know how you are!" I told him I appreciated his unceasing optimism, but I wanted him to be honest with me. What was it like to be paralyzed and fighting for breath? Wasn't this getting to be too much? I needed to know the truth.

"It's not bad," he told me and his voice was sincere. "I don't know how long I'll feel this way. Now, if I lose my ability to swallow – that will be difficult. Or if I can't speak – that would be very hard if I can't tell people my needs. And the breathing of course. If the breathing gets real bad... You know, you never really realize how great breathing is until you get in this situation. Breathing is... better than sex!"

Richard considered my question. "I don't know why this is no big deal for me. You just adjust to it somehow. Or at least I do. One thing I tell myself is other people have died before. Other people have died of ALS and it didn't kill them."

I frowned.

"I don't know. Maybe it's just me. I guess I've trained myself for this sort of thing my entire life. I've meditated and I've practiced what we've discussed before – contemplative prayer."

Richard suddenly started talking about the catacombs in Rome. He said that inside the catacombs, are some hieroglyphic pictures of early Christians. The Christians are holding both of their hands up to the sky.

"The way I see it," Richard explained, "they weren't holding their hands up to plead and beg to God. They were reaching up to receive all of his blessings. We do the same thing when we say Mass as priests. We hold up our hands. And Evangelical Christians also do that. You see them praying and singing with their arms in the air. For me, life has been like an endless stream of gifts raining down from the heavens. Even now, how can I feel sad when there are so many wonderful things happening all around me?"

## Tim

Tim McDaniel spent a lot of time at Marty's Place. He lived in Oakland, but he drove over to help us several times a week. When Tim was with us, he really put his time to good use. It was not uncommon to find him crawling under furniture fixing some electrical outlet, or bathing Plumita or shaving Richard.

Tim was a big, burly Irishman with a flock of white wavy hair. He looked more like a lumberjack than a once pious seminarian. He and Richard had known each other since their days at the Santa Barbara Mission. Tim eventually dropped out of his clerical studies. He ended up marrying, and had worked for years as a probation officer.

He didn't seem to regret leaving the seminary, and he spoke fondly of his wife and son. Still, I couldn't help but think he'd make a wonderful priest. When I told him so, he replied, "A priest is only a title. It means nothing. We can all live 'priestly' lives in whatever we do. We can be parents, teachers, nurses, whatever – and still bring to our work some core values."

Tim loved his former job as a probation officer, and he sounded good at it. The clients adored him, even if he was hauling them off in handcuffs. He told me stories of hardened criminals crying on his shoulder, or inviting him to their weddings or their GED graduations.

"Things have changed a lot in that field," he admitted. "They used to call probation officers 'social workers with badges,' and now they call them 'cops without guns.'" Tim said that due to cutbacks, probation officers have a bigger work load now and they deal with tougher cases. "But working when I did – it renewed my faith in human goodness. People aren't bad," he said. "They just do stupid things and then get arrested. And often they do these things because they come from screwed-up backgrounds. I did encounter a few *really* bad people, but only few. Maybe about 10 out of hundreds of clients I've met."

I asked Tim if he still considered himself a Catholic.

"I'm a Christian, but I don't go to church, except for special occasions like Easter or a wedding. I do believe in the teachings of Jesus, because they make sense. Be kind, be helpful, be honest... these lessons are a good model for living."

Tim often went camping by himself in the wilderness. He wasn't a friar anymore, but he still felt a call to peace and silence.

We talked about the big mess that the Pope had gotten himself into. This was during March of 2010, when Benedict XVI was being implicated in some of the priest sexual abuse cover ups. The Pope was saying nothing, despite rising criticism.

"The Vatican is trying to preserve the structure of the church," Tim explained, "but it's losing its basic principles. That's the problem with structure. Just like with Saint Francis. Francis had this great idea about living and working with the poor, but what he did wasn't institutionalized. Structure is sometimes good, but you've got to watch out. When you create an organization out of a movement, you don't want to lose the movement's original meaning.

"It's like marketing my grandma's apple pie. She made this killer pie, but she didn't follow a recipe. She just threw in a little of this and a little of that... You could never duplicate what she did by writing it down.

"It's like what Richard is doing here. After he dies we could preserve this building and continue his work, but it wouldn't be the same. All you would have would be the building – the structure. So it's good that they're giving Marty's Place away to another AIDS organization."

Richard suddenly interrupted our conversation. "I'm hungry!" he exclaimed.

"Well, what do you want for lunch?" Tim asked.

"I don't care," Richard replied.

"Well, if you don't care," said Tim, "then how about a cat turd on a stick? Jeez... I get so sick of trying to figure out what I'm supposed to feed you!"

This was the way the two men talked to each other. They were constantly giving each other a hard time and throwing insults back and forth. One time Tim told me about one of his camping trips. "The place was so open and isolated," he said, "I just took off all my clothes and bathed in the river."

"I hope there weren't any bears around," said Richard. "Because if they saw you with your clothes off, you would have scared the hell out of them."

Another time, Richard was telling a long story and Tim interrupted. "I've heard that story a million times. *Cállate!*" Shut up.

They loved each other dearly, but that was the way they talked.

## Choosing to be Gay

"Someone once asked me," said Richard, "if I had a choice – would I choose to be born gay? I answered, 'That's a no-brainer. Of course I would choose to be gay.'

"I've always liked the word *queer*," Richard continued. "Some Irish authors liked it too. James Joyce used it a lot. It means *different, special.* It just has a ring to it. And as far as being gay – it can be a gift not to be accepted into the mainstream. It's a challenge to grow."

Then Richard spoke about his $50^{th}$ high school class reunion in Montana. He had officiated at the reunion's Mass. During the sermon he shared a gospel passage. It had to do with the years that Jesus lived with his parents. "The gospel tells us," said Richard, "that Jesus lived with Mary and Joseph where he grew in age, wisdom and grace."

Richard explained how he had incorporated this scripture into the sermon for his former classmates. "I started out with the concept of age, because we were all growing older. It had been over 50 years since many of us had even seen each other. I told my classmates that age is a blessing, that living through years is a good thing. And then I spoke of wisdom. I quoted Socrates, who said that the heart of wisdom is to know yourself. And Jesus asked 'What good does it do to gain the whole world and forfeit your soul?'

"And then right there during Mass, I said, 'And for me personally – I didn't know I was queer until I was 21.' You could have heard a pin drop. Mind you, this was Montana! Some of these people were from the back woods. But I kept on talking. I said that back then, I was probably the only one who didn't know I was gay. Even Sister Mary Jean, our beloved teacher, used to always say, 'Oh Dickie, you're such a queer duck!'"

The congregation howled with laughter, and one woman in the front row began to weep. "Tears literally poured out of her eyes," said Richard. "Later she came up to me and gave me a big hug. She said that was the most wonderful sermon she had ever heard. I guess maybe my words had brought up some personal realization, something within herself that she had never confronted."

I shook my head with amazement. "Richard, you are too much." Then I asked, "What about grace? What did you say about grace?"

"Grace," he explained, "is realizing that we are good, valuable, and surrounded in light. That we are special. Grace means that we are the Christ. That each of us is the anointed one."

## March 21, 2010

On March 21st, Rebecca, Rogelio and I drove Richard up to San Damiano for another Day of Dialogue. We put the BiPAP in the van and plugged it into the cigarette lighter. This was the first time my girlfriend Rebecca had accompanied me to San Damiano, and I was pleased to have her along. She too had grown to love Richard, and she suspected that this might be his last public appearance.

When we arrived, only a handful of people greeted us. Perhaps they were out enjoying the beautiful spring day.

"It doesn't matter," said Richard when he saw the small turnout. "We always have a good time no matter who is here."

Ma and Pa Kettle were present, along with Elizabeth, the Filipina lesbian; May, an older woman who had a gay son, and of course, Neil.

Rogelio plugged the BiPAP into an electrical outlet and adjusted Miss Piggy's long hose. Neil stared at the hose, and then told Richard, "You look like an elephant."

"Which end?" Richard shot back.

The subject of backsides came up again when Richard was sitting beside me. I glanced at him, and I was struck by how much he was shrinking. Richard had always been quite buff, but he was losing muscle mass. He seemed to be slowly deflating, like a tired balloon.

"Is he getting lighter?" I asked Rogelio.

"I guess so," Rogelio replied. "I think he's getting flabby."

"Yeah," Richard concurred. "Somebody told me that my ass looks like two lace curtains blowing in the wind."

Elizabeth began the discussion. She said that her parents, who lived in the Philippines, had stopped pressuring her to marry. She hadn't yet come out to them, but perhaps they were beginning to take a hint. "They still want me to have a baby," she laughed. "The other day my mother phoned and asked how much it would cost to preserve my eggs. I guess she thinks I'm getting too old too fast, and wants insurance that she'll be a grandmother. When I told her it might be $10,000 or more, she actually offered to find the money."

Rogelio shared a story about the difficulties he'd had in coming out to his own Mexican-American Catholic family. When he first revealed he was gay, all three of his sisters cried. And then, after sniffling and wiping away tears, one managed to ask "What do two men do together in bed?"

"*Hermanita!*" Rogelio had exclaimed. "I don't ask what you and your husband do in bed! *Ay Caramba*! Nosey people!"

We all laughed, then Rogelio became more serious. "But I do come out to my family. I come out because I have so many nieces and nephews, and my cousins have children and grandchildren. And I know that some of them are probably gay. I want them to know that their *tío* is a proud gay man. If they have questions, I want them to know they can talk to me."

Rogelio had a special place in his heart for children. He worked as a teacher's aide in a special needs class. The kids were extremely challenging. Many had severe mental disabilities or behavior disorders. But Rogelio never spoke disparagingly about the children. He loved them and his job, and like a proud parent, he would talk about the children at any opportunity.

"When I think about homophobia," said Rogelio, "I think about the problems that I sometimes have with the kids at school. Homophobia is a problem. It's a behavior I don't like, just like I don't like the way my students sometimes behave. But the experts say that when dealing with children, you correct them just once. You don't nag. If you keep going on and on, and focus on the negative, what you're teaching is counterproductive. You say it, and then move on. And you hope that what you've said, or the example you've set, will someday take root. It never happens overnight.

"It's the same with coming out. You come out once, and then you move on to other things. You have no control over how people will react when you come out. But if you live with integrity, then maybe things will be okay."

Rebecca agreed with Rogelio's take on coming out, but she added, "Sometimes we have to fight. A lot of where we are with social acceptance of gays today has come from hard-fought battles. Look at Stonewall. Sometimes you really have to go against the grain in order to create change. I mean, where would we be with racism if it wasn't for the civil rights movement?"

One of Rebecca's main passions in life was political activism, so I wasn't surprised when she steered this discussion into the topic of social justice. She even managed to bring up the health care debate. Congress was voting on Obama's health care bill that very afternoon. Rebecca talked about the years she lived in England, where she had free healthcare.

Much of Rebecca's political efforts highlighted the unpaid work that women do everywhere every day. Cooking, cleaning, caring for the sick and for children – and in some countries, even growing most of the food is often done by women. Yet these women don't get paid. And many parents have to abandon their children to work in terrible jobs just so they can afford certain necessities – like health insurance.

I mentioned the care that Richard was receiving. Because of his unique situation, he had plenty of help. And thanks to Aurora Dawn, he was dying in a beautiful place with dignity. As a nurse, I knew that millions of people didn't have access to that kind of care. And even if they found it, it often led to financial ruin.

Everyone listened to Rebecca and me, and then Helen asked, "How long have you two been together?"

"Ten years," I said.

Ted and Helen had been together for over 50 years. Helen changed the course of our discussion by sharing something she had learned about marriage. "To love one another is a decision. Essentially, there are times when you don't agree, so loving each other is something you repeatedly decide to do."

Richard surveyed the room. When it was his turn to speak, he started where Helen had left off. "If you've never been in love, you're in deep trouble. You don't know what life is. Life is love and great relationships. Any right relationship lasts only through surrender. Both people in a relationship have to surrender. I realize it might sound masochistic, but each person has to become the servant of the other. When you talk about getting close to the quick of life – that's what life is. Surrender.

"'But I don't believe that,' you might argue. Or 'I don't want it that way.' Or 'I'm right and I can prove it.' Then you should be the first to surrender.

"Otherwise, there's no way you can keep a love affair going. There's no way, because our pride, our lack of forgiveness, our know-it-all attitude, and our judgments will keep the fires stirred up... the fires of discontent, anger, frustration and resentment. And pretty soon, that will be the end of it. You might live together. You might pretend you're friends. But love ain't there. So what's the good of it?

"In every moment and every action of our lives with others, we need to compromise. As we sit here now, during the health care debate in Washington DC, we should talk about compromise. Somebody refuses to compromise, and that's why we're in the mess we're in. There's no surrender. 'I'll kill you before I'll give you anything. I won't give an inch.

I'd rather cut my nose off to spite my face than give any person what they justifiably deserve.' So that's where we are.

"We all must compromise. We're not going to get very far in life if we don't. We won't have a good life. We'll be brittle. We won't be able to bend with the wind. We won't have many friends and we won't have love.

"None of us have all the answers. We might think we do – but they're not the answers for everybody. So for me, the word for today is surrender. In all things, give up your control and judgment of the way things should be. Because they are not always that way."

## March 30, 2010

It was Alejo's birthday. Max cooked a delicious meal, and the evening's guests included Alejo, Tree, Angela, Gary, Felipe, Juan, Rebecca, me, and Charles, a visiting Indonesian Franciscan priest.

Charles visited Marty's Place every year, and on this visit, he and I had a long talk. He told me that the first time he encountered Richard was in the mid-90s. Charles was visiting a Franciscan parish in the Bay Area, and Richard and Max showed up. Max was wearing bleached hair, earrings and a brightly colored shirt. He looked obviously gay, and Charles was taken aback by his appearance.

Charles struck up a conversation with Richard and Max, and they told him about Marty's Place. Charles was intrigued with the way Richard talked about the gay men at the house. Richard was matter-of-fact and nonjudgmental about the whole thing. This was new to Charles, since in Indonesia, homosexuals are considered sick.

Since meeting Richard, Charles' opinions on homosexuality had changed. He said that in recent years, when young Indonesians confided to him that they were gay, he was much more sensitive to their plight.

"They're usually in a lot of pain," he said, "and considering the climate of our culture, I can understand why. One thing I tell them is to study hard and succeed. If someone is successful, if they have a lot of money, it matters less if they're gay. This is unfortunate, but it's the way things are."

Through the years, Charles and Richard became very close. In fact, Charles chose Richard as his special spiritual advisor, and invited Richard to visit him in Indonesia.

Charles described an occasion when he took Richard up to the Papua Highlands near Wamena, to visit the Papua Natives. "One day, some of the Papua invited us into a tribal hut and showed us the mummy of their ancestor," said Charles. "Richard later emerged from the hut saying that he could 'feel the power… an eternal, peaceful power from the spirits.' He could feel it and smell it. He was so happy."

As Charles anticipated leaving San Francisco after this last visit, he feared that he would never see Richard alive again. He told me something Richard had said earlier that week. Richard was explaining to Charles that even though he had ALS, he didn't fear death. "The soul has no limitations in space," Richard said. "I will be able to go anywhere freely. I will come and visit you in Papua or Jakarta and accompany you if you need me."

Charles had started to cry.

"Don't cry Charlie," Richard said. "No matter what happens, I'll still be alive."

As Charles and I talked, Max prepared dinner and Juan dressed Richard. Plumita sat on a chair at the set table, like a human waiting to be served. Since Richard always shared his meals with her, she was more than ready for the party to begin.

Over the years, there had been many of these celebrations at Marty's Place. "We were always partying," Richard told me. "Even the men who were dying in the bedrooms – as long as they could eat, we'd bring them food, and they'd be partying too. And the food was always superb, only the best."

Didn't I know it. These gay guys could cook!

Plumita became very excited when we sang Happy Birthday. She panted and waved her tail.

"She recognizes Happy Birthday," Max explained. "She knows it means she's going to get cake."

## Rogelio

Rogelio's school was having a day of silence. Those who didn't speak were demonstrating their support of gay and lesbian students. We were discussing this one afternoon at Marty's Place – how wonderful it was that young people, both gay and straight, had participated.

"A day of silence?" Richard asked. "Do you think even *Rogelio* stayed silent?!"

We all laughed, for we knew what Richard meant. Rogelio loved to talk. The previous night he had come to my apartment for dinner, and three hours after the meal, we were still sitting at the table. Rogelio chatted nonstop. I didn't mind, since he was a great storyteller.

I had known Rogelio for several years, but that night he told me some more details about his life. I learned that even though he was gay, he'd once been married to a woman.

"She thought she could make me straight," he said. At the time, before he stopped drinking, part of him hoped that she'd succeed.

But it didn't take long for him to realize that this marriage business wasn't going to work for him. "No offense," he told me, "but I have a hard time understanding women."

He described a time when his wife had flung herself onto the bed, sobbing.

"*¿Qué te pasa, Maria?*" he had asked her. What's wrong?

"*¡Nada!*" She told him. Nothing.

"I was so stupid," said Rogelio. "I didn't understand women, and I took what she said as literal. She told me nothing was wrong… so I went back into the living room and watched TV. Pretty soon, she appeared in front of me with her hands on her hips, completely exasperated. 'Uh….' I told her, 'Could you please move away from the TV? I can't see the screen.' Man, did she get angry when I said that! She got angry a lot of other times too.

"She'd get so fed up with me, that she'd frequently pack up and leave. It happened so often that I could see it coming. So one time, I packed her bag for her. Not in a mean way. Not like I was kicking her out. I was just trying to be helpful."

Rogelio pantomimed packing a bag, in the precise and thoughtful way that some gay men might do. "I knew what she always took with her," he said. "A clean pair of underwear, socks, her toothbrush and soap... "

He also told me more about his friendship with Richard. The two men had met in Arizona in the early 80s. Even though Rogelio was part Yuma, he was living near the Pima reservation where Richard worked. Rogelio was only 18 when he started going to Richard's church.

"The services were beautiful," said Rogelio. "And people loved Richard. He's always been about living in simplicity and spreading joy. The people in the desert were beautiful too – so generous and yet very poor." Richard hired Rogelio to do odd jobs around the church, and in time, Rogelio moved into Richard's house. There were others living there too, Rogelio recalled, including the Central American refugees who Richard had helped smuggle north. "It was all about living in community," said Rogelio. "Just like today. That was Richard's life."

Rogelio confided that he felt some sadness these days when he saw how Richard's spiritual beliefs had evolved. As Rogelio spoke, he fingered a gold crucifix around his own neck. "Back then, Richard was more of a Christian. Now he says he doesn't believe in God, and that is sad to me. But on the other hand, he's still living as a true follower of Jesus."

Meeting Richard changed Rogelio's life. Richard started him on a path that, 30 years later, Rogelio is still walking. Like Richard, Rogelio lived for a while in a Catholic Worker House in New York City. It was there that he came out as a gay man. And as with the Native Americans in the desert, Rogelio spoke very respectfully of the Catholic Workers.

"They were the most wonderful people. A lot of them were very educated and had other options in life. But they chose to live with the poor."

It was no accident that Rogelio ended up in San Francisco. Through the years, he never lost touch with his old friend, Richard Purcell, who was eventually instrumental in helping Rogelio give up booze.

Rogelio then told me about the children at his school. "Those disabled kids are something else," he said. He mentioned the children who were severely mentally challenged. "People get frustrated with them because they do inappropriate things, like run up and down the hallway, or like this one little girl who is always sticking out her tongue. But who is to say what is appropriate and what isn't? Who makes those social rules? What some people really miss about these kids is that they are filled with joy. I can see it when their bus pulls up in the morning. It is the *ka-razy* bus! You can hear it coming. You can hear the laughter and the squeals and you can see these kids bouncing up and down. What I see in those children is that they're happy. They're excited about life and joyful. Some very highly functioning people wouldn't recognize joy even if it was standing right in front of them."

Then Rogelio returned to talking about his wife. He felt sad for Maria. "I told her I wanted the best for her. I wanted her to be loved in the way I knew she deserved. But I couldn't do it. I was a gay man, and, at the time, a practicing alcoholic.

"After I left, she continued to call me. She would ask *'me quieres?'* Do you love me? I told her yes, but not in the way that she wanted."

## Gold Teeth

Bootsie and Jim were in town and we were all sitting in Richard's room, telling yarns. Richard told us about a time when he still lived on the Rez, and he visited San Francisco. A friend treated him to a marijuana brownie, and after an evening of driving around and talking, the friend dropped him off at St. Boniface, where Richard was spending the night. "I had a key to the entrance," said Richard, "but after my ride left, I realized I didn't have a key to the front gate. I couldn't get in and it was after midnight. So there I was, with no money or phone, and stoned on marijuana.

"I started to walk the streets, and I had this weird sensation that my legs were different lengths. One was normal and the other was cut off at my knee. My foot was coming out where my knee should have been. Can you imagine walking like that? But I had to – so I walked lopsided like that all night, wandering the city."

We were shaking with laughter as Richard told his story. Then we gradually became more serious. Somebody brought up the question that remained on all of our minds: When and how would Richard die? We hoped he'd die in his sleep. Sometimes with ALS, it happened that way. Too much carbon dioxide would upset the patient's gas exchange, and he or she would silently drift away.

"I just don't know," somebody said, "what I'd do if it was me who walked in the room and found Richard dead. I just don't know what I'd do."

"I know what I'd do," said Richard.

"What?" We asked.

"I'd quick get a pliers and pull out all his gold teeth," Richard replied.

## The Women

Through the help of Carmen Madriz, a social worker on the Aurora Dawn Board, I was able to visit the Women's Program at Ward 86. Located on the campus of San Francisco's General Hospital, Ward 86 is a world-renowned clinic for people with AIDS. Aurora Dawn contributed to the clinic's Women's Program by offering a free breakfast there every Thursday morning. The foundation also funded a bi-annual weekend retreat for the women, and free vouchers for food and clothing.

Long-term survival with HIV depends a great deal on a patient's health care and standard of living. Since women tend to have limited personal or political power, they have less access to resources. Women are also frequently mothers and caregivers who often put their family's needs ahead of their own.

Paying for housing is an enormous challenge in San Francisco, and most AIDS shelters don't accept children. Thus, it's not uncommon for women with HIV to give up their kids in order to find a place to live. And often the housing that they find is substandard or in unsafe neighborhoods.

The Women's Program has social workers, psychiatrists, medical doctors and case workers who address many of these issues. But when Carmen invited me for the first time to Ward 86, I wanted to focus mostly on one thing – the free breakfast. Compared to other programs, it wasn't much, but it allowed women with HIV to sit down together in a safe place and talk openly about their lives.

The breakfast was set up in the clinic's waiting room, where clients also waited for appointments. On Thursdays, the room was sealed off for women only, and any men seeking medical care were directed to another waiting room at the end of the hall.

Karina, one of the social workers showed me around and then led me to where the women were eating. "This is Susan," she announced. "She's writing a book about the man who helped finance this program. Please come and talk to her if you're interested in sharing your story." The women stared at me with blank faces. Karina went back to her office and I was on my own.

The clients were grouped together by race. Some black women were in one corner looking aloof and guarded. A few Latinas were in another corner, whispering in Spanish. A couple of transgendered females sat in front of the room, clutching their purses and waiting for their appointments. All of the women seemed to have a lot on their minds.

One white woman sat alone. She looked homeless and displayed signs of a psychiatric disorder. Another woman looked well dressed, educated, and very professional. The HIV virus, I realized, did not discriminate.

It took a while for anyone to talk to me, so I sat and observed. I felt out of place, but decided I wasn't leaving. I managed to say a few things. "How are you?" "Beautiful day, huh?" "*¿Qué te pasa?*" And then, finally, the ice broke.

Gradually, women began to approach me and open up. When one spoke, others listened, and then they too joined the conversation. Soon several of us were talking, until we became an impromptu rap session. We started moving our chairs around, until we formed a circle. As people began to chat, the hours sailed by and I lost track of time. The women were quite candid. I heard stories of drug addiction, prostitution, rape, homelessness, accounts of losing kids, and being rejected by families. I realized that "Women do not get AIDS" is a prevailing myth. And because there is so much ignorance around this issue, the women had to deal with rejection and stigma as well as the disease.

Despite the tragedy of their lives, these women were still able to laugh that morning. They managed to find humor in their stories and have a good time. And I sensed Richard's fingerprints on all of it. This was what Richard did, I realized. This was his recipe. You take human beings and put them in a safe place and give them something to eat. This works especially well if you find people who have no other place to go, like with the gay Catholics at San Damiano or the homeless men at Marty's Place. And now these women. You give them a protected area where they can be themselves. You add food, get them talking, and voila! They find strength and solace, if only for a while. And what I also heard from these women was spirit, intelligence, courage and humor. They were overflowing with all of it.

"We struggle," one told me. "We have dark times, but we love this place. It means so much to come here and connect with one another."

One white woman was very thin, and her skin was wrinkled from too many years on the street. She currently lived alone in a room in the Tenderloin, and was on methadone. She told me she'd been diagnosed with AIDS 20 years earlier, and in the mid 90s, she'd been given three months to live. "I was in this shelter for people with AIDS," she said. "It was a racket. The owners of the shelter would take people's money and resources, knowing they were going to die. The undertaker was always hauling bodies away, and they figured that I'd too be on one of those gurneys."

But she survived. Once she even survived getting hit by a car. "I was out walking one day and I got run over and they took me to the hospital. I had an emergency surgery, and they said I died on the operating room table. They honestly thought I was dead. In reality, I think I was just on a bad combination of drugs."

If her story was true, the woman had fooled death, and probably on a number of occasions. She escaped from the shelter where they were giving her too much AZT. She was introduced to some holistic medicine, and that turned her health around. She said she was on some AIDS drugs now, but the newer ones, and not too many.

"You have to take control of your own life," another woman told me. "You can't just take the pills and expect they're going to fix you. I work hard on my health. I'm dying to live, not living to die."

I wasn't the only white woman in the room with a notebook. There was another stranger present – a researcher from Stanford. She had announced earlier that she was conducting a study. She was trying to determine whether having a social network improves a person's health.

As I watched her, I thought about something that had always seemed very odd. I could never understand how academics used up so much time and money trying to answer some perfectly obvious questions. I wondered why research dollars weren't better spent on more practical needs – like in setting up more breakfast programs. Richard never had much use for the academic world. He chose instead to spend his life actually doing something.

## The Farm

The Earth Abides Land Trust (also called the Catholic Worker Farm), is located near Sheep Ranch, California. Among other charitable activities, the farm holds weekend retreats for people with HIV. Richard had started these retreats, and at the time of this writing, the program is still going strong.

Richard was a dear friend to Father Josef Trochnow, one of the farm's board members. Josef belonged to Richard's Franciscan province, and one day Josef invited me up to the Catholic Worker property.

At 74, Josef had broad shoulders from his many years of working outdoors. He possessed a ready smile, and a warm and engaging spirit. Because people were always calling him for counseling or support, he constantly wore a Blue Tooth. He also drove a 2001 Prius, which had been given to him by his brother.

"Do you get to keep the Prius?" I asked, as we prepared for our trip, loading up the car at Josef's home at San Damiano.

"No," he said. "We friars don't get to keep anything. The car belongs to the province, but I get to drive it."

"That must be hard at times," I said, referring to his lack of personal possessions.

"Do I look like I'm suffering?" he laughed, and I had to admit, he didn't. He lived in a beautiful place, reveled in his current ministry (serving people with AIDS), and drove a nice car.

One of Josef's greatest callings was that of a gardener. He was in charge of the landscaping at San Damiano, and the grounds were well-known for their beautiful flowers and organic fruits and vegetables. Josef extended this same love of gardening to the land trust, and made the three hour drive to Sheep Ranch almost every week.

When I opened the back of Josef's Prius, I spied dirt, tools, potted plants, and a plastic bin that held water and a large live turtle.

"I'm bringing the turtle up to the mountains," Josef told me. "I think he'll be happier there."

As we pulled onto Interstate 680, I asked Josef why he chose to be a Franciscan. He said he was first drawn to this life as a child in Los Angeles. He'd lived on a busy street and his pets were always getting run over. He'd lost several dogs and cats that way, and one day he saw a picture of St. Francis.

"He was surrounded by animals," said Josef, "and I thought to myself, 'If I were like him, then my pets would be safe and all around me.'"

He began his clerical studies in junior high, and never looked back. Like Richard, he said it had been a good life, which had led him to serve the poor in Guatemala, immigrant farm workers in California, and now people with AIDS.

As we climbed the foothills toward to the Western Sierras, Josef pointed excitedly out the window. He identified different trees, and wildflowers which were blooming at every turn. When we found the farm itself, it was shrouded in a magnificent forest of ponderosa pines.

Gradually, over the course of two days, I learned the history of the place. It was started in 1976 by a group of people, including Chris and Joan Montesano, who still lived on the land. Like Richard, Chris Montesano had worked with Dorothy Day in New York City, and in 1971 had started the St. Martin De Porres Catholic Worker Soup Kitchen in San Francisco's Mission District.

The farm was also built on Catholic Worker principles. Like Marty's Place, it strived toward communal living and serving the poor. It had sheltered battered women and their children, hosted retreats for foster kids and the developmentally disabled, and had provided retreats for recovering alcoholics and people with AIDS.

On my first morning there, I helped Chris do chores. Although a good decade older than me, he was muscular and strong. His face was stern and leathery, with a thick gray beard and clothes that were caked in dirt. He seemed firm in his convictions, and weighted down with the tremendous responsibilities he had taken on over the years. And as we shoveled compost and talked, I also discovered a man who was thoughtful and kind.

Chris inquired into Richard's health, then talked about the project that Richard had started – bringing men and women with AIDS to the farm. Most of them had no money, so offering them this beautiful place was a real gift. Richard used to drive them up in his van, and in recent years, Josef had taken on this task.

We talked about the vision of the property. One of its goals was sustainability. The workers grow organic food, raise chickens, and the sole power source for the 80 acres is solar.

Chris spoke fondly of Dorothy Day. He also had tremendous respect for Peter Maurin, who helped co-start the Catholic Worker Movement.

As we worked, Chris told me Maurin's story. Marin was a Christian brother, a draft resister, a hobo and philosopher. He was a prolific thinker and speaker, and envisioned a new world that was not dominated by industrialism and greed. He proposed a "green revolution," and a three point program of action which included round-table discussions where thought could be clarified, houses of hospitality where the needy would be served, and "agronomic" universities where people returned to the land. Now, well into the 21$^{st}$ century, people like Chris Montesano were still carrying on this vision.

Later that afternoon, as the sun descended, I walked across an open meadow with Josef. He pointed to various trees and flower bushes that had been planted in memory of people who had died of AIDS.

I told Josef about my brother Jay, and about a book I'd once read. It was called *A Grace Disguised: How the Soul Grows after Loss,* by Gerald L. Sittster.

Sittster's mother, wife, and daughter were all killed in 1991 in a terrible car accident. After this tragedy, Sittster noted a tree in his back yard that had been cut down. The severed trunk symbolized his loss; it seemed to represent the scar in his broken heart that he knew could never be repaired.

He began to plant flowers and other foliage around the trunk. These plants grew greater, stronger, and more beautiful as the years went by. Sittster's point was that some wounds in our hearts will never heal, but renewed love can always be cultivated.

"Since the loss of my brother, love is being cultivated," I said. "Especially with many of the people I've met through Richard."

Josef was one of those people, and so were these new friends on the farm. When I said goodbye, I was certain I'd seen them again... because I definitely planned to come back.

## Gay Pride

Edmund White, the gay writer, once suggested that the rules of homosexuality are determined by different societies. He felt that same-sex attraction was probably biological, but what we describe as gay has varied meanings.

I was interested in this perspective, because even though I enjoy many aspects of gay culture, much of it has nothing to do with my own life. For one thing, I struggle with the extreme emphasis on sex in the gay press or in the gay pride parades. In addition, I dislike the fact that LGBTs are often defined by their sexuality, when sexual orientation is such a small aspect of our being. We are, in fact, all complex and unique individuals, and yet so often we end up being labeled.

As June descended on San Francisco and the streets were alive with Gay Pride, I tried to explain some of this to Richard. After a while, I pointedly asked him "Are you really gay?"

"Damned right I'm gay," he said without hesitation.

"Well, what does that mean?"

"It means absolutely nothing. It's like asking me if my eyes are blue or if my skin is white. I'm attracted to other men. End of story. The only reason we're talking about sexuality is that it's caused so much pain for so many people."

Richard's analogy to eye color was in tune with the words of another author. In *Spirit and Flesh: Sexual Diversity and American Indian Culture*, Walter L. Williams discusses some Native Americans' historic perspectives on homosexuality. The Navajo felt that becoming a *nadle,* or gay person, was solely a reflection of a child's inner nature. Likewise, the Zapotec believed that one's character or spirit was one of the most important elements of homosexuality. This philosophy appears in other tribes, including the Lakota, who called their gay people *winkte*. One Lakota claimed, "It's obvious from infancy that one is a *winkte*."[14]

Since Richard was drawn to indigenous cultures, we talked about the book. Williams wrote that some Native Americans considered it good fortune to have a gay person in one's family. The *winkte* were looked upon as unique personalities with admirable gifts. One Navajo stated, "The *nadle* know everything. They can do the work of both a man and a woman.... If there were no *nadle*, the country would change.... You must respect the *nadle*, they are somehow sacred and holy."[15]

Some gay Native Americans held sacred positions in certain ceremonies, or were viewed as spiritual teachers or healers. Because they often understood the perspectives of both genders, gays at times served as counselors to married couples.

"It seems that LGBTs were woven into the fabric of these communities," I noted. "They had a place and they fit in."

Richard agreed, then added, "It goes along with the Native belief that we are all part of everything."

"What you think about Western gay culture?" I asked. I mentioned the things I disliked about it, including the exaggerated stereotypes that even the gay community itself sometimes perpetuated.

"You'll find that in any culture," he replied. "If you think of any group of people, you'll come up with stereotypes. But if you get caught up in them, or if you're part of that group and you identify with them, then you're setting yourself apart. You're practicing dualism or separatism, and it's not healthy. That's the reason I don't wear my Franciscan robe when I'm out in the world. And I never put bumper stickers on my cars. I don't announce my beliefs to the world like those evangelists with their bullhorns on Mission and 24th Street.[16] Of course we do have to stand up for civil rights, but the way I see it, the less said about gay identity the better."

## Who are We?

July came with more changes. Felipe returned to Mexico, and we missed him immediately. After that, a Franciscan postulant named Eric moved in. Eric was 30 years old and had dark hair and olive skin. Although people mistook him for Latino, he was in fact, part Pueblo Indian. He was taking a leave of absence from his studies, and he decided that for a while, he wanted to help care for Richard.

Eric spent his first morning at Marty's Place laughing for hours in Richard's room. The two men were so loud that I poked my head in the door to see what was going on. Eric looked up at me and smiled, "We're bonding!" Later, he took me aside and confided, "That Richard is something else!"

Richard's body continued to deteriorate, but very slowly, like a tortoise climbing a steep hill. By July he needed the BiPAP 24 hours a day, and he kept getting weaker. Fortunately, he could still turn his head and show facial expressions. He could still talk and eat. He also had some miniscule movement in his fingers and, if someone helped him, he was able to operate a computer mouse and a TV remote control. He could adjust the volume of his little radio and ring his call bell. But he struggled to do any of this, and often we'd intervene when it became too painful to watch him trying.

For the most part, he did nothing physical. And in seeing this, I began to really consider the importance of my own body and limbs. I'd read, have a cup of tea, take a walk, get a snack, see what was on TV, check my email, and do the other endless things that one does during the day. And frequently, I'd think about Richard, just sitting or lying there, dependent on others for almost everything.

"How is this for you?" was my refrain. Despite his optimism, I imagined his life to be pure torture.

"It's really okay," he'd tell me again. "A lot of this is about knowing who we are. We're not our bodies. If we identify ourselves as our bodies, then we're going to be in a hell of a mess."

"Who are we?" I asked him.

"We're spirit," he said, then added, "A Navajo woman once told me that the spirit doesn't live in the body. The body lives in the spirit. We swim in it, like an immense ocean."

## July 4, 2010

On July 4th, Rogelio got Richard out of bed and into his electric wheelchair, then left for the holiday. I was to watch Richard for 10 hours until Juan arrived in the evening.

Rebecca came over to keep me company, and we wheeled Richard onto the patio. When the sun got too hot, we tried to move him into the shade, but the wheelchair malfunctioned. It wouldn't budge, even when we tried to push it. Rebecca and I were unable to transfer Richard into his manual chair, and nobody was available to help us – so there Richard sat.

We pondered all this, then realized our first priority was to get Richard out of the sun. We constructed a "tent" out of a sheet and hung it over him. Then, as the hours wore on, and the air cooled, we wrapped him and ourselves in blankets. We chatted, read to one another, and eventually Rebecca went out to get us some *pupusas*. After we ate, I found myself becoming rather bored and restless, and wondering when Juan would show up.

"We're camping!" Richard suddenly declared, referring to our makeshift tent. There was a little gurgling fountain on the patio, and Richard nodded toward it. "We're camping beside a babbling brook."

## August 1, 2010

It was time to go to San Damiano again. I drove and Eric did the lifting. Frank, a guy with AIDS who had been hanging around Marty's Place for years, joined us for the ride.

"I'm not Catholic," Frank mentioned as we headed east toward the Caldecott Tunnel.

"You don't have to be Catholic to be part of the group," I assured him. "You just have to be seeking."

"I'm not seeking either," he laughed. "I'm single and I want to be sought."

*Richard and his mother in 1947*

*Richard in 1961*

*Richard at ordination*

*Richard and Groody circa 1976*

*Marty Purcell*

*Richard at Catholic Worker Farm*

*Chandika*

*Tim and Plumita*

*Jane and Richard painting his cardboard coffin*

*Joseph Enos and mourners at Richard's grave*

Frank had a sad story. His father was a famous politician and his family had feared that Frank's coming out would harm his father's career. This had pushed Frank deeper into the closet, and had caused some major rifts between him and his father.

As we drove, Frank shared with me why he hated churches so much. They were places where his father would go to solicit votes. "My father would tell the congregations whatever they wanted to hear so they would vote for him. He'd alter his rap to please whoever he was talking to. My Dad never believed any of the stuff that came out of churches – they were just a means to an end for him. That made me very cynical about religion."

Frank was pretty much estranged from his family. He lived alone in an apartment, dealing with AIDS as best he could, and he spent a lot of time visiting Richard. Richard had become a lifeline for him, and he didn't have to be asked twice to go up to San Damiano. If Richard was going, Frank was happy to tag along.

When we arrived, we were pleasantly surprised by the turnout. It was large, with many new faces. We got Richard situated, and then it was time to begin.

One woman especially needed to talk. She had grown up Catholic, and had always deeply loved her faith. As a lesbian mother, she was raising her two children in the Church. Previous to having children, she had never had problems reconciling her faith with her sexuality. But now things were shifting. The children were going to catechism and starting to ask questions, and the woman was having a hard time aligning her own beliefs with what her sons were learning. Their questions, and the Church's stance on homosexuality, were playing havoc with her head. She seemed troubled and confused, and as she tried to explain all this, Richard quietly listened. Finally, he spoke:

"Some of you have suggested that you are at a crossroads in your life. You don't know which way you'll go. Each of us is always on the road, and I've found in the turns that I've taken, especially in my interior life, and in my attitudes about the other – the power that runs the universe, the energy of life – that if you don't change, you won't get to first base. Life is change, period.

"Fundamentalism is rampant in the world today. The reason a person is a fundamentalist is fear of change. For people like that, change is hell. For example, if you were born, baptized, confirmed, and married Catholic, perhaps you believe that you need to stay Catholic. Well guess what? Perhaps something along the way tells you to try something different.

"Many of us were supposedly born heterosexual. We acted heterosexual and some even married a person of the opposite sex. Well guess what? We discovered something else along the way.

"The Franciscans that I admire most are those who have the courage to change. Maybe a man has been with us for 25 years. Maybe he's a priest, he's ordained, and he's worked hard. For all practical purposes, everybody thought he was straight. But he was not. He was gay, and he had the guts to leave and to try something else. That is such a tremendous example of really living.

"I always thought there was a God like the one I learned about in catechism. He was a man, and he was sitting up in the stars somewhere, and he had a big black book. He was taking notes, and he was gonna get you if didn't watch out. I believed that, and as a priest I even taught it from the pulpit. I believed others, and I was teaching it to others, and they believed it. What a horror! Especially from a man who was supposed to know about life. I feel so bad about doing that. And I wonder how many people have committed suicide physically, emotionally, mentally, and spiritually, over the superstitions which we believed. We were afraid to change – personally, as a church, or as a community. That's what sin is.

"Someone recently asked me why I no longer believe in God. I said, 'It depends on how you spell it.' I don't believe in the God I was taught to believe in growing up – not G-O-D. But if you want to spell it D-O-G.... now I do believe in that. Because Plumita is my little goddess at this moment. She's faithful, forgiving, kind, helpful, constant... she brings me hope, love and peace. So there she is... my little God. But even that will change. Something else will come along. But that's how I see God at this moment.

"Family is vitally important. But Jesus himself said that community is even more important. At one point in the New Testament, a messenger told Jesus that he was being summoned by his mother. Jesus asked the messenger, 'Who is my mother and who are my brothers?' He then pointed to the crowd sitting around him, and answered his own question. He said that these people were his mother, brothers and sisters. So it's really about community. That's what it's about. That is supposedly the main reason for church.

"Allegedly Jesus never heard of church, never heard of Christian or Christ. None of the above. And he got killed because he bucked the institution. He told the high priests where to get off, and they didn't like it, so they said, 'Let's get this sucker.'

"And from then on, people who lived in high places, or wanted power and control, took that message of Jesus and distorted it, and that's what we have today. So we have to go back to zero.

"What's more important than church? My own spirit, my own integrity. My integrity as a person. If church is connected with it, fine. If it lifts me up and satisfies me, sends me out to bless others – beautiful. Keep it up. If it doesn't, drop it. And Jesus said this too. What good does it do to gain the whole world and lose your integrity? The real you never stood up. Why? Because of the teachings of the Church?

"Can you imagine taking the beautiful person of Jesus, reducing his message – which is true love – and putting him in a gold box, and feeding people something that looks like fish food?[17] Can you imagine the horror of doing that? And some big Daddy up there will decide whether you're good enough to get a piece of fish food? We've been at it for so long. Over 2000 years. That's a hard habit to break, but unless we ourselves, as individuals, forge ahead to save ourselves and our own integrity... if we don't do it for ourselves, then who will? And we have to start some place. We have to.

"All of us know these things, but who is going to do something about it? I couldn't go to church if I had to. Every day I am fully grateful that I have Lou Gehrig's disease, because it has kept me from going back up in front of a congregation to continue telling the same lies that I'd been telling for years. And I didn't have the guts to get out of it. Well, the spirit is full of surprises. It took me by the tail and said, 'Try ALS for size. Now you won't be able to get up there and tell lies anymore.'

It's very powerful, scandalous stuff, these sacred things. They're full of power.

"Some of you will come to the end of your lives and say, 'I stood up for my integrity, for who I was as a person,' or else you'll say, 'The Church said, the Pope said, people might say...' They're saying it about you now! 'Well, I don't want to scandalize.' Scandalize! Jesus is a scandal. Absolutely! That's why he got killed. And if I don't scandalize because I am the Christ, I am the chosen one, then Jesus doesn't mean anything. So a big part of this is overthrowing, getting rid of... changing.

"We must ask ourselves, 'Do I really believe what I've been up to in the past years in my spirit life? Is it really what I want?'

"So you know, I can only speak for myself. But in church I used to ask people, 'Why are you here listening to this fool jabber on about things he thinks are important? Are you here because the Pope sent you? Are you here because you were told to come as a child?' Well, you're not a child anymore. And it's not only Catholics who are blindly following things they've been told. It happens in plenty of religions. That's how it is. It's the same way with our sexual orientation. If I'm straight, then I need to be the best straight person I can be. If you have another orientation... why wouldn't you be what you are? Why wouldn't your integrity form your life?

"If any of you are confused about who you are, you might want to pray for ALS. Then the real you will stand up and say, 'Wow, this is what I needed!' We often don't know what we need until we let go and let Dog take over. When we try too hard in this spiritual business, it doesn't work. But if we let go and let God, wonderful stuff comes up.

"It's just about having the guts. And so many of you have done this. You were married, and you had the guts to get out. You were headed in one direction, and realized that this wasn't for you, and you took a turn. That's the divine. And it has nothing to do with church."

## August 25, 2010

I had been out of the state for several weeks, and I'd never been away from Richard for this long since his diagnosis. When he first got sick, his friends were so terrified that he would die, that for a long time, we were taking shortened vacations. But by the summer of 2010, we had all begun to wonder whether Richard was really in the process of dying at all. He seemed instead, to simply be living with ALS, which in his case appeared to be a slow, chronic disease.

So like others in our community, I began to venture away for longer periods. But after this latest trip, I was anxious to get back to San Francisco. I missed Richard and everyone else at Marty's Place.

Much to my delight, Michelle had returned from South America. She was still on good terms with her Peruvian boyfriend, but she had decided she wanted to live in the states. She moved into her old room and was immediately back in action, cooking her delicious meals and helping fill in the caretaking schedule. She shared the upstairs with Eric, and the two became fast friends.

When I walked in the door after my vacation, I received hugs and kisses from Max. Max was very physically affectionate, and he was also always showering me with terms of endearment. "*Mi Corazon!*" He'd say. My heart. Or "*Muñeca!*" Darling or doll. And sometimes I was "*Guapa!*" Handsome woman.

On this day he had a new one. "*Doncella!*"

"Doncella?" I asked. "What does that mean?"

"It means a virgin who is destined to be a queen!"

"Let's not get carried away," I laughed.

"I have other names for you," he told me.

"Perhaps some that are more accurate?"

"*Si, Maricóna.*"

A female gay. Now that made sense.

"Or *Marimacha,*" he added.

I pulled out a Spanish dictionary. "A robust, masculine woman?" I read aloud.

"*Si,*" he insisted. His final handle for me, at least for the day, was "*Machorra.*"

Again, I leafed through the dictionary. "A barren ewe!?"

"*Si,*" he replied. "It can also apply to a woman. A woman who has never had children. Like a *burra.* A donkey cannot give birth."

I frowned and turned the book's pages to "*burra's*" definition. "A stubborn, ignorant, and un-teachable woman," it read.

"Max," I suggested. "I think we need to quit while we're ahead. Please... no more Spanish lessons for today."

*"Bien."*

I followed him outside to the patio where he brought Richard a smoothie. Richard was soaking up the sun on a hot day. His electric wheelchair was tilted back, and his robe was wide open. He was literally sun bathing in the nude, and the fact that I could see him, didn't trouble him in the least.

*"Hola Susanna!"* He smiled as I kissed him on the forehead. "Welcome back!"

Max dramatically plucked a leaf off a fig tree and placed it over Richard's privates. "There," he said, "Now you're decent."

"I'm always decent!" Richard argued.

If seeing Richard decked only in a fig leaf wasn't enough to remind me that I had returned to this beloved (but zany) environment, Tim suddenly appeared with a bedpan on his head.

"Hello Susan," he said. He bowed and tipped the bedpan as if it was a hat.

"Hello Timothy. What the hell are you doing?"

"I'm trying to illustrate a point. This is Richard's new piece of equipment. He has a name for it. He calls it a fireman's helmet. What do you think? Do I look like a fireman?"

"I think you look like a *loco*. Is that thing clean?"

"Yep. I scrubbed it out with bleach this morning."

"Good," I nodded. So Richard had a new piece of medical equipment. And like his other gadgets, he had given it a name.

Later that day, Tim filled me in with some details. Richard was using the bedpan because it was getting too exhausting for both Richard and the workers to get him on and off the toilet. Now when Mrs. Murphy called, he preferred to do his business in the fireman's helmet.

So the disease was progressing. It was slower than any of us could detect on a daily basis, but when we took note of these types of changes, we knew that it was still crawling forward.

## September 19, 2010

A meeting had been called between the caregivers and the Aurora Dawn Board, and we guessed that something big was going on. We knew that there was going to be an important announcement when we gathered downstairs outside of Richard's room.

We also took the occasion as an opportunity to celebrate Angela's birthday. Guests arrived with a cake and gifts, and chatted excitedly before settling into a circle. Present were Richard, Tim, Julio, Annie, Angela, Tree, Rogelio, Juan, Michelle, Eric, Max and me. Also present were four of the board members: Carmen Madriz and her physician husband Ken, George, the board's lawyer; and Asli, the Aurora Dawn accountant.

Carmen opened the meeting by expressing her extreme gratitude to the caregivers for our work. Then she gave a special acknowledgement to Angela for all of her efforts, and wished her a happy birthday. Finally, Carmen got to the point of the meeting, which had to do with money. Most of us guessed that this was what the gathering would be about. The foundation was running out of cash, and they couldn't keep Richard at Marty's Place indefinitely. Since the shelter no longer housed men with AIDS, the foundation wasn't receiving HIV funding, nor was it accessing the many donations that Richard had helped solicit while he was well.

The bottom line, Carmen told us, was that unless Marty's Place received some miraculous donation, the foundation could only continue to run the house for another six months. After that, they would have to turn it over to Dolores Street Services.

Following a long search, Dolores Street had been chosen as the lucky recipient of the old Victorian. Dolores Street was another nonprofit agency that housed people with AIDS, and unlike Marty's Place, it had a paid staff and received government funding (which brought with it a lot of government bureaucracy and regulations). Marty's Place and Dolores Street were different in many ways, but Richard and the board had decided that the two nonprofits shared similar visions. And Dolores Street appeared to operate with significant integrity.

So in six months, Carmen explained, Delores Street would move in. It could then take on the house's huge costs, such as insurance, utilities and maintenance. If Richard was still alive at that time, he'd need to be transported to a nursing home in Oakland.

The announcement didn't come as a surprise. Most of us had wondered how Marty's Place had survived this long without clients. At the same time, we knew that the shelter was still serving a serious purpose. It was helping Richard die at home, and it was also providing a center for the many people who passed in and out its doors.

After Carmen spoke, she turned the meeting over to Richard. She asked him, in the wake of these changes, how did he feel?

Richard spoke through his BiPAP, and I pulled out my tape recorder. "I feel, "he began, "joyful, at peace and without fear." Then he continued:

"I've always known I will be well taken care of no matter where I am. The board is wonderful and always has been. I think it's just a perfect situation. There's no more a person could ask for. Really. When I will croak, I don't know. It might come sooner or later. But I have a hunch that by the time the six months is up, I'll be gone to La-La Land. That would be good, because then I won't have to move my shit across the Bay Bridge.

"I just think it's a good deal. I really do. I'm so grateful to the board, and I have respect for their feelings just as they are.

"I know everyone has strong feelings about this, and I suspect they are different than my feelings. As for the caregivers, who could ask for better guardian angels to gather round their bed, day and night, other than this motley crew? They are just beautiful people, and each one so different from the other.

"These have been the best years of my life. The reason being is that the other years I was so busy. First, as a pastor, and it's no fun being a pastor, because you have to deal with the system. I loved the people on the reservation and I loved the work, but the burden of being a pastor was tough. And then I got Marty's Place started. I had no idea what was coming. It was just – plop… it was on my back. So for 20 years I had a lot of responsibility helping people transition into another way of living. I loved it, but I didn't know how to get out of it. I was stuck.

"And so, when I was diagnosed with ALS, I didn't realize what was going to come down the line... but I know now what a tremendous gift this diagnosis is for a 72-year-old man who has to croak. What a gift, to be able to say, 'I'm sorry, I'm not responsible. You pay the bills, you do the dirty work... You do this and that because I can't.' It's great. Not everybody gets a gift like that.

"I never suffer. There's absolutely no suffering at all here. I believe in karma. I believe that what you give is what you get. And I believe that if people have given their lives for others, they have a peace and a joy on the inside that nothing on the outside can hurt.

"That's how it is. We're not bodies after all, we're spirits. Our spirit is in our body, or maybe we're swimming in the Great Spirit. Maybe that would be a better way to put it. Sooner or later the body stops, but the spirit still surrounds us. There's only one spirit. There aren't individual spirits, and there's no coming and going. No beginning and ending. These are just my thoughts, but to me, that's how it is. It's all about life and it's all about love. And if I've given my life and love to others, well that's what I'm here for.

"So don't feel bad for poor Richard, because poor Richard is extremely rich. I'm very satisfied no matter what happens. It's like I always say; 'I don't give a shit.'"

In his last sentence, Richard was alluding to one of his favorite comments. Whenever any of us asked him what he wanted – for example, "What do you want for dinner?" "Should we turn on the TV?" "Shall we read to you?" ... his common reply was "I don't give a shit." He never said this disparagingly, as if he didn't care or because he was depressed. He said it because no matter what was going on, he seemed to be content.

## October 3, 2010 – Back to San Damiano

It was time to go to San Damiano again, and Eric got Richard out of bed, onto his wheel chair, and into the van.

The two of us also dealt with the complexities of the BiPAP: lugging it around, untangling its wires, then hooking it first up to the van's cigarette lighter, and then to the San Damiano outlet. We had to do all this quickly, since Richard was able to spend less and less time without his mask. We rushed around during the moments he was unhooked, like race car mechanics at a pit stop. It was exhausting work, but all worth it to have Richard with us at San Damiano at least one more time.

After we arrived, we unloaded our cargo and gathered for introductions. Then Richard began to speak:

"What we have here is a beautiful bouquet. We have straight people, lesbians, gay men, a bisexual woman, and a transgendered man. That type of diversity is natural in the garden of life. That's how it's supposed to be. The trouble is, some plants take over a garden and crush out other plants. Scotch thistle is a good example. It's taken over hundreds of miles of land.

"I think meetings like this give us support and courage because we know that can happen to us. Because of our sexuality, we've often been pushed aside by the majority. We're trying to overcome this problem, and little by little, we're making headway.

"Some of you came to this meeting to talk about how God or spirituality relates to us and our sexuality. Personally, I've come to the conclusion that there is no God, or at least what we've been taught about God. He's not a man in the sky and he doesn't keep track of sins. He didn't get mad at us, and send part of himself to this world so he could die, and he wouldn't be mad at us anymore. Foolish myths. Crazy myths. That's my opinion.

"But there still is a God. We're surrounded by God. We live in and breathe God. We are God. And what is the number one attribute of God? Love. And what is love? Love is right relationships. Love is a well-ordered relationship between two people, or between a person and any part of creation.

"You can meet someone and say, 'Man, he's cute! I'd love to have him as my boyfriend.' You can go out with him for a while and you can say, 'Oh, I just love that guy!' That's puppy love. But if you want to stay with him, then you have to choose love. The first is a feeling and the second is a choice.

"'He stinks,' you might realize. 'He's mean sometimes. He doesn't come home when he's supposed to. He doesn't clean up the house. I sure don't like a lot of things about him. But guess what? I choose to love him.'

"So the bubbles have gone out of the wine. Puppy love is gone. But I choose to love and give of myself to that person. That's the main attribute of what we call love. And the love between people is the main attribute of what we call God. God doesn't exist out in the stars someplace. God doesn't have a mind. We make God exist by loving.

"What is the second attribute of what we call God? Beauty. So if we recognize beauty... first of all, when we wake up in the morning and look at ourselves with curlers in our hair... We could say, 'God, she's cute. She's a cute gal!' And recognize how beautiful we are – no matter what the world says. The world might say, 'You're too fat or thin. You're too black, white, old, or young. You don't match up.' No matter what the lies tell us, we still believe we're beautiful. That's all. We simply exist. We don't have to achieve or do a damn thing in life. That's not where we're here for. We're not here to get our name in the paper or make money. We're here to be beautiful. To be. Not to do.

"If I recognize myself as being beautiful and a part of the divine, I can see the beauty of others. I don't have to put them down or push them out of my life or expect things out of them that they're unable to give. They are God. God is acceptance. God is right here before me always, if I can see that beauty all around me and respect that beauty."

## Glenn Burke

Glenn Burke was a professional gay baseball player who contracted AIDS in the early 90s, and ended up at Marty's Place. Burke had an intriguing background, in that he was a talented athlete who helped bring the Los Angeles Dodgers to the 1977 World Series. Despite his athletic prowess and promising future, he was traded after rumors of his homosexuality surfaced. Legend has it that homophobia contributed to his ruined career, drug addiction and homelessness. In 1995, at the age of 42, he died.

Because of his remarkable history, Burke became the subject of a Comcast SportsNet documentary called *Out. The Glenn Burke Story.* As the producers searched for people who knew Burke, they discovered

Richard. Consequently, the film crew came to Marty's Place and interviewed Richard, who lying in bed with "Miss Piggy" on, became an important part of the movie.

The producers were so impressed with Richard that they decided to donate all the proceeds from the premier of the movie to Marty's Place. Thus, for many reasons, we were all very excited when the film opened on November 10, 2010, at San Francisco's Castro Theater.

The premier was sold out, and the theater was filled with an odd combination of gays, professional athletes, slick broadcasting personnel from Comcast, and a sizable African American contingent connected with Glenn Burke's family. Among the gays, there was a collection of old timers; friends of Burke, who had survived the AIDS epidemic. Likewise, some of the athletes present had known Burke back in the 70s at the height of his baseball career.

By uncovering Burke's story, the film's producers had lifted up a rock, and a strange mix of characters crawled out. These people had lived through an incredible time, but had never been allowed to voice what they had witnessed. In most cases, they had never talked with each other. Yet they now were altogether, beneath the ornate and massive domed ceiling of the Castro Theater.

The movie itself was great, and when Richard appeared on the screen there was jubilant applause. Many in the audience recognized him, and I couldn't help but believe that his presence cast a spell over the Castro that night. Before and after the show, people were talkative and friendly, and seemed to come together in a magical way. Barriers between queers and the world of professional athletes had been broken down.

I reflected further on the film when I was discussing it later that week with Richard, Annie, and my grown stepson, Curtis. Richard had watched the DVD at home, and the night of the premier, I'd been with Curtis and Annie in the theater.

Curtis surprised me by saying that he had some problems with the documentary. "The film was about this talented athlete," said Curt "who got kicked out of the major leagues because he was gay. End of story. But the filmmakers brought in all this stuff that wasn't relevant, like the fact that Burke was hanging out with gay guys after the games.

So what? That's what gay guys do. Straight players would be going off with women, so what's the big deal?"

Richard chimed in. He said he didn't care for the panel discussion (which he also saw on DVD), that took place after the movie. The discussion was about accepting gays into professional sports. Some athletes on the panel brought up that tired old paranoid fear – that queer athletes might be looking at them in the locker room. "And they kept using the term 'sexual preference'," Richard added. "When it's not really a preference. Preference means you've got a choice. It's an orientation, for chrissake."

Annie believed that there was definitely a progression in attitude between the older and younger athletes on the panel. The younger ones seemed more open-minded and comfortable with the whole subject.

I was proud of Curt, and intrigued with his views of the movie. He could be very macho and was undeniably heterosexual, yet he was raised in San Francisco by lesbians. He saw gay relationships as more natural and healthy than even many of us did.

"It was really something," I said to Richard as I described the evening at the theater. "All these important people came down to the Castro and made us feel like we were special."

"But we *are* special," Richard retorted. "And why should we leave it to others to define who we are anyway?"

## Richard's 72nd Birthday

Richard's birthday in November was another exciting event, but this year, he didn't come upstairs for his party. He simply stayed in bed while people stood in line outside his room, waiting for a turn to pay their respects. They brought armloads of gifts, and one Mexican man showed up in a mariachi suit to serenade Richard with the song "*Las Mañanitas*."

To everyone else who was having a birthday in November, Eric passed out decorative wooden eggs. He had found them in an old box when he was going through the house packing up things for Goodwill. In a speech before dinner he declared that the eggs symbolized "birth and renewal."

Throughout the morning, four of us women prepared food in the kitchen. Michelle commandeered the production, and her crew consisted of me, Bootsie, and Chandika Tazouz , the artist from Tucson who had returned to San Francisco for the event.

Michelle was in an especially foul mood. She hadn't been feeling well that week, and she was growing irritated with so many people coming in and out of the house. The constant flow of guests made things interesting for most of us, but since Marty's Place was her home, for Michelle, the lack of privacy at times got old. She also felt that as one of the few women around the house, she often assumed more than her share of household responsibilities. She complained to us, and later that day, she griped to Richard.

Richard listened patiently, then encouraged Michelle to talk to the people she was having problems with. "Let them know how you feel," he suggested. "They won't be the first diva queens around here to get their asses kicked."

## Chandika

Chandika had flown back to Tucson. That was the way it was with her. She would come and go like a bird, lighting down quietly in our midst and then disappearing. It wasn't unusual for me to walk into Marty's Place and unexpectedly find that she was back in town.

I was stunned at one point to learn that she was pushing 80, since she didn't look it. Although her brown face had been carved with smile lines from years in the Arizona sun, her body remained lithe and lovely. She was a vegan, but mostly ate raw food and practiced something called "sungazing." She meditated while looking into the sun as it rose or set. "Sungazing," she explained, "is living on Prana, an energy directly from the sun that fills the body and heart with light. It supposedly helps with longevity. And it also takes away one's appetite for food, as the body gets nourishment directly from the sun."

Coming from anyone else I might have been skeptical, but Chandika had a way of convincing me that what she was saying was true. Perhaps it was the way she said it. She just seemed so sure of herself.

She was definitely sure of the way she chose to live. She had taken a leap of faith in life many years earlier, and had never turned back. She loved to paint, so that's what she did. When I met her, she'd been supporting herself as an artist for 50 years.

As a painter, Chandika was especially drawn to images of indigenous people. She'd traveled extensively, and her work reflected native cultures from all over the world. "I found the most honest way I could represent these people was to live with them, and learn from them," she said.

She lived with the Tohono O'odham, and she writes of them on her website: "I discovered a People whose shyness is overcome by their humor, whose gracefulness shows in their dances and whose hearts are warm and accepting. Seeing within and beyond became even more important to me during the eight years I lived among the Desert People, and it was there that I learned the true meaning of silence."

"Is that where you met Richard?" I asked.

"Yes," she smiled. "He opened my heart and melted all the icicles."

Richard made such an impression on Chandika that she continued to circle around him for the rest of her life. Not intrusively, but just in her light, birdlike way.

On one of her visits to the Pima Reservation, Richard asked her to stay. "Why don't you live here and teach art to the O'odahm children?" he suggested.

Chandika was thrilled with the idea. She immediately said yes and proceeded to move into Richard's house. This didn't last long. Some of the church authorities caught wind of what was happening, and that was the end of that. I had to laugh as I envisioned the whole scenario. This beautiful, and at the time young, hippie woman moves into the priest's quarters – and Richard thinks nothing of it. He sees it as no big deal, so he's surprised when it causes an uproar. Needless to say, Chandika had to leave.

## December 1, 2010. World AIDS Day

In an effort to perform some symbolic ritual in remembrance of my brother, I made a rare visit to church. Most Holy Redeemer was having an Advent Vespers service, and a small crowd had gathered, bundled up for the cold winter night.

I sat quietly, listening to the beautiful voice of a cantor. Then Reverend Jay Emerson Johnson took the podium. Johnson was an Episcopalian priest at Berkley's Pacific School of Religion. He began his talk by saying he had never spoken in a Catholic Church before, but having heard of Most Holy Redeemer's reputation, he felt honored.

He said he was "hoping for a cure," and that he wanted his friends back. He added that he could have been talking about a cure to so many things – world hunger, breast cancer, war – but on this day, he was referring to AIDS.

He mentioned the recent suicides of gay youth that had been in the news. And he referred to all of us when he said we were paving a path. We were not leaving religion in the hands of those who might use it to hurt others. We may not see the fruits of our efforts in our lifetime, but what we were doing at Most Holy Redeemer would save lives. "Don't be mistaken," he said. "This is the truth."

## December 23, 2010

A year earlier, we thought we were celebrating Richard's last Christmas. "We were wrong," Juan told me, as he again supervised the season's decorating.

Michelle and Julio were planning the meals for Christmas Eve and Christmas Day. "You're having two parties?!" I asked Richard.

"Sure," he exclaimed. "Why not?" Then he added, "I don't need to do any of the work. I can just lay here and listen to the reindeer prancing above my head."

He was referring to the fact that he spent most of his days in bed now, directly under the kitchen. And from there, he could frequently hear footsteps, pots and pans banging, and squabbles when there were too many cooks involved in the house's proverbial stews.

Despite the merriment of the season, I had some worries. Richard had been having more trouble breathing, complaining that there was something wrong with his mask. But when we tried other masks, they didn't work either – not Darth Vader, Miss Piggy, Tortuga, or his latest models, Pillow Talk and Bongo.

I phoned Lee, the respiratory therapist, and she told me, "His lungs are getting stiffer." She also said that the BiPAP was nearing its maximum capacity. I knew what that meant. Once the BiPAP no longer worked, Richard would have to be switched to a ventilator or die.

After this conversation, I confided to Michelle, "Perhaps it will be good if Richard is transferred to a nursing home. He'll receive better care there." I mentioned that in addition to the breathing problems, he appeared to be developing a bedsore – something we had diligently tried to avoid.

"No!" Michelle disagreed. "He needs to stay here with Plumita and Pinto. Richard doesn't want to leave."

I also told Max that if Richard moved, Max would be able to get some sleep. Max had just worked three night shifts in a row, despite the fact that he was having trouble sleeping during the day.

"No, I don't want him to go into a nursing home," said Max, and he refused to give up any night shifts.

In suggesting that Richard go to a nursing home, I wondered whether I was being selfish. "I just don't want to watch him die," I said, "at least not like this. To have him suffocate when he's alert and aware."

"None of us do," said Michelle.

Both Max and Michelle stared at me in silence. Nobody wanted to discuss what had been on all of our minds, so we decided to go back to work. Michelle returned to cooking and Max to his vacuum. I went downstairs to check on Richard.

I had given him some morphine earlier during a bout of breathlessness, and he had drifted off to sleep. Now he was awake and feeling much better. In fact, he was full of his same old shenanigans. As I approached his bed and peered over him, he pretended to sleep. I was looking down at him nervously, studying his respiratory rate, when he suddenly popped open his eyes and shouted, "What are you looking at?!" I almost jumped through the ceiling.

"Thanks a lot," I grumbled, feeling rather embarrassed. Richard was laughing.

I shook my head and held the straw from his water bottle to his lips. Then I tidied up his room. It was a small room that was crowded with the gifts that people were constantly bringing. Flowers were a big item, as were cards, candy, DVDs, handmade artwork (which plastered the walls), and my personal favorite, new and fascinating books.

I studied the recent titles that had accumulated on his desk and asked Richard if he wanted me to read to him. He immediately said yes, requesting *Spiritual Envy: An Agnostic's Quest,* by Michael Krasny. In it, Krasny claims to be an agnostic who envies those who believe in any kind of spirituality – whether they're Christian, Muslim, Buddhist, participants of Native American drumming circles, or even New Age healers like Gerald Jampolsky. Krasny says he is envious of these people because they've found some comfort in their beliefs in the face of a brutal world. Still, he remains a steadfast nonbeliever.

"Would you call yourself an agnostic?" I asked Richard after I had finished a chapter.

"Perhaps," he replied. "I don't use the word atheist because it's too severe."

Using Krasny's own words, I asked, "How do you explain 'spiritual hunger,' or the need for every culture throughout history to seek or try to define God?"

"I think it's like what we've discussed before," he replied. "We all yearn for beauty."

"So do you believe that the myths and rituals that cultures design around a higher power are meaningless?"

"No, not at all. We need myths and ritual. They help us try and make sense of why we're here."

"But if you don't believe in God, then what's the point of any of it? Why be charitable or selfless?"

"It's like I said before," said Richard. "I guess I believe that God is love. But we ourselves have to form and fashion love. God doesn't come from a spirit on high. God is inside each of us. So getting back to myths and rituals, if our rituals are beautiful, they help us form beautiful acts. And it's through beautiful acts that love emerges. That was one good thing about old Catholicism – the beautiful rituals. Protestants don't have that, and Catholics have less of it since the Ecumenical Counsel. Now mostly all they have is a bunch of words."

"You quote Jesus a lot," I mentioned.

"That's because he says some great things. I love to quote people. I'd quote Peter Pan if he said something significant."

I wiped Richard's eyes with a Kleenex. Those of us who cared for him instinctively watched for the fuzz and moisture that often accumulated around his eyes. Without being asked, we would perform this simple task that he could no longer do for himself.

"I guess," Richard went on, "what I truly believe in is transparency – in thought, in speech, and in spirit life. So that light can come through, to get rid of what is opaque. This isn't about finding the right answers. In fact, the more answers you have, the more trouble you're often in. You don't need a lot of answers or spiritual teachings, except to live by the Golden Rule: to do unto others as you would have them do to you. That's all you need."

Maegly entered the room, and Richard and I switched our conversation to Spanish. Maegly and I changed the sheets and put lotion on Richard's skin. As we worked, I remembered a patient I once cared for who had advanced multiple sclerosis. Like Richard, he used to lie paralyzed, flat on his back.

"He referred to himself as 'the old cadaver,'" I remembered aloud. "He used to say after we were done helping him, 'Okay then, just cover up the old cadaver.'"

Richard listened and then nodded. "Yep. That's about all I am now too. An old cadaver."

Maegly tenderly brushed his wavy white hair.

*"Pero amamos a nuestro viejo cadaver"* (but we love our old cadaver), I said.

*"Porque todos son necrofilios,"* Richard quipped. Because you are all necrophiliacs. "A bunch of cemetery queens."

## January 9, 2011

Richard continued to endure some nights of severe shortness of breath. He was starting to use morphine more often, and because it required too much effort, he was no longer getting out of bed. Except for some tiny movements in his right thumb, he was also now completely paralyzed from the neck down. Since it was often hard for him to ring his call light, his caregivers had taken to spending entire nights in his room by his bed.

Despite these changes, Richard was in bright spirits when I arrived for my Sunday morning shift.

Rebecca stopped by and brought a book which Richard had requested. It was called *When the Body Says No: Understanding the Stress–Disease Connection,* by Dr. Gabor Maté.

Rebecca read aloud a chapter about ALS. In it, Maté cites anecdotal and scientific data, and he hypothesizes that significant numbers of ALS patients are exceedingly "nice people." He uses this research to suggest that ALS victims may cluster at the most pleasant end of the personality spectrum.

Aside from being nice, Maté' notes that many of these patients live selfless, hyper-busy lives where they suppress their emotions, including their rage. Case in point was Lou Gehrig himself, who sacrificed a great deal for his fans and his teammates. He played so hard that he broke bones in his hand, and he refused to take a vacation from baseball, despite excruciating injuries.

Maté goes on to question whether the personality traits of people with ALS might cause them to succumb to this illness. The author ponders whether a lifetime's accumulation of stress, brought on by repressed emotions and not taking care of one's own needs, may contribute to the destruction of the ALS patient's nervous system.

Richard was captivated by the book, and after Rebecca finished, he told us in all earnestness, "This is me! This is my life 100 percent!" He also said that he had heard similar impressions of ALS patients from some of the staff at Forbes Norris, an ALS research center in San Francisco.

"So do you think there is some connection between your personality and your getting ALS?" Rebecca asked.

"Oh, absolutely!" Richard said. Then he repeated something he sincerely believed about his disease. "I got it because I didn't know how to quit working. I was stuck in situations that I didn't know how to leave until ALS gave me a way out. For example, now that I'm paralyzed, I don't have to do so many things anymore. Like run this household or say Mass. As far as not showing emotions," he went on, "that's also me. I seldom cry."

"And you're selfless," I added.

"I'd say I'm more self-contained than selfless," he said. "But you're right, I don't like to ask for help."

"What about suppressed rage?" I wondered. Then I mentioned the rare times I'd seen him get angry. His occasional shows of anger had been forceful and even hurtful because they were so out of character for Richard, and so unexpected.

"Yes indeed," Richard nodded. "Beware the rage of a patient man."

"Well, why is that? Was it your upbringing?"

"Probably. Maybe. Who knows? I'm not one to analyze things. I don't really care, because I don't live in my head. That's why I never did well in school. I live in my heart and gut and groin. My sister Bootsie is the one who analyzes things. She'll talk to me for hours, trying to figure out why people behave the way they do. I listen to her, but I think it's a waste of time."

"But if you did analyze yourself," I suggested, "maybe you could... who knows... maybe you could... get better!"

"Why would I want to do that?"

"Why wouldn't you?" I thought. The logic of his question completely escaped me. Or maybe my question had confused him. I was proposing that if he changed his way of thinking, he could possibly be healed and rise up like Lazarus. But Richard wasn't interested.

I suddenly realized that I may as well have been asking him to get rid of his right thumb or his fondness for Earl Grey tea. ALS was a part of who he was. It was an enormous part of his present reality. And if he'd been telling us the truth for the past four years, it was a blessed reality. He looked at me like I was being preposterous.

I took another approach. "If you think that these personality traits caused you to get ALS, then, in retrospect, would you have lived your life differently? Like... would you have shown more emotion and been less selfless?"

"I doubt it," he said at once. "No, I don't think so. Because it's been a great life."

## Into the Mist

I was reading a book to Richard – *The Mist Filled Path: Celtic Wisdom for Exiles, Wanderers and Seekers,* by the shaman, Frank MacEowen. In it, he describes the beliefs of the ancient Celts. They felt that that the world was upheld and sustained by a single melody called the Oran Mór. MacEowen encourages us to seek the Oran Mór, or what he also refers to as "The Great Music." This music, he states, vibrates "...through all of life, from the microcosmic level of electrons, atoms and cells to the giant swath of whole galaxies..."[18]

He also writes that most indigenous or religious traditions have a creation story. These myths provide an "anchoring point of identity," and an explanation of how we and the world came to be. The Celts however, have no such myths. MacEowen believes that this is because creation to the Celtic people is a living experience. "...a story that wants for each of us to remember it. In other words, no matter how much we look, we will not find a story outside ourselves.... We are the story and it continues to unfold."[19]

One way this story arises, the author explains, is through the Oran Mór. MacEowen proposes that the Oran Mór is part of all mystical, spiritual and religious traditions, and that it can be accessed through chanting, drumming and singing. He also says that we can find this music in the cries of a bird, in our own heart beats, in the gurgling of a stream, in the rising and setting of the sun and moon, and in the rhythm of the sea tides and waves. He urges us to look for it everywhere.

As I read, Richard drifted off to sleep and started to snore. I thought to myself, "Perhaps this too (Richard's snoring) is the Oran Mór."

MacEowen also wrote of the "mist," and how much of our spiritual journey is about moving into a mist of "not knowing."

When Richard awoke, I said to him, "Maybe you're moving into the mist." I was referring to his frequent lapses into slumber.

"No," he disagreed. "I'm leaving the mist."

## Canticle of the Sun

I received a phone call from Luz's daughter, Daniela, with news I didn't want to hear. Luz was in the hospice program at Laguna Honda, dying.

Daniela was a wiry and tough Chicana dyke who had done quite well with her life. She had come of age in the Portrero Hill housing projects; and without the financial assistance of her family or a man, she now had a successful career and owned two houses. Aside from that, she was a wonderful human being. So much of this had to do with her mother. Luz had instilled in her daughter an inner strength and healthy self-esteem. No matter what happened, I knew that Daniela would be okay.

Luz opened her eyes when I came to see her. She recognized me and smiled, and we chatted a bit. She especially wanted to hear how Richard was doing. She chuckled when I told her of his latest comments and antics, then she drifted off to sleep. A few days later, our Secular Franciscan group from Most Holy Redeemer came to the hospital together. Luz was unconscious by then.

We didn't know if she could hear us, still we told her what was new, and we told her that we loved her.

"We need to pray," I realized, as I appreciated like never before the meditative value of ancient prayers. I wanted to grab hold of one like a banister, and repeat it with my Franciscan brothers.

Greg was way ahead of me. He passed out some books and we recited St. Francis' Canticle of the Sun.

*Be praised, my Lord, through all your creatures, in the first place for the blessed Brother Sun who gives us the day; and enlightens us through you... for Sister Moon and the stars...*

*for Brothers Wind... for Sister Water*
*so necessary, yet humble...*
*for Brother Fire*
*who lights up the night.*
*He is beautiful and carefree, robust and fierce....*
*for our sister, Mother Earth*

*who nourishes and watches over us*
*while bringing forth abundant fruits and colored*
*flowers and herbs....*
*for our sister, bodily death*
*Whom no one living can escape....*[20]

## January 21, 2011

Luz's funeral Mass took place at St. Anthony's Church on Cesar Chavez Street, near where Luz had grown up. On any day, Cesar Chavez is lined with day laborers waving to passing cars, hoping for work. When Luz was well, she used to serve these men free breakfast in St. Anthony's Parish Hall. This was only one of the countless ways that she had given of herself in her life.

It was an evening Mass, and as I walked down the dark and gritty street, I longed for the light she must have brought to this place. The church wasn't crowded, but it held a devoted gathering of family, friends, and, of course our entire secular group. As part of the ceremony, several people got up to speak.

The words they used to describe Luz rang true to those of us who knew her well. "She was generous, loving and always uncomplaining, even in the face of a devastating disease. " "She was my best friend." "She saved my life."

I had thought that the bond I had with Luz was special, but in hearing these words, I discovered it wasn't. I realized that this is how it is with light; it has the power to shine on many faces. And I thought, what true wealth this is, to have so many people sincerely weep at your wake. All the money in the world couldn't buy those kinds of tears.

Luz's body had been transferred to a local funeral home to await cremation. In her refusal to be a burden on her family, she had already paid for these arrangements in advance. But when Daniela spoke to the funeral director, he said, "Our fees have increased since your mother paid us. You owe us more money."

"Can you believe it?" I said to Richard after I told him the story.

"Mmmph," Richard grunted. "Now you know what we need to do? We need to lob a Molotov cocktail through the mortuary window. That will take care of the cremation."

Pure Richard. And if Luz was around, she would have thoroughly enjoyed the line.

## Changes

Max was not the only person I knew who referred to Richard as a saint. And as Richard dealt with his deteriorating body with such peaceful grace and humor, this title seemed all the more apropos. But Richard was in many ways, just like the rest of us. He might have done saintly things, but he was also just another human being. And like all humans, he had his own share of faults.

For a long time I refused to see Richard's faults, and this didn't serve either of us very well. My inability to see his weaknesses made me have some unrealistic expectations of how he should handle his death.

Richard was not perfect, and in some ways, the ALS certainly didn't help matters. It's understandable that under stress, everyone's character defects have a tendency to magnify. And what Richard was going through – becoming a quadriplegic with a decreasing ability to breathe – certainly qualified as stress.

At the same time, I was still stuck in the conviction that Richard would sail through his death with a Buddha-like serenity. And he had done nothing to dissuade this belief. Since his constant refrain was, "I'm fine and dandy, sugar candy," he had convinced me that he was not suffering.

To this day, I'm not convinced that Richard was extensively suffering. ALS was a terrible disease, but Richard had an uncanny ability to compartmentalize things in his life. If he had a bad moment or day, he was quick to set these feelings aside and move forward. "I take things one day at a time," he told us.

He also explained that since childhood, he had possessed a sunny disposition and an innate ability to feel happy and at peace. He took no personal credit for this quality. He said it was part of his nature, just as chronically depressed individuals weren't to blame for their gloomy moods.

On the other hand, Richard admitted that he did have problems voicing his needs and openly expressing his frustration. "Growing up Catholic, I probably saw that as sinful," he said. Richard's frustration could only be suppressed for so long however, before it finally erupted in explosive anger.

When this happened, it caught me off guard. When he lost his temper, it seemed to come from out of nowhere, as Richard was usually such a calm and peaceful man. And his outbursts could be especially hurtful when they got personal. He had a sharp tongue, and if he was angry enough, he could rip you to shreds. These episodes didn't happen often, but when they did, they were ugly.

Max blamed a lot of this on the morphine. "Richard used to get mad before he started taking morphine," Max told me, "but he never got mean."

Others claimed the cause was a lack of oxygen. "We're dealing with the same Richard," Angela explained, "but with the hypoxia, his inhibitions are gone. He's always had this problem of repressing his frustration until he explodes, but now nothing is holding it back. And who knows how much he's been suffering with the ALS. He says he's not suffering, but I don't believe it."

Bootsie recognized some personality changes with her brother beginning around January of 2011, but I was slower on the uptake. This was because for the most part, throughout his illness, Richard seemed lucid and in overall good spirits. He also continued to be quick with jokes and verbal play, and he was never outwardly depressed. He just had these rare episodes of rage, and on occasion, at least from my perspective, he could seem unreasonable. This could have been due to the morphine or hypoxia, or simply from the burden of enduring ALS for so many years. In truth, these changes were probably caused by a combination of things.

Richard's irritability was mostly related to his nursing care; but he also started to become prickly when I interviewed him. Previously, I could talk to Richard about anything. I'd throw out a topic and he'd readily discuss it from every conceivable angle. Suddenly however, some of his responses became short and hostile.

Most of the volunteers took Richard's outbursts with a grain of salt. Richard barked at Juan once, and Juan simply smiled, continued to tenderly bathe Richard, and started singing a Spanish ballad.

"So what if he yells at me?" Tim asked. "If I were in his position, I'd probably blow everyone away with an AK-47."

When Richard's anger was aimed at me, I was not so philosophical. Initially, I was shocked and hurt.

As a nurse, I should have been better prepared for what Richard was going through. After all, on my job, I was used to dealing with these issues. I could recognize cognitive changes, even when they were subtle, and I'd seen patients hurl their most vitriolic rage at their caregivers or at the people they loved the most. I knew about Elizabeth Kubler-Ross, who claimed that when people are dying, their anger is often projected onto others almost at random. I knew these things, but this knowledge failed me when it came to Richard.

I'm not sure why. Perhaps it was because I had become so personally involved with him. With my patients at work, I was able to maintain some professional distance, but I viewed Richard as a good friend. And like a lot of people, I admired Richard, which led me to have these expectations of him that just weren't realistic.

So beginning in 2011, the waters around Marty's Place began to get rough. And it would take a while for both Richard and me to find our sea legs.

## The Day from Hell

One afternoon, Richard really lost it. He was angry at the way I was caring for him and he started ranting and shouting at me. Then he became downright vicious.

These types of scenes had gradually begun to accumulate over the previous weeks, and by this point, I'd had enough of what felt like abuse. I told Richard to stop; if I had done something wrong, I was willing to make amends, but he needed to knock it off.

He didn't quit.

"You can't talk to me that way," I said again. "You owe me an apology!"

"SORRY!" he said with flippant sarcasm. Then he added, "But it doesn't mean anything."

That did it. Now I'd really had enough, and I told him so in no uncertain terms. I also announced that I was leaving. "If you want to behave like that," I said, "you can take care of yourself!"

I kicked open the door and marched onto the patio. Rogelio was out there gardening, and he had overhead our conversation. "It's not about you," he told me. "Don't take it personally."

Eric echoed this sentiment when he came out to join us. "Richard is changing," he said.

"He's fighting for his life now," said Rogelio. "His anger is one of the only things he has to hold onto."

Neither of their words meant anything to me. They didn't alleviate the pain I was feeling. Max, who had been outside with Rogelio, added, "Don't listen to Richard. He can be that way."

I looked at the three men. If I left, then one of them would have to take over my shift. Since they had their own shifts and obligations to deal with, I knew I couldn't do that. I couldn't cause a big scene and then walk out because my feelings were hurt. So, reluctantly I returned to Richard's room.

The day lasted an eternity, with Richard and I barely speaking to one another. The air was exceedingly tense, and I was grateful when it was time to leave. As I pulled on my jacket, Rogelio grabbed my arm, "C'mon Susan," he said. "I'll walk you home."

It started to rain, and Rogelio ducked under an awning to light a cigarette. As we stood there in the darkness, he tried to give his own explanation for Richard's behavior and for my reactions. "You're disappointed with your own expectations of him," he said. "Maybe you think he's some holy guru, but he's not that person."

"Who is he?" I wanted to know.

"He's a dying man," said Rogelio. "He's gasping for breath and it's ugly. He's in pain so it makes sense that pain is going to come out his mouth."

I was the nurse, and should've known these things, but I didn't. Not in this situation. And even when Rogelio spelled it out for me, I refused to accept it.

"Who is he?!" I asked again. "You've known him longer than anyone. I don't know him. I thought I did, but I don't."

Rogelio tossed his cigarette butt into a puddle and we continued on our way. "This is what I know about Richard," he said. "I recall climbing mountains in Arizona with him when we were both vibrant young men. And I remember us singing in church on the Indian reservation. 'This is the day the Lord has made; let us give thanks and be glad in it.' That's what we sang together. It was beautiful. But this... this is death. Who celebrates death? Richard says he does, but now that he's facing it, can he truly do that? I don't think so. He's terrified. And there's nothing we can do to save him. We can feed him and change his sheets, but we can't save him."

We had reached the front of my building and Rogelio joined a crowd that was waiting for a bus. Through the rain and the dim streetlight, Rogelio looked at me from beneath his baseball cap. "Things are just getting more real," he said. "We all have to face that." The number thirty-three pulled up and he climbed on board. I watched while the bus disappeared into the foggy wet San Francisco night – a night following a day from hell.

## Beauty and the Beast

The next morning Michelle called. She said Richard wanted to speak to me. I was still reeling from the previous day and Richard was the last person that I wanted to see. Still, I longed to resolve the hard feelings that existed between us, so I walked over to Marty's Place.

I spoke to Michelle before I went downstairs to see Richard. Since they were housemates, Michelle had become one of his closest caregivers. He felt comfortable with her, and she seemed to be protective and sympathetic toward him. She had heard about our argument, and although she admitted that caring for Richard lately could be difficult, she justified his behavior, saying it was related to his deteriorating health.

Like Michelle, most people continued to dismiss his outbursts as a symptom of his illness. Intellectually, I agreed, but emotionally, I'd been wounded and was still angry.

I stepped tenuously into Richard's room and sat down at the foot of his bed. He spoke to me in a slow and patient voice, explaining a problem he had struggled with his entire life. He said he had trouble asking for his needs directly, and then resentments built up until he finally exploded. Richard said that he'd also recently verbally abused others in the house, and his hospice nurse had told him that this was due to a lack of brain oxygen.

I listened quietly to what sounded like an apology, or rather half an apology. I had a hard time believing Richard, especially about the brain oxygen, because for the most part, he seemed extremely alert.

Then I took a few deep breaths and tried to summon some compassion. I remembered Rogelio's words. This was a dying man. And he was completely paralyzed, living an existence that I couldn't even fathom.

"I'm sorry you're suffering like this," I told him. "It must be terrible."

"But it's not!" he almost laughed. "I keep telling you... I'm at peace. I'm fine."

This was what was driving me crazy – this extreme contradiction between his words of "acceptance," and the fury he'd clobbered me over the head with.

"Richard," I decided to ask. "Are you angry about the book I've been writing?" By pushing me away with anger, I wondered whether he was he trying to sabotage our writing project.

"No, not at all," he said. "In fact I was just thinking about the book this morning. I was thinking, 'This is the part where the beast comes out.'"

"Yeah," I nodded. "You've definitely been a beast." Then I tried again to speak with compassion. "But listen, if things are starting to get ugly... if this anger is a symptom of your illness... I won't include it in the book. I want people to remember all your wonderful qualities. We can skip this part."

"No, no, no!" he exclaimed. "You have to tell the whole story. You can't have the beauty without the beast."

## Decisions

Nobody expected Richard to live this long. Yet day after day, thanks to the BiPAP, he continued to breath.

"I have healthy organs," was his own explanation of his survival.

"In addition to all that," Angela reasoned, "Richard has a strong life force."

For the most part, life went on as usual at Marty's Place. People kept lining up to visit Richard and, overall, he appeared in good spirits. His previous bouts of anger seemed to have blown over, but I feared that at any moment, they might return.

I could rationalize Richard's anger, but I was still concerned about again being its target. I began to question whether I wanted to continue volunteering at Marty's Place. And then I got a surprise phone call.

We had expected Marty's Place to close in March, and after that, Richard would be transferred to a nursing home. Then one evening Angela called to say that the board had scrounged up some extra money. Marty's Place would tentatively remain open until May 31.

After Angela spoke, she heard my silence on the other end of the line. "It's a mixed blessing isn't it?" she asked.

"Yeah..." I had to admit. "How do you feel about it?"

Angela hesitated, then replied, "I think it's good. Richard wants to die at home and this will give him some extra time."

I sensed some ambivalence in her voice, and if anyone deserved to be ambivalent, it was Angela. She had been overseeing and scheduling 24 hour nursing shifts at Marty's Place for almost three years. She worked some of these shifts herself every week, including overnighters. In addition to this and other volunteer work, she also held a waged job.

I had my own share of ambivalence. Beyond my recent conflicts with Richard, I had other problems. A family member was facing foreclosure, and I had taken on a third job to help him out. I was extremely busy. And I wondered whether my one day a week at Marty's Place was really holding the Circle of Care together.

"If I gave up my Sundays," I asked Angela, "do you think somebody else could fill in?"

"Probably," she said. Angela felt that perhaps Maegly could cover my Sundays, but she wasn't sure about some of the other shifts. Richard's care was growing more physically demanding, and many of the volunteers were showing signs of fatigue. Nobody complained openly, but I did hear comments about how difficult the work was becoming. The Aurora Dawn Board was trying to provide more money for caregiving, as Angela was having a harder time filling in the volunteer schedule.

The board members were tired too, and painfully aware that the foundation was running out of cash. When Richard and the board decided that the house would be donated to Dolores Street Services, Richard also insisted that Delores Street be given a year's worth of operating costs. The agreement was that Richard could live in the house for as long as the foundation existed – but that was back when a lot of people expected Richard to die in 2009. Now, two years later, most of Aurora Dawn's money had been used to keep Richard at home, and the foundation was getting closer to its dissolution date. Marty's Place still served as a community center, particularly for men with HIV, but the price of operating that center wasn't cheap.

The following workers remained on the nursing staff: Angela, Tree, Gary, Juan, Max, Alejo, Annie, Michelle, Eric, Julio, Tim, Maegly, and me. Another caregiver, a Franciscan brother named Mike, also occasionally filled in shifts. This was a slim crew for 24-hour shifts, seven days a week, especially when several of these people had other jobs. We weren't really in a position to pull in any new volunteers because Richard's care had become too complicated. We had all been carefully trained in the intricacies of his needs.

The board held fast to the new May 31 deadline for keeping Marty's Place open. Whether Richard could remain there was another matter. The biggest question was, could they fill the nursing shifts? So, they decided to have an alternative plan in place.

In late February the Board sat down with Richard to discuss looking into a skilled care facility. Richard had told the board in his typical calm manner that he would be at peace with whatever happened. If he went into a nursing home he'd be fine, and if he stayed at home, he'd be okay too.

I took Richard at his word. Of course I knew he'd prefer to remain at home, but in many ways, the nursing home option made sense. Some of the volunteers felt that Richard might fare better in the structure of a medical facility. He would have licensed staff caring for him and the shifts would always be covered. Mercy Center, which was the nursing home available for friars in Oakland, was not a bad place. We also knew that Richard's present caregivers and friends would continue to travel to Mercy Center to offer their help and support.

Other people at the house thought differently. They argued, rightfully so, that it was far more humane for someone to die at home. The people who cared for Richard, as beleaguered as they were, truly loved him and were willing to give him the gift of their labor. Then there were Plumita and Pinto. Nobody could envision Richard without his pets, or they without him.

## February 28, 2011

At the February 28 Circle of Care meeting, changes were in the air. Two hospice social workers and Carmen Madriz, the Aurora Dawn social worker, planned to attend. Angela also insisted that every caregiver be present. We all crowded into Richard's room, with some of us pouring out into the hallway.

Carmen opened the meeting. Carmen was a small and stunningly beautiful Venezuelan woman who was always impeccably dressed. She had worked for many years as a social worker for people with AIDS, and she had served on the Aurora Dawn Board since 1996. With her Spanish accent, she announced that we had much to talk about. First, she confirmed that Marty's Place could stay "open" until May 31. Whether or not Richard lived here, Eric and Michelle were welcome to remain in the house until that date. She also referred to the discussion that Richard and the board had earlier that week, when Richard had agreed that he was ready at any time to go into a nursing home. "Isn't that right Richard?" she asked.

Richard cleared his throat and looked at Carmen over his BiPAP. "I've changed my mind," he said quietly. "I'll tell you about it later."

Carmen frowned, and the rest of us glanced quizzically at one another. Richard's response was totally unexpected. Not sure where to go from there, Carmen turned the meeting over to Angela. Angela thanked people for coming, then noted the increasing challenge in filling the schedule. She asked us to go around the room and express how we felt about the new May 31 closure date, and what our commitment was to this process.

As each individual spoke, they declared their undying loyalty to Richard and their vow to stick this out to the end. Everyone but me. I had decided by then that I would only work through March 13. I'd given the Board three week's notice, but I hadn't told Richard and the other caregivers about my decision. I'd resisted telling them, but now I was in a situation where I had no choice. I said what I had to say, but added that if Richard really wanted to stay at home, and my leaving was going to make a difference, then I'd reconsider.

You could have heard a pin drop and I was starting to sweat. "I need a break," I told the group. "Maybe I'll fill in as a back-up in April, but for now, this is what I need to do."

I had been so frightened to say those words and afraid of how people would take them. But nothing happened. Everyone just sat there. The room was silent.

Then the hospice social worker looked at me. She thanked me for being honest and knowing my limits. She'd had a lot of experience in working with hospice caregivers. She knew we had an important job, but we also had to take care of our own needs.

Her words were somewhat comforting, but I still avoided looking at Richard.

When it was Michelle's turn to speak, she began by vowing to hang in there with Richard until late May. Then she changed the tone in the room by digging deeper. "There's been some tension around the house lately," she said. "Richard's been stressed out and I think I know why."

She said she was apprehensive about the possibility of Richard being transferred to a nursing home, even if didn't happen until May. She didn't understand why Richard couldn't remain at home. Dolores Street now legally owned Marty's Place, but since its mission was to house sick people, why couldn't Richard stay? Perhaps, Michelle suggested, we could continue to take care of Richard downstairs while Dolores Street used the rest of the house.

Michelle was a very direct woman, and I sensed some accusation in her voice. Accusation perhaps, toward the board, who seemed to be moving in the direction of the nursing home plan. Carmen responded to Michelle's tone in kind. She voiced indignation at any suggestion that the board was trying to kick Richard out.

"We've bent over backward trying to keep Richard here," Carmen declared, "but the fact is, we're running out of money."

Then Richard spoke, and he sounded angry. "I have something to say," he said. "And I cannot continue on this journey unless I speak the truth."

Then Richard surprised us by suddenly accusing the board of mishandling the entire situation. He said they had been "jerking him around" by changing the date of closing Marty's place, first in March, and now not until May. But more than that, he said, the board hadn't been forthcoming around their finances. He refused to believe that they were running out of funds. He implied that they were insisting he leave Marty's Place for no reason. And even if he lived past May, he believed that there was still enough money for him to stay at home.

I was startled by Richard's words, especially since Richard himself had told me that he'd been part of the decisions that led up to the May 31 closing date. And one of the board members had informed me that Richard had reviewed all of Aurora Dawn's financial statements. Based on what I'd heard, Richard should have known how much money was left. I could certainly understand why he wanted to remain at Marty's Place, but a lot of what he was saying, at least from my perspective, didn't make sense.

Richard insisted he was right, and his charges were aimed directly at Carmen. He laid into her in a fashion similar to the time he'd gone after me. Carmen was a petite woman, whose speech and manners revealed a very refined background, but she stood up to Richard like a pit-bull. "How dare you accuse the board of this?!" she demanded. "Especially when you've been part of these decisions every step of the way. You said yourself only a week ago that you were ready to go into a nursing home!"

Richard wouldn't back down. His face was red with anger. He was not only angry; he seemed to be in some kind of psychic agony. He threw his head back and I thought he was going to cry. "How could the board be thinking like this?!" he asked. "Sending a dying old man to a nursing home!"

He then insisted that the board had two chunks of money: the funds that were now running Marty's Place, and another $50,000 that had been set aside. Why couldn't this money be used to keep him at home?

Carmen said that she understood his concerns, but there was no such extra money. Jane joined the fray by backing Carmen up. Jane had served on the board for several years, and had recently rejoined it during the dissolution process. It was possible, the women suggested, that Richard was referring to some money that the board had set aside for closing costs and unanticipated expenses. But there was no $50,000.

Richard just kept asserting his opposing views. He was loud, and the women raised their voices in defense. They had both known Richard for years, and it appeared as if other conflicts they'd had with him were suddenly coming to a head. Jane complained that Richard was continuing to do what he'd done before: he was refusing to voice his needs until they finally overwhelmed him, and then he was attacking other people.

"Why haven't you said all along that you didn't want to go into a nursing home?" she asked. "You've never said that you had any problems with it. You've always said 'no matter what happens, I'm fine and dandy, sugar candy.'" Then Jane couldn't help but add, "I get so tired of that phrase!"

"This whole thing with Dolores Street has already been set up," Carmen added. "It involves lawyers and a lot of complicated details, and you've been part of the whole process all along."

I was struck with the huge dilemma that Richard was facing. He had told the board he was ready to go into a nursing home, but obviously he wasn't. He was resisting the idea, and it made sense that he would. He was frightened, as any of us in the same situation would certainly be.

He was also angry, and his anger was aimed at Jane and Carmen. And because they had been so unnerved by his sudden outburst, they fought back. The rest of us just stared in disbelief. At one point, because of the way Richard was talking to her, Jane asked for an apology. And as he'd done with me, he refused to give one. He did say however, that we all needed to stop worrying about the future and be present in the moment. He started to philosophize about the dilemma, perhaps because that was what he did so well.

When he tried to do this, Jane let him have it. "I don't need a goddamned sermon!" She snapped.

I suddenly became aware of Max, who was frantically signaling for Jane to quit talking. Max pointed at his own head, insinuating that Richard was not thinking clearly. "I just gave him some morphine," Max whispered to Jane.

Carmen and Jane backed down, perhaps remembering that they were dealing with a very sick man.

Max's warning finally brought the argument to an end. Tree proposed that we get the board to show Richard a record of all the finances for Marty's Place, so he could see for himself how much money was left. Everyone, including Richard, agreed to this, and then Angela changed the subject. She wanted to piece together the caregiver schedule for March. I slipped silently out of the room. I had already stated my availability for the next month, and I didn't want to draw any more attention to my resignation.

Slowly the meeting broke up. People scattered about the house, lost in individual conversations. Michelle apologized to Carmen for appearing not to trust the board. "I don't feel that way at all," she said. "I just didn't understand what was going on and why Richard couldn't stay in the house."

Carmen accepted the apology, but she looked exhausted. The meeting, especially Richard's anger, seemed to have taken its toll.

## March 6, 2011

On my next Sunday shift, Richard slept though most of the morning. I had been avoiding the other caregivers since my announcement on February 28, but on this day, Michelle cornered me in the kitchen. She gave me a hug and asked me how I was doing. "You haven't been coming around much," she noted.

I told her about the misgivings I had after deciding to leave the Circle of Care. And my fear that the other workers would blame me for jumping ship.

"Nobody feels that way," Michelle assured me. "And Maegly has already picked up Sundays. She enjoys working here and she can use the money." Michelle also said that I would always be part of the circle, whether I cared for Richard or not. Her words meant a great deal to me.

When Richard woke up, I started his morning routine. We were pleasant to one another, but I tread cautiously into our conversations. I didn't want to bring up any tender topics, and I especially avoided talking about what had occurred on February 28. So Richard surprised me by bringing it up himself.

"That was some 'Circle Jerk,' huh?" he said. Circle Jerk was the moniker he'd given our Circle of Care meetings.

"Yeah," I said. "Quite a scene."

He then proceeded to take delight in recounting every detail of the meeting, repeating things that people had said with astounding accuracy.

I listened, amazed. Since he appeared to be rather unreasonable at the meeting, I had begun to question his mental clarity. Yet his memory seemed sharp as a tack. His moods had become more labile, but he was still the same old Richard... alert, funny, and more than willing to stir up a pot of gossip and drama.

He still clung to the belief that Aurora Dawn was holding onto an additional $50,000, but now he didn't fault the board; instead, he claimed that there must have been some misunderstanding.

He did blame Carmen personally for other things, though. "Did you hear what she said?" he asked. "Claiming that I was accusing the board of trying to kick me out? I never said that. I love the board. But I do believe Carmen's confused around this money issue."

Then he asked me about my book. "How is it coming?"

I told him I hadn't written for a while. I was still trying to digest the previous weeks. "I think what's gone on around here lately... it's going to take time to make sense of it all. Time and distance."

He knew what I meant. I was referring to his angry outbursts. "You can tell the readers that it had to do with Elizabeth Kubler Ross," he said, implying that his anger might have been related to the stages of dying.

"Is that why you're so angry?" I asked.

"You mean is that why I've *been* so angry?" he said. "I'm not angry now, and I have no idea where all that anger came from. Maybe I'm going through these stages on an unconscious level, but mostly I feel fine."

"And dandy, sugar candy," I mumbled.

"That's right."

His words irritated me because I felt he was minimizing his anger. He acted as if it had been as benign as a sneeze. On the other hand, I envied how he was able to compartmentalize things in his life. He knew life could be terrible, but for the most part, he chose to focus on the good. Yes, he'd been mad, but so what? Now it was over and he wanted to move on.

"What about bargaining?" I decided to ask. "Bargaining is supposed to be another stage in loss, and I'm wondering if that's what you've been up to with this nursing home issue?"

"How so?"

"Well, you said you don't care if you go into a nursing home, yet now you're making a big deal out of this $50,000."

"I don't care if I go into a nursing home."

"That's not what you said on Monday."

"No, what I said on Monday is that I don't believe we're running out of money."

"Fine," I sighed, and I looked at the clock. I was hoping my shift would end soon. Richard was wearing me out, and not only physically. He, or perhaps he and his disease, were also pulling me through an emotional roller coaster.

## April 5, 2011

I kept my distance from Marty's Place for a couple of weeks, then slowly drifted back. I missed the people and I wanted to see what was going on. Things were still tense between Richard and me, but now it was a different kind of tension. Neither of us was angry anymore, just a little embarrassed and shy about meeting one another's eyes.

We were polite and rather formal, with Richard asking about my life and me wondering about his health and Marty's Place.

He said he was fine (and dandy, sugar candy), of course. As far as the house, the board had clearly convinced Richard that they were indeed running out of funds.

"They can't afford to keep me here," said Richard, and I knew he believed it.

I liked our new relationship. I wasn't his nurse now, and that felt good. I could simply be his friend and the two of us went back to working on the book. I read to him some chapters, and he gave me his feedback.

Carmen had given Richard a new radio, so I realized that the two of them were still friends too.

"I've been talking to Jane," Richard told me. "She mentioned this problem I have about never voicing my needs until I blow up. She suggested that maybe this is why I'm still alive, because I haven't worked it out yet. I haven't been able to tell people what I need, and perhaps I have to learn this before I croak."

"What do you think of that?" I asked.

"I think... that Jane is one smart cookie."

## April 8, 2011

The Dolores Street staff had started to move into the house. They occasionally had meetings in the living room and they had begun to clean out the garage.

Max was somewhat peeved with the nonprofit's intrusion into our lives. "Richard is dying downstairs," he complained. He felt that their coming around was in bad taste.

At the same time, Dolores Street owned the building, and it made sense that they could no longer put their work on hold. Richard said he didn't mind that they were there, and Eric believed that their presence was good for Richard.

"He gets to see the fruits of what he's passing on," Eric told me. Eric also said Richard was very concerned that the Dolores Street people were comfortable. "He keeps asking me to offer them something to eat, or to put a log on the fire for them if it gets cold."

Still, Max looked sad when I found him staring at *Caso Cerrado* (Case Closed), an afternoon court program on Spanish TV. Not only was Dolores Street moving in, Marty's Place as we knew it was thinning out. Visitors had begun to remove furniture and other objects, including paintings off the wall. They'd ask Richard, "Can I have this?" and he'd say "Sure." Because whether he died or moved into a nursing home, he sure wasn't taking any of it with him.

"It's getting very depressing around here," Max told me.

I could see what he meant. Marty's Place was fading away and this was going to be a major loss for many people. It would be a loss for me too, but since I was hanging out there less often, the pain was less acute. The pain was still there though. In looking around the emptying house, I could definitely feel it. And I was somewhat grateful that Richard and I recently had a bit of a falling out. Our quarrel had provided a little distance for me, distance from him and from the reality of what was now taking place.

## May Day

Michelle talked Richard into having one more party before Marty's Place folded. He was reluctant at first. He was growing weaker and had even told Tim, "Sometimes I feel I could just sleep 24 hours a day."

"Then go ahead and do it," Tim advised, but instead, Richard continued to see visitors, and finally conceded to Michelle's party plans.

"We'll have a celebration," Richard announced. "And we'll call it The Gratitude Party."

"Gratitude!" I had to laugh. "And coming from a man who is about to be sent to a nursing home to die."

"Yeah," said Michelle, "that's Richard."

I'd been away again for a couple of weeks, and as Michelle and Maegly prepared tamales for the fiesta, Michelle filled me in on all the news. Apparently, in a short space of time, the dust had been kicked up again around Marty's Place. More problems.

"Part of it was my doing," Michelle admitted. She had been one of the most vocal supporters of Richard dying at home, and she had gone to the board again to see if the May 31 closing deadline could be delayed. She even discussed the issue with Dolores Street. One of her arguments was that Dolores Street wasn't immediately intending to use the building. They didn't have enough funds yet to start their own homeless shelter, and they also had to renovate Marty's Place to bring it up to legal codes.

Michelle wasn't the only person who was concerned about Richard leaving. A couple of AIDS activists also started to whip up a crusade to keep him at home. They too went to the board, to Dolores Street, and to Father John Hardin, the current provincial of Richard's Franciscan order. They even threatened to contact the press in order to draw attention to the fact that Richard was not being allowed to remain in the house. Other volunteers sought out private donors, hoping to collect enough money to keep Richard at Marty's Place.

The board asked Richard if he was behind some of these campaigns, and he vehemently said no. Carmen told me that the board believed him, but Richard had his own take on the situation. He felt he'd been unjustly accused of something that he hadn't done. He got very angry again and directed his anger at some of the members of the board. This was painful to watch, as these individuals really loved Richard. And although they tried to see his point of view, they were still quite hurt. Their distress was compounded by the fact that they had to deliver a final and very difficult decision. They insisted that Richard needed to go.

As I witnessed all of this, I was left with only one conclusion. I felt that although there were many viewpoints, everyone involved in this conflict wanted Richard to die in peace. And both the board members and the Circle of Care had worked extremely hard to make that happen. In fact, in spite of these disagreements, people continued to function as a team. Everyone's main objective was to keep Richard as comfortable as possible, as the ALS continued to take over his body.

After the February 28 Circle of Care meeting, Richard never again publically indicated that he didn't want to leave Marty's Place. If he expressed any anger, it was at individual board members for other things. What those things were, I never completely understood. But one thing was certain, Richard was angry.

Richard also told Bootsie that he was scared. It made perfect sense that he would be. He was totally at the whim of whoever was caring for him. Nobody in his position would want to abandon the comfort of his home or his familiar nurses.

On May 1, when I arrived for the Gratitude Party, I found Bootsie and Jim talking with John Hardin. They were discussing the house's recent turmoil, and the fact that Marty's Place needed to close.

John and Richard had had a long talk that morning, and had come to a final decision. Richard was going to a nursing home. They had decided on Coming Home Hospice, a facility in the Castro District. That way Richard could stay in the city. There would be no more discussion on the matter.

The pets had been a major sticking point for Richard, but that issue had been resolved. Through the help of a social services agency, Juan had moved out of the Tenderloin, and he now had a studio apartment in the Western Addition District. He could have pets there, and was adopting Plumita. Max would be inheriting Pinto.

## May 14, 2011

Max was preparing Richard for bed and he chatted with me as he worked. He told me that Richard was starting to have periods of confusion. "He forgets where he is," Max said. "The other day I told him we were here at Marty's Place, but he insisted we were at San Damiano's. Another time he claimed that he was on Main Street in Helena, Montana."

"Well..." I said, "That sure beats being paralyzed and stuck in bed. You get to travel all over, huh Richard?"

"Yes!" he smiled. "It's wonderful!"

"Maybe that's what death is like," I pondered. "You just take off and you get to fly."

"Yes, yes!" Richard agreed. "I can't wait. I can't wait to just fly away." He looked truly happy and excited.

## May 17, 2011

I stopped by Marty's Place and found Tim sitting in the hallway outside of Richard's bedroom. I could hear Richard snoring.

"Richard's getting ready to go," Tim told me.

I wasn't sure what Tim meant. I knew that Richard was indeed literally preparing to leave Marty's Place. Within a week, he was trasferring to Coming Home Hospice. Tim also believed that Richard was getting ready to die. He was sleeping a lot, and he was becoming more confused. He'd say, "What's that big green thing over there?" Or, "Why did they move me out of my room?"

"You're in your room," Tim would assure him, and Richard would slip back into his dreams.

Tim assured me that Richard was very comfortable. He wasn't struggling to breathe, and he seemed at peace. Annie and Michelle told me that although Richard was becoming disoriented, he was still very sweet. One night he woke up and started singing songs to Annie that he recalled from his childhood.

Richard had been taking more morphine, and I assumed that was why he was so sedated. "Do you think you guys are giving him too much?" I asked Tim.

"It's a pretty low dose," Tim insisted. "And we give it to him because that's what he wants. He requested it."

I wondered out loud, "Maybe he's trying to kill himself before he has to leave the house."

"I thought the same thing," said Tim. "I suggested this to Angela and she disagreed. She doesn't think Richard will die *until* he leaves Marty's Place. She thinks that he cares too much about what goes on in this house. He's been running this place for over twenty years, so he may not be willing to give up control until he physically leaves."

## May 22, 2011

As it turned out, the excess morphine for Richard wasn't a good idea. One morning, when he was thinking clearly, he told the team to hold the doses. He explained to us later that the drug had been no joy ride.

"I was having terrible hallucinations," he said. "I was completely disoriented and it was frightening. It was a nightmare."

We realized we'd been wrong. We had guessed he was comfortable, and yet we really had no idea what he was going through. I wondered again whether he'd been taking a high of dose morphine so he could die before he left Marty's Place. I cautiously asked him if that was the case.

"No," he told me.

"Are you angry about having to leave Marty's Place?" I couldn't help but ask. "Are you frightened?"

"Absolutely not!" He exclaimed. "No to both of those questions."

## Coming Home

Richard was transferred to Coming Home Hospice on May 24. He told me later that he flirted with the ambulance drivers as they carted him away. "They were these big, handsome, hunky guys," he said. He also bitched to the drivers about his recent nemesis – certain members of the Aurora Dawn Board. He said he was glad to get away from Marty's Place because it meant he could get away from *those people.*

The image of these strangers listening to Richard complain seemed pretty bizarre. It also underlined how little I understood about what Richard was going through.

For the following days, the community around Marty's Place waited to see what would happen next. Everyone except the immediate Circle of Care. The board had asked that the volunteers stay with Richard for a while longer and fill in their regular shifts. They would do their routine nursing tasks and introduce the Coming Home staff to Richard's specific needs.

For the first few days, while he adjusted to his new home, Richard accepted no visitors. By May 29, I figured enough time had passed for this adjustment, and I walked down to the Castro to see him.

Richard's room was extremely small, with no bathroom and barely enough space for only two straight-backed chairs. My heart sank. My immediate impression of the room was that it looked rather bleak. It did, however, have a window. Richard said he was very happy about the window, since one problem with his room at Marty's Place was that he couldn't see the sky.

I asked him how he was doing.

"Great!" he exclaimed. He then went on to tell me about all the people he had met at Coming Home. The nurses, nurse's aides, housekeepers and cooks... He told me of a little drama that he had already gotten himself drawn into. And lots of gossip.

Later, the Circle of Care workers confirmed that what he was saying was true. New people were being enchanted by Richard, and he was making more friends. His room had become a gathering place for many of the Coming Home staff, who would listen to his stories or tell their own.

"He's spreading his magic around in another place," said Tim.

As we chatted, Richard again brought up the board members who he'd been angry with. By now, he wasn't angry anymore. He tried to explain why, but to me, his words didn't make a whole lot of sense. It wasn't that he was confused; it was just that I never fully understood what the controversy was about to begin with. So I also decided to let it go, and I took comfort in the fact that Richard seemed relaxed and at peace.

"Everything is new," he said of his life at Coming Home. "The people, the building, the birds...." He was referring to the birdhouse that Tim had hung outside his window. "Every day is always new and filled with more surprises." Richard looked at me and asked, "Isn't that amazing?"

I suddenly realized that Richard had taken a giant leap. Like so many of us do when encountering change or loss, he had faced his fear and then moved forward. He was like the fluffy seed head of a milkweed when it blows off into the autumn breeze. He'd sailed and then landed on fertile ground, and now he was sprouting roots.

"And what about Marty's Place?" I decided to ask. "Do you miss it?

"Snip!" He said. I knew what he meant. He was imitating the sound of a scissors cutting something free. Marty's Place was part of his past. Now he existed in new surroundings, in another moment in time.

## The Saging

One June 5, 2011, it was time for the rest of us to also let go of Marty's Place. So we gathered there for a "saging" ceremony. Dolores Street had changed the locks on the doors, but Eric let us in. Michelle had returned to South America, and Eric was living in the house alone. Gradually, several of the volunteers showed up; Angela, Tree, Rogelio, Annie, Tim, Juan, Max and me. We found much of the furniture gone, and that Dolores Street had ripped out some of the carpets.

Plumita was with Juan, her new constant companion. After being separated from Richard, she had first refused to eat, but now she was doing better. She seemed happy to see us, and later, when we traversed the house for the ceremony, she followed us from room to room and up and down the stairs.

Annie explained how the saging worked. We would walk through the house, sharing thoughts and memories of what occurred in each room, and burn sage as we went along. In so doing, we'd release the old Victorian from those who had been there before, and we'd bless the place for its future inhabitants.

As I followed the group, I stayed mostly quiet and listened. I realized that I had known this old building for such a brief time. Angela and Max held its longest memories. They spoke of men who had died in the house – names that even through Richard I had never heard of.

When we saged the patio and kitchen there were no specific memories. Just talk of "so many parties, and so much laughter and good food."

We arrived back where we had started – in the dining room – where we sat down at the table. Annie read a poem – one of Richard's favorites by Hafiz, who was a Persian poet from the 14th century.

*We have not come here to take prisoners,*
*But to surrender ever more deeply*
*To freedom and joy.*
*We have not come into this exquisite world*
*To hold ourselves hostage from love.*
*Run my dear,*
*From anything*

*That may not strengthen*
*Your precious budding wings.*

*Run like hell my dear,*
*From anyone likely*
*To put a sharp knife*
*Into the sacred, tender vision*
*Of your beautiful heart.*

*We have a duty to befriend*
*Those aspects of obedience*
*That stand outside of our house*
*And shout to our reason*
*"O please, O please,*
*Come out and play."*

*For we have not come here to take prisoners*
*Or to confine our wondrous spirits,*

*But to experience ever more deeply*
*Our divine courage, freedom,*
*and Light!* [21]

As we were winding up the afternoon, Jose walked in the door. Jose was a 37 year old Mexican man who we all knew very well.

Jose had first come into contact with Richard via another friar. The friar had found him when Jose was a homeless teenager – an undocumented immigrant who had wandered into this country alone. The friar had introduced Jose to Richard, and asked if Richard could take the young man in. True to Richard's own philosophy of welcoming anyone who showed up at his door, he gave the youth a roof over his head and a place to sleep. This was when Marty's Place was still on Hartford Street. When Richard acquired the Mission Marty's Place, Jose was one of the main people who helped him move.

On this day, Jose reminisced about that period of time. "Richard had just gotten this house," Jose recalled. "He looked at it and told us, 'I don't know if I can make this thing work, but I'm going to try.'

"We knew we were all going to bust our butts trying to pull it together. And as we worked, Richard said to me, 'After you've helped us, and this is all completed, then I want you to relax. I want you to move into one of the empty rooms here and go back to school and learn English.'"

That's exactly what Jose did. He learned fluent English and got a trade.

A year after the Mission Marty's Place opened, some serious funding started to come in. Richard then informed Jose that he had to leave. Jose didn't have HIV, and due to monetary restrictions, he couldn't remain in the shelter.

"Jose was fine with it," Richard himself had told me. "He packed up and found another home."

Throughout the years, Jose continued to stay close to the Marty's Place community. "I will always love Richard Purcell," he said. In many ways, he owed the priest his life.

As Jose spoke, he was well-dressed, and I knew that he lived in a nice apartment. He had achieved full US citizenship, and he had returned to Mexico several times over the years to reconnect with his family and help them out financially.

As I listened to him, I thought about Richard's fluctuating moods and the recent household wrangling. I realized that none of it was important. None of it really mattered. What did matter, however, was what Richard had done with his life, and the lives he had touched.

And now we too would be like milkweed seeds sailing off into different directions. Some of us would stay in touch, but the pod that held us together, an old Victorian called Marty's Place, had changed the locks on its doors.

## Gay Pride Again

One bonus of Richard being in the Castro was that he was now directly across the street from Most Holy Redeemer Church.[22] Visiting

Richard brought me into that neighborhood more frequently, and consequently, I increased my involvement with MHR. Occasionally I went to Mass and participated in other parish activities, including a women's organization and a meditation group. I also remained connected with the Secular Franciscan Order. So like millions of other Americans, it appeared as if I'd found a church. But for me, the church was the individuals I met at MHR; it had little to do with the Catholic hierarchy.

I thought about all this in late June when it was once again time for Gay Pride. And I decided to attend a talk on pride by MHR's pastor, Father Stephen Meriwether. The lecture took place in the parish hall, and I gathered there with a large group of parishioners. As he took the podium, Father Steve looked relaxed in an open-collared shirt and jeans.

He began by talking about the word pride itself. He said that in religious circles, it was given a bad rap, as one of the seven deadly sins. But he also said that pride is a good thing, and that as human beings we have much to be proud of.

For example, he told us, we have a lot to be proud of as Catholics. The Church has had, and still has, many flaws. But it also has done good things, such as serving the poor, building schools and hospitals, and helping create a sense of community. We humans also have flaws, he said, but we are also God's handiwork and each of us is a gift to the world.

"People are very diverse," he continued. "We speak different languages and are of different races and ethnicities. We also have different sexual orientations. This is a good thing. It is not something to be frightened of, for diversity enriches society.

"Your being is a gift of God," said Meriwether. "At our core we are a reflection of that divine being. Not a perfect reflection... yet even though we may be flawed, we don't lose the goodness, love and care of God."

Meriwether brought up the gay pride parade. He suggested that a lot of people who condemn the parade have probably not watched it very closely lately. The celebration has had some blatant displays of sexuality over the years, but these days, the parade is composed mostly of "families with small children, main line sponsors, and every politician who can find a convertible.

"By and large, the parade consists of people who say, 'We are who we are. We have faults and failings, but we're proud of being people and being part of society.'" Meriwether noted that most people at Pride don't go there with thoughts of religion. "But for some of us, our life and all we do, is an expression of our faith. We live, breathe, communicate, socialize, and are part of the world. So it's good for people to celebrate their being. Their existence."

After the lecture, I crossed the street and walked into Coming Home. Richard greeted me with a smile and invited me to pull up a chair. At this point in our relationship, our interviews had ceased. I no longer wanted to write down Richard's words, but I still enjoyed being with him.

I told Richard about the talk on gay pride that I'd just heard at MHR. And as I recounted Father Steve's words on "human imperfection," I thought about some of the imperfect events that had happened in the preceding months. Richard and I been through some rocky times.

Although things had calmed down between us, I still struggled with some feelings. For one thing, I wondered about my decision to quit the Circle of Care. At times I felt that I had failed both Richard and myself by leaving. I felt this, even though no one in the circle ever criticized my decision. And Richard never lacked for good care. He continued to receive excellent nursing from the workers at Coming Home and from Angela, Eric, Max, Juan, Julio, Tim, and Annie, who came to the hospice to volunteer their services. Nevertheless, my feelings of failure lingered.

There was no perfect death, I realized. Although I sought some meaning in Richard's death, at times, the process was simply difficult. And as we moved through this process, any shortcomings in either Richard or me, were understandably bound to be amplified.

Pema Chödrön, an American Buddhist nun, writes about the negative things in ourselves and others. She claims that we often cling to these things, but they are not worth clinging to. Because they never touch our basic wealth. "They are like clouds that temporarily block the sun," she says, "but all the time our warmth and brilliance are right there."[23]

I wasn't so sure about warmth and brilliance, but I did know that at least for the moment, I felt at peace. Richard seemed to feel the same.

So we talked, looked through the room's lone window, and enjoyed the beautiful day.

## July 27, 2011

In July, Richard began to suffer from severe nausea and vomiting. At first we thought his intestines were blocked, and then later we blamed the morphine. He was still taking it in low doses and it had begun to make him really sick, so his medical team switched him to Phenobarbital.

I hadn't seen Richard in two weeks when I stopped by Coming Home on July 27. As I opened his door, I was shocked. Because frankly, Richard looked... wonderful. He had a rosy glow about him and so did his room. That tiny room, that had so depressed me on the first day I'd seen it, had now taken on vibrant color and spirit. Sunflowers and irises sat in a crystal vase, and the sun shone through the open window. Directly across from Richard, on the wall, someone had hung a woven maze with the little stick man, I'itoi (Earth Maker), in his Ki (house). This was the same Native American design that was on the top of Richard's coffin. Below the maze, and looking directly up at it, was the painting of a Native American on a horse with his hands outstretched toward the heavens. The picture was a replica of Cyrus Dallin's famous sculpture, "Appeal to the Great Spirit."

I sat down and asked Richard what was new. He recounted a recent conversation he'd had with Lee, the respiratory therapist. She'd told him that he was at a crossroads. Apparently, the BiPAP was on the verge of no longer being able to help him breathe. He needed to make a decision. Did he want to be hooked up to a ventilator or did he want to die?

Richard already knew what he wanted to do, and so he began to do it. He had stopped eating, and although he was still taking small amounts of water, he planned to stop drinking as well.

"You and Cesar Chavez," I said, referring to Chavez's many hunger strikes.

"That's right," said Richard, "and our friend Lou-Lou." He was alluding to the fact that his brother friar, Louie Vitale, had gone on fasts for both spiritual and political purposes.

"How do you feel?" I asked.

"I feel... *great!*"

"But you've had some bad days lately," I said, referring to the vomiting.

"Yes, it was horrendous! I was getting ready to join Elizabeth Taylor at Forest Lawn... wrapped in my furs and diamonds."

He still could make me laugh. I held his flaccid hand and felt a deep and warm connection. We talked for a long time, just the way we used to. Richard was alert and well aware of everything that was going on – not just at Coming Home or among his friends, but with what was happening in the world, as he still watched the news. And when I shared with him some of my own recent personal problems, he gave me wise and sound advice. We just had a lovely time together.

PART IV

# DOCUMENTING A DEATH

"Death is like a mirror in which the
true meaning of life is reflected."[24]
– Sogyal Rinpoche

## The Final Days

The last time I saw Richard was on July 30, 2011. I asked him how he was doing, and he said he was fine. Then he comically feigned that he was crying, and whined, "I feel so sad that I can't feel sad!" He hadn't eaten in over a week, and he was waiting for Bootsie to return to San Francisco. After that, he said, he would quit drinking water.

Bootsie and her husband Jim showed up on August 2, and so did 23 other visitors, including some Pima from Arizona. Richard had become extremely weak, but he still managed to speak. Aggie Apkaw, one of the Pimas, described this conversation she had with him:

"When we spoke, we knew that this would be the last time we'd see each other. As we said our goodbyes, he cried, and it was from the heart. I told him when he saw my brother in heaven, to say hello, and that I missed and loved him. He said he'd do that, and he asked me to tell my mother to set a place for him at her table on All Souls Day.

"I told him that it was alright for him to go, that everything would be okay. He wanted to make sure I took care of myself, and he was also glad that I found a job. He told me that he'd been praying that I would find a job.

"I asked him, 'Who am I going to talk to now that you're leaving us?' He answered, 'I'm not leaving you. All you have to do is come to the grave and talk, and know that I'll still be there for you.' Then he said, 'Aggie, see that jacket over there? Get my wallet out and count the money inside.' I counted $139.00. He said, 'Take it and use it for gas for your trip home. I won't need it where I'm going.' When I tried to refuse, he insisted. 'No take it,' he said. 'I love you guys.'"

Michelle had been in Peru when she heard Richard had stopped eating, and she made a split-second decision to fly back to see him. On August 3, following a long flight, and exhausted from lack of sleep, she walked into Richard's room.

"As soon as I saw him," said Michelle. "I knew he was a dying man." Richard had begun to fade. He had been too weak to speak for most of the day, but when he saw Michelle, he managed to thank her for coming. He also said, "I love you."

The next morning, August 4, Richard silently left this world. Max was at his side, holding his hand.

John Hardin and some other friars drove over when they heard that Richard had died. After they lovingly dressed Richard in his Franciscan robe, they placed him inside his cardboard box. Then they lifted him into the back of John's pickup and drove him over to St. Boniface Church. For the next two days, Richard lay in state in the church's small chapel.

I arrived at St. Boniface on August 5. A bouquet of beautiful yellow gladiolas lay over Richard's body, and at the head of his coffin sat a vase of bright yellow sunflowers. Yellow was his favorite color. Later that day, someone placed a pair of kitschy yellow sunglasses on his face – a joke that Richard himself would have loved.

I stared at my old friend, and decided that this corpse didn't look like Richard at all. It looked like an empty vessel... a shell. The real Richard had flown away. Yet as I stood there, I knew that Richard's powerful spirit had not been extinguished; that would have been impossible. His spirit would continue to exist in laughter, in beauty, and in so many of the other things that he had taught me to cherish. And it would certainly live on inside all of our hearts.

Later that night I spoke with Bootsie. She expressed how grateful she was that Richard had been her brother. And she was thankful, too, that he was finally freed from the ALS. Then she revealed to me something that Richard had once said. He'd told her that he never wanted to die suddenly - from a heart attack or an unexpected accident, for example. He wanted a lingering death, so he could experience the process. He certainly got his wish.

## August 13, 2011

Richard's funeral Mass took place at St. Boniface Church on August 13. He had specified what he wanted at the funeral, including the music. His chosen recordings included *Old Man River* by the Brazilian artist, Milton Nasciemiento, *Brother Warrior* by Kate Wolf, *That's What Friends are For* by Dionne Warwick and *Guardian Ang*els by Mario Lanza. "My Guardian Angels" was the nickname that Richard had given the Circle of Care.

John Hardin gave the eulogy. He told us something that we all already knew, that Richard had taught us how to live and how to die. John also mentioned Richard's frequent refrain, "I'm fine and dandy, sugar candy."

Once, Hardin recalled, a friend had asked Richard, "How the hell can you be fine and dandy when you can't do anything for yourself?"

Richard's response was... "I am."

It suddenly dawned on Hardin why Richard was fine and dandy. "Although he was totally helpless," said John, "he had a rich inner life. And that was where he lived in these past several years... in that inner world."

John asked us to look around at one another. The church was filled with many different types of people: different colors, ages, nationalities and sexual orientations. "He had a magnetic personality..." said John, "and he drew us in. Even in his two months at Coming Home, he charmed his nurses. They would have done anything for him, and they were crying as we picked him up and brought him here in his box..."

In conclusion, John said, "I believe that Richard died not of Lou Gehrig's disease, but because his frail body couldn't hold his big heart."

Joseph Enos, a spiritual healer from the Tohono O'odham Nation, was also part of the ceremony. With a gourd rattle, he blessed Richard's coffin, and the four corners of the earth. Then, in his native tongue, he chanted the "The Song of Light."

As the Mass ended, a band called "The Dixieland Dykes Plus Three" belted out a brassy tune. They played loud New Orleans Jazz, while the friars who carried Richard's coffin, followed the musicians out the front door of the church.

## Arizona

I knew I would eventually have to witness first hand, the center of Richard's heart and being. I would need to travel to the desert, where he had lived for so many years.

A few days before he died, he talked to Chandika on the phone. "It's beautiful out here," she told him. "It's really warm."

"Wonderful!" he said. "I'll be there soon! I can't wait to be placed beneath the warm Arizona earth."

After the funeral in San Francisco, it took everyone a while to re-group and plan for more ceremonies at the Tooham O'odham and Akila O'odham reservations in Arizona. By September, many of us were able to make that journey. On September 30, a Mass and procession with the Tooham O'odham took place during the day in Covered Wells. Later, people traveled north to Santan. There, the Akila O'odham held an evening Mass, followed by an all night vigil and the burial of Richard's ashes at daybreak. After that, they hosted a feast.

I was amazed at how the Native Americans had organized such extensive and beautiful ceremonies for Richard, especially since it had been so many years since he'd lived among them.

"If the O'odham love someone," said Chandika. "They never forget."

"Richard was one of us," one Pima woman explained. "He spoke our language."

I was unable to make it to Covered Wells during the day, but I did make it to the Akila O'odham reservation at dusk. As I drove alone in a rental car from the Phoenix airport, the desert's effect on me was immediate. The sky was massive and outlined by blue, jagged mountains. The earth was alive with creosote, mesquite, saguaro, tomatillo and salt bush. I opened the window and inhaled the plants' wonderful smells.

When I arrived, the outdoor Mass was already in session, and over one hundred people had gathered. As the stars appeared, they were joined by a warm, dry and shifting wind.

I spotted Chandika and gave her a hug. She whispered, "Richard said to listen for him in the wind." Then she added, "As usual, he's talking a lot tonight."

Father Ed Fronske, who had known Richard from their seminary days together, gave the eulogy. "I dared call him a mystic," Fronske said of Richard. "He was very close to God and very much in love with God." Then Fronske quoted the theologian, Gregory Baum: "Religion is essentially a relationship with God, or else religion is playing games and keeping busy."

When referring to Richard's ALS, Fronske cited St. Paul in his second letter to the Corinthians: "'Therefore, we are not to become discouraged; rather although our outer self is wasting away, our inner self is being renewed day by day... for we look not to what is seen but what is unseen.'

"That was Richard's focus when I visited him or called him on the phone," said Fronske. "I had never seen him as joyful as I did in those last months."

After Mass, I searched the crowd for familiar faces. Bootsie and Jim were present, along with other members of the Purcell family. So were Angela and Michelle. I asked Michelle what had become of Max and a few of the other guys from Marty's Place who I knew planned to join us. Michelle shared some bad news. That day, while riding together from Covered Wells, Gary, Max, an African American man, and Michelle, had been pulled over by the border patrol. Perhaps their California license plates and skin colors attracted some undue attention.

The travelers were detained, and it was discovered that Gary was carrying marijuana. Gary showed the agents his medical marijuana card, but since it was issued in California, the Arizona border patrol was not impressed.

The others in the car were released, but Gary was locked in a cell for several hours. He was interrogated, and one agent's attitude indicated that this detention was not just about pot. The officer started making disparaging comments about liberals from California. He even went into a diatribe about why our country needs to wage war and stockpile nuclear weapons. Gary, who was behind bars, could do nothing but sit and listen. When he was finally released (after it was ascertained that he indeed had a legal right to smoke marijuana), the cops refused to return his stash.

When Gary showed up at the funeral, he looked clearly traumatized. He shook his head and sighed, but then took comfort in the beauty of the evening. I felt safe here too – in this remote place, which was far away from so much craziness.

I recalled something that Chandika had told me. One thing she really loved about the O'odham was their silence. "White people are too loud," Chandika complained, and that was why she kept returning to these reservations.

The O'odahm were very quiet on this night. They spoke in hushed tones and at times they sang. They sang Christian-folk, as well as O'odahm songs, all heartfelt and moving.

"Why do you stay awake all night?" I asked one Akila O'odham woman.

"Because," she said, "when someone dies, we want to spend as much time with that person as possible before we send them on their way." Then she giggled that the O'odham had been joking earlier. They had said that Richard was probably standing at some gate, wanting to be released on his journey, but the people were delaying his departure. "We could just see Father Richard," she smiled. "And we figured he'd be saying, 'I want to get moving, and all of you are holding me up, having so much fun telling stories and singing.'"

As the night wore on, I heard some of these stories about Richard's time in Arizona. Once, he tried to speak Toohno O'odham, and ended up botching the language. He had meant to say to a woman, "I like your dress," but it came out as, "I like your ass."

One woman said that her son so admired Richard, that the boy wanted to be a priest. The boy presided over funerals for pets when they died, and he also hung his grandmother's frying pan in a tree, and banged on it like it was a church bell.

Other stories contained the same emerging theme, about how Richard had deeply touched the individual lives of these people, and changed them on a profound level.

"Before Richard came, many Indians had given up on the Catholic Church," said an older woman. "They had lost hope."

A man explained that Richard had incorporated the O'odahms' own religious beliefs and practices into what he was teaching. This was something that the people really appreciated.

It was clear that Richard's effect on these tribes had been extraordinary. He had planted seeds here that were still in full bloom. One person said that it was Richard who first brought the Cursillo movement to the reservations.

I had never heard of this Catholic movement before, and certainly not from Richard. Thus, I was surprised to hear that he had introduced it to the tribes. As I inquired more into the meaning of the movement, I understood why Richard was drawn to it. The Cursillo (translated as "course"), had begun in Spain in the 1940s, in the years after the Spanish Civil War. A pilgrimage was planned at that time to the shrine of Saint James at Compostelas. The pilgrimage grew out of a spirit of restlessness among various Catholic action groups. Many of the pilgrims sought to confront their dissatisfaction with the Church, and kindle a spirit of renewal within it.

The Cursillo is difficult to explain, but it is basically about learning to bring the light of Christ's teachings into our daily lives. It was also part of other Catholic movements that occurred just before the Second Vatican Council.

The Cursillo's emphasis on the spiritual growth of individuals (not institutions), made me understand more clearly why Richard was attracted to it. And the Native Americans had taken the movement much further than I'm sure Richard had expected it to go.

Some of the O'odham wore rainbow colored lariats and t-shirts with a picture of a rooster. These are all symbols of Cursillo. The rooster, with its many colored feathers, represents the rainbow in the Old Testament where God makes a covenant with his people. The colors also refer to De Colores, a Spanish folk song associated with the movement.

Legend has it that when groups of pilgrims were one day returning from a Cursillo, their bus was held up by a thunderstorm. After the storm passed, the sun came out, and the countryside was alive with color. One of the men pulled out his guitar. He started to sing De Colores, and other pilgrims joined in. The song tells of the many colors of nature, and of the exquisite joy of just being alive.

And on this night in the desert, as the sky grew lighter, this is what the people sang:

*All the colors, all the great, glowing colors*
*that we see in the sky at sunrise,*
*All the colors, all the colors are seen*
*in the thousand reflections in sunlight,*
*All the colors, all the colors are seen*
*glittering in a diamond ring,*
*And that's why a great love of the colors*
*makes me feel like singing so joyfully….*

## Morning

The stars began to fade and the mountains became more visible. People who had gone home or who had crawled into their cars to get a little sleep, returned. A larger crowd gathered, more musicians arrived, and the singing grew louder. As daylight emerged, we sang *Mañanitas* to Richard, to bid him a good morning.

Then, as the steeple bell rang in the village's little white adobe church, we gathered flowers in our arms and walked silently across the desert toward the cemetery.

The dry and dusty graveyard was filled with many weathered crosses. Very few of the graves were marked with any names. Yet people obviously knew who was buried there, since individual grave sites were adorned with flowers and gifts. The unmarked graves made me think of the O'odham themselves – humble people, whose allegiance lay with each other, and less with the extreme individualism that is so rampant in my own culture. And today, this allegiance, along with so much love and sweetness, was also extended to us and to Richard.

Max held Richard's ashes in a box, and Joseph Enos, the Native healer, performed a blessing with some prayerful songs. Then Richard's ashes were tenderly placed inside the grave with other gifts. Branches of creosote, a medicinal herb that Richard often drank as tea, was also lowered into the hole. As the sun burst over the eastern horizon, we each tossed handfuls of sand into the grave. Then the tears began to flow.

We filled the grave with dirt and placed a large wooden cross above it as a marker. The cross held Richard's picture, his name, and the dates of his birth and death. Richard had asked to be buried with Marty, and with the other men from Marty's Place, but the O'odahm wanted something else. They preferred to give Richard a strong and visible memorial – and his own special grave. After the hole was filled in, we covered it with flowers.

I thought that perhaps now I finally understood what Richard meant to these people and what they meant to him. Richard loved all of us at Marty's place, and he enjoyed his life in San Francisco, but the Tooham O'odham and Akila O'odham were his family in the deepest sense of the word. And now he'd finally returned to them for good.

## Flying Home

I left Richard in Arizona, because that was where he wanted to be. And in many ways, I no longer required him in my life. He had already taught me what I needed to learn from him, and he had given all of us his blessing to let go and move on. In fact, he left these words of wisdom for us in a letter that he had written before his death:

"By the time (this message) reaches you, I will have danced and whistled my way beyond the blue horizon. That's why I want to get this written now before that happy day comes....

"I've had wonderful examples of living the spirit life, both from my twenty years with the Native Americans, and from other ingredients. Thus, I've arrived at a joyful acceptance of life as it is, not what it should be...

"When you get the news that I've moved beyond this physical form, cry your eyes out, and then get off the ground... and dance your asses off!

"I've always felt that despite all the dogma, morals, control, power and bad example that organized religion has shown the world over the centuries, the real messages that Jesus, Buddha, Mohammed, and the other prophets brought us are these two things: first, do not be afraid and second, always live in love."

After I flew back to San Francisco, I returned to the Mission District. Like the rest of my life, my ragged little barrio still had its problems. So little had changed since I had moved there almost ten years earlier. Yet everything had changed. And I couldn't help but feel lucky that this place was my home. Not only had I gotten to know many of the people in my neighborhood, I'd also had the wonderful fortune of knowing Richard Purcell.

PART V

# RICHARD'S TRANSCRIBED JOURNALS

"What is there to do when people die – people so good and rare – but to bring them back by remembering."[25]
– May Sarton

## February 4, 2007

The letter kills and the spirit gives life. We need to respect certain laws and rules, but only to a point. Then the spirit needs to take over. What is our spirit? Our inclinations and our deepest soul. We need to be obedient to our souls and not let outside influences take over our lives.

The fruits of the spirit are patience, charity, joy, peace, dignity, long suffering, mildness, faith, modesty...

What is charity? A benevolence. An openness to every person – allowing them the spaces and resources they need to be a full person – in whatever way they choose, so long as it's not impinging on others. These resources could be material, spiritual or emotional; whatever builds up appreciation for each person, no matter what they do or don't do.

What is joy? Joy is not happiness. Happiness, like sadness, is something that happens on the surface of a lake. Joy, like despair, occurs in the deeper part of the water. Joy is more of a constant thing. And even in sad times or disturbed times, we can continue to have joy. Joy comes from meditating, from sitting in silence, and from having an attitude of gratitude. It comes from knowing that we are not in control of anything... except whether we'll react in hurtful ways when things don't go as we wish.

## June 10, 2007

So many Christians engage in a form of idol worship in their constant reference to Jesus. It's terrible, using poor Jesus for these purposes. Holding Jesus on a pedestal and bowing down in front of him, and forgetting that Jesus is really sitting on a curb in some old man who can't walk and doesn't have a place to live... in some young woman who doesn't know how to feed her children... in some transvestite prostitute. Isn't that Jesus?

The name of Jesus and person of Jesus is so glorified in such anti-Jesus ways, and so neglected in other ways. It just doesn't hold water for me and hasn't for such a long time.

## September 28, 2007

Abbe Pierre and Dorothy Day were two people who really influenced me in my early life. They became my heroes, my saints. Another one was Dom Hélder Câmara, an archbishop from Brazil. Hélder Câmara once said, "When I give food to the poor, they call me a saint. When I ask why the poor have no food, they call me a communist."

He was a powerful voice for the poor and homeless all through his life. He should have been praised by the people in Rome, but instead, they gave him nothing but trouble. Because he gave the rich people in power, who were neglecting the homeless, the men who were killing off the poor, he gave *them* trouble.

## October 10, 2007

I can't believe the world is so filled with such wonderful people. I can't understand why people can concentrate on the negative. Maybe there's too much newspaper reading and TV watching. The negative just hasn't been my experience. I recognize that tragic things happen. That's reality. But to balance that off, there are all these good and positive acting people. All we have to do is scratch the surface. One on one, meet people. Talk to someone. Expose ourselves to somebody. Expose our wounds and others are willing to meet us half way, and show their woundedness too, and sometimes help us in our situation.

For some reason, the cream hasn't risen to the top. I guess it's our love of money, or that corporations have taken over, instead of well meaning folks who want to lead. That is very disheartening. It's thrown into our faces all the time by the media – stuff that's just tragic and really evil that's done by people in high places – who have killed off others to get to the top of the hill. It seems so hopeless, negative, ugly, destructive and hateful. And so many people are ignorant of what goes on or what should go on. Sometimes it seems like we'll never get out of this mess.

But like Dorothy Day said, it's not individuals. You can kill off every capitalist in the world and still have the mess. It's not individuals – it's the stinking rotten system. It's the structures that allow people to do these things. And unless those structures change or are changed, as they're not going to change themselves, these systems will continue to produce leaders who have greed, power and control in mind.

## November 18, 2007

Why wouldn't somebody be proud to be as old as they are? It's all blessing. What are you supposed to do with a blessing? Put it under a bushel basket? That's not what Jesus says. That's why I really like my birthday. I want to celebrate it for as long as I can.

## November 28, 2007

If you go to a tree and not only touch it, but get a stick or a board and hit the tree; it stimulates new growth. It somehow energizes the tree. I guess it gets the sap flowing.

Circulation is the secret of life in plants and animals. Plumita and Pinto, my dog and cat constantly want to be pet. With blood, sap, and a lot of other things, it's all about circulation. If things don't circulate, they stagnate and die. So receiving body treatment is so important.

Some people have never had a massage in their life, never had body work, or never had anyone touch them. That's strange. In our family we never touched. Maybe it's part of the Irish thing... but I don't remember touching. There wasn't hugging in those days. At least none that I knew about. There wasn't holding hands or kissing. It takes its toll.

It definitely builds up, because we're creatures who need that. All creatures do. If we're deprived of it, imagine what bad things can happen. You can't put 10 pounds of mud in a 5 pound bag and hope that it's not going to split open. The 10 pounds of mud comes from the stuff that builds up inside of us and isn't released in ways of touching, in ways of sexual expression, in holding things in, in denying and fearing things, and in pretending we're not human. It comes from being in the head instead of in the heart and the bowels and the groin.

That's the story of our lives as Christian Catholics... the fear of the body. And certainly in religious life, because we were trained in very strange ways. Custody of the eyes – you had to look straight ahead. You had to guard your vision so you didn't see anything. That might pull us away from what we had vowed. And I don't know what we had vowed. Not to be human I guess.

And you couldn't have what was called a particular friendship. You couldn't have a friend. And if it was noticed that you were friendly with somebody, or you and another person were talking too much with each other... then you'd be called in and warned. You'd needed to stop having that friendship, or you were going to get booted out.

So no wonder we were crippled creatures in religious life. And no wonder terrible things happened in the area of sexual abuse. Because people can go just so far. They either lose it mentally, emotionally or physically. And how can you have a healthy spirit life if your body is so crippled and locked in a cage? I think that happens in other religions too.

## May 14, 2008

I've had days when I've been down, but they've passed. If I did something wrong, I felt shame or guilt for a while, but it's not something that hangs over my head. I've felt hated and criticized. But if anyone does anything in their life, if they take a different path, of course they'll be criticized. That's just how it is. You go into these situations knowing that you better have broad shoulders and not be thin skinned. That's the case if you want to do anything worthwhile in life.

I've been reading *The Life you Save May be Your Own* by Paul Elie. It's about Thomas Merton, Dorothy Day, Flannery O'Connor and Walker Percy. These people were beacons of change. They were also highly criticized, misunderstood and debunked. They caused a lot of jealousy and fear because they were so far ahead of themselves. I've seen the same with many of our friars. Those who have done something worthwhile in their career – meaning something that was truly them, that wasn't institutionalized, that was part of the unknown and different, or that was controversial or radical. With these people, criticisms and jealousies have happened.

Some people have stepped outside of the comfort zones of institutional or social thinking and tried something different. They weren't satisfied with the status quo. They were always pushing against – not to alienate, but because they had to or they would die.

Life is relationships. I can see why people are depressed because of their lack of relationships or because their relationships are not satisfying. I'm not putting blame on anyone, but the more self centered we are, the less happy we are. This doesn't mean we shouldn't take care of ourselves. It just means that if you stay there, the mirror is going to crack and life will lose its salt.

Jesus is supposed to have said, "You are the salt of the earth. You are the light of the world." If salt loses its flavor, then what good is it? You can salt forever and it won't make life taste good. If you are the light of the world, and you hide your light under a bushel basket, what good does it do? It's supposed to be put up on a lamp stand so all can be blessed by your light. We do lose our salt, our savor, if we become selfishly focused.

I know a lot of people that this happens to because of things that have happened in their lives – hurts and traumas and worries. These types of people, I always surround in prayer. I don't see them as depressed, dour, sometimes mean, angry and insolent. I picture them as radiant and with a smile, and standing tall. That's my prayer for them. It doesn't need any words. Except that I say I am fully grateful that so and so is beautiful, confident, loving, healthy and recognize that they are loved. Those things work, although what they might just do is give me a different perspective of that person. But on the other hand, maybe it does work, because of the energy that I send, forms these people in a healthier way. I don't think we realize how psychic we are. It's one of the senses that we don't realize we have.

## February 19th, 2008

If we selfishly make demands of processes, if we come to conclusions faster than we should, we get into trouble. That's when the end product is worse than the first. I realize that we have to be in charge and take care of things – but we can't direct things that are part of the natural course.

I think that the little creatures in the world are so smart. They are so innately intelligent about living. When they're tired, they drop, when they're hungry they eat or try to find something. When changes come, they don't scream and kick and holler. They simply slow down and let nature take its course. I guess I can be that way too. I guess any of us can, if we're patient enough. The most important virtue is patience. It's so necessary and so hard to do. Especially in today's world when there is so much hurry up, hurry up, hurry up and now, now, now and me, me, me. But to be patient and wait things out is so important. Not to force, demand or control.

## February 29, 2008

I bless the syndrome of ALS and befriend it. This doesn't mean I welcome it, or that some things would be easier without it. But what is the sense of condemning and hating and making an enemy of anything? By having an attitude of gratitude and by being open and generous – it's a lot easier to walk with a smile in my heart and on my face.

## March 5, 2008

When we are kids, a certain pattern is imposed on our brains and hearts. We grow up in a family that has beliefs and ways of doing things. One of these is the perception of what we grow up to call God. When we're little kids, we don't question any of this, and probably those who taught us this didn't question it either. So by the time we're teenagers, we might realize that things have been imposed. Such as the imposition of baptism. How could anyone impose Baptism on a baby? We might have some kind of welcoming ceremony into the tribe, or some kind of blessing. But baptism is supposed to be a choice we make when we want to make a commitment in our lives to follow a certain way. And to make matters worse, when you grow up, you realize you have to follow these things because you're baptized.

By the time we're young teenagers, they come up with another thing. They say that in order to seal that baptism, you have to be confirmed.

*"Well, I don't want to be confirmed."*

*"Well, you're going to be confirmed."*

*"Well I don't believe in that way."*

By then, we start to assert our individuality.

*"Well, you're going to do it. Otherwise it will be a terrible blot on the family and what will the neighbors say and everyone else in your class is doing it."* And then we're forced into other things.

Some people resist. Some young people say *"Nope, I don't care, I'm not going to do it."* And that is the beginning of something great in their spirit life if they work on it.

I'm not trying to judge, because I don't know the people, but by the looks of it, so many Catholics have really never investigated anything. St. Paul said, "When I was a child, I spoke, acted and thought like a child." Well, I ain't a child anymore so my childish ways have to go. And for me, one of the main childish ways is our belief system. That means that I have to investigate and find my own spirituality. I can't follow Mom and Dad's. It has to be something that works for me.

When I was a teenager, I never questioned any of this. I was always the pious one. Then I got to be a young man and I followed the party line right down to the hilt. Then I got to be a Franciscan and I didn't question anything. I just went through the motions as most of us do. I read something out of a book that somebody else had written, but it didn't mean anything really.

When I lived with the Native Americans, I started thinking different things about life, about my spirituality and about God. That's dangerous if you're a preacher, because if you don't preach the party line, the big shots can get you. And because I didn't preach the party line the big shots got me. And because I was the member of a team, the whole team got blown out of the water. A bishop in Tucson kicked us out of the diocese and I felt sorry for the other people on the team. They got dragged in because they supported me as the pastor. They could have resisted and said they were not part of this, but they were faithful to me, and they put their necks on the chopping block.

So this doubt kept growing about God and the Bible stuff. And it's scary because you don't know where it's going to take you. If you really are faithful, you don't know what it's going to do with your life.

The important thing is to be an integrated being – an honest being. A being whose identity is owned personally and who isn't twisted and turned by what others demand.

One important thing about the spirit life, is that there is no plateau. You don't climb, and then sit up on a flat rock and relax forever. No, because when that happens, you slide off the rock, and down you tumble again. So it's constant movement, evolvement, and becoming. As you climb, and you might do a little sliding – the Baptists call it backsliding – but then you just get up and go again. It's like anything in life... like children getting up and walking. It's like addicted people falling off the wagon and then getting back on and going further. It's the same with our spirit life.

The reason I can't call it God, is because God is way too limiting, too power and control driven by people who use religion to keep others under their thumb. Promises of pie in the sky if you follow the rules...

Looking out at congregations I've seen over the years – doctors, lawyers, merchants, and priests sitting there... I've wondered, these are schooled people, yet in the notion of spirit stuff, just infants. Never having gone past kindergarten. I could never figure out how that could happen. That one box, of all the boxes that make up our lives. That one box is so neglected, while others are moving at such a break neck speed.

## May 23, 2008

I am closer to a final exit than somebody who is younger or in better health. People have asked me, "Have you ever thought of suicide?" I never have. There was no need for it, as I was always in good shape. I've never been ill. Besides, because of my strong background of anti-suicide, and how bad suicide is, it never dawned on me.

Euthanasia is a whole different thing as far as I'm concerned. And even suicide seems different to me today.

I still don't feel I would actually do some type of violent harm to myself. As far as euthanasia – I think that's a good idea. Why should we help four legged creatures: dogs, cats, whatever, be relieved of their suffering, but not do it for human beings?

## June 19, 2008

There is some kind of screwball Christian outfit, including the Catholic Church, which is fighting for a revision to be put into the state constitution; words that only a man and a woman can get married. That's supposed to be on the ballot in November, so we'll see what happens.

I could never figure out Schwarzenegger, the governor, when he vetoed this subject when it came up in the legislature. He said "Well, it's up to the people to decide." I couldn't figure that out. It's like saying of women's suffrage, back when women couldn't vote – it should be up to a vote of the people. *Men?* All men voters? Until that was made law, it was never going happen.

The same with interracial marriage. People, being as ignorant as we are, as stupid and prejudiced, would never say, "Give interracial couples the right to have marriage." Same way with slavery. People who owned other people were never going to say, "Oh yeah, no more of this." It had to be done in the legislature. It's the same with sexual orientation. It's so crazy. But I guess all things that are worthwhile have their process.

We have to be patient and little by little gnaw away at things that aren't right.

How people of religion can be so evil in their actions and thoughts is beyond me. Like the Bishops of California. And some of them are nice guys. But coming out and making pronouncements about stuff like birth control, using condoms and same sex unions? It's just crazy.

## October 9, 2008

I think there is this danger among religious people in that "we are in the world but not of the world." We're kind of isolated in a way. There's a ghetto mentality that we pick up on and we just fall into it as young Franciscans. There's a jingoism, jargon, ideas, notions, and expectations that are very ghettoish. It separates us from what's going on in other places. It helps with fraternity, but for the sake of keeping balance in our lives, I don't think it's healthy.

If you get any group of people together – people that separate themselves from others through their dress or the way they talk... I often feel that way not about only Franciscans, but also about other Catholic groups. It doesn't have to just be religious orders – but Catholics in general. It's not as apparent today as it was in the 50s and 60s... but there are still ideas, whether they come from higher or lower levels – ideas that are odd, strange, not helpful and not even very real. They don't come from reality. They come from dreamland.

We see it in this political situation – Catholic bishops getting involved. They are so strong on priests not running for public office and separation of church and state, and yet they make pronouncements, and stick their noses, and make demands in areas that are beyond their domain. And they may have the Catholic faithful by the nose, but they can't have the whole world by the nose. But they influence a lot of people. Like this thing of gay marriage.

The Supreme Court of California decided that people who are gay had a right to be married. Well the lid blew off the pot on that one. The Mormons and some Catholic bishops got their heads together, and pronounced that the whole thing was evil. Then this group started a campaign to put a constitutional change in California that says only a man and a woman can get married. This is very shallow to me, very not thinking. It's interfering. If you do say you're for gay marriage, then the bishops come down on your heads. Just like they did with the abortion thing, and not giving communion to certain Catholic politicians.

It's just crazy, hurtful stuff. It shows the ghetto mindedness of living in a glass house and having a whole pack of stones you're throwing all the time. It's a scandal and it's very hurtful, and shows a shallowness of life and spirituality. No wonder people leave the Church in droves.

## October 15, 2008

Being infirm is a blessing in many ways. It can help people be naked. Being naked is very important. When we started out as humans, perhaps in Africa, we were naked. Many tribal people still are naked. As we started to wear clothes, that became kind of a curse.

Being clothed can be dangerous. What we do on the outside can affect what happens on the inside. That includes notions, ideas and feelings, etc. I've always said that being immodest means drawing undue attention to yourself. Nuns, priests, and people who wear strange uniforms in the middle of people who are clothed differently, are drawing undue attention. That's immodest.

If you're having trouble with your health and you can't take care of yourself, then you better be unafraid to be naked. To get rid of the masks or the pretense is the only way we grow in our spirit lives. When we can do that, and it comes with honesty and change, it's so wonderful. That's why 12 step programs work. People have to admit, strip down and become naked, tell the truth about themselves, and live the truth, because secrets kill us. And the bigger the secrets we have, the more our outside demeanor is like layers of clothes. So people can't see us, or hurt us or find out who we are.

I've never been afraid of being naked. I figure everybody's got a penis or vagina or sometimes they have both. What's the big deal? So it doesn't bother me to be naked in front of caregivers.

## November 5, 2008

All good things come to those who wait. Patience is the number one virtue. This doesn't mean that you wait lazily, or without effort. But you choose your battles, let nature take its course, and you don't interfere too much. And things often work out.

If I had limited my life to living in a Franciscan institution, I have a pretty good hunch that by now I would have been farmed out to some rest home. I see that happening almost daily to many of our men. I'm not trying to judge, but if we Franciscans allow ourselves to live together as brothers; the most important thing in our lives is to care about each other.

I was talking to a Christian Brother the other day, and I asked him whether in their fraternity, they had close emotional contact with each other. Like when a brother died, did they cry or if someone was ill, would they be inquiring? Were they really involved in their brothers' lives? He said no.

Sometimes, it's the same with us. I don't know if it's the way we're trained. We're not supposed to have specific friendships, but that should have gone out years ago. But these days, not showing intimacy? It's something we're scared to death of. It makes for a very lukewarm, weak brew of a fraternity.

Instead of really embracing each other, especially those who are down and out... those who have personal troubles in their life, be it physical, emotional, mental or addiction problems; or things that they've been called on the carpet for, that the public knows about. Those are the ones that I like to be closest with, because they're the ones that need the most love and understanding. I've always tried to concentrate on those people, to let them know I'm thinking of them. Why concentrate on propping up the well and the rich? That's something I could never figure out.

But if someone dies in our province, I've noticed, it's as if they were here yesterday and they're gone today. Don't talk about it. We have money to make or jobs to do, houses to build, etc. It's a very strong example to me of how things have replaced beings. I think it's from the structures we have.

When you get locked into the systems that the world holds dear, such as corporate systems, or corporate ways of doing things – which we do as modern day "religious" people – you suffer the consequences. You run the risk of being no better than those who run General Motors or Del Monte. It's that way for anyone in a bureaucracy, and God knows, the Catholic Church is the biggest bureaucracy in the world. And as a religious order, we're part of that whole mess.

A lot of religious women have fought to get out of this muddle. They could teach us so much if we'd listen to them. But there aren't too many left, and many of them are teetering also. I don't think it's going to last too much longer for any of us. But before the ship goes down to the bottom of the sea, maybe we can have a square dance on the deck, and see if we can get some happy times going.

In spite of this, I'm so convinced that if I had to live my life over again, I'd do the same thing. It's been a rich life; a wonderful, good life. I've done what I set out to do which was to be a servant of the servants. I've concentrated on living my life with the poor, the downtrodden, the sick, the underserved – people who have been looked down on by others. That has been my joy and salvation. I've had to fight upstream around the whole deal, and I realize that in some areas, I'm seen as a rabble rouser.

But it doesn't matter. What matters is that you make a commitment. Not in a brittle way, where you get locked in, but rather, you sway with the breeze. You stay rooted, but your branches can sway. You stay rooted in honesty, courage, friendship, hospitality, joy, peace, and in bucking systems that enslave, and in respecting even the ones that do the enslaving.

You don't respect people for titles. You let go of all titles. Like Jesus said, "Call no man father." That's a title. To me, anyone with a title puts him or herself above or below the rest. It's supposed to be an even playing field according to gospel values. And that's supposedly what Francis had in mind.

A letter just came out of our provincial office. It said that in the year to come, we're supposed to address the subject of poverty and our response to our promise to live a simple life. We're supposed to talk about it. Those in authority want to see if we're hitting the mark or not.

The last time we went through this whole thing was probably in the late 60s and early 70s. I was living in Arizona. My God, it was a war zone. People were slamming doors, pointing fingers, calling names and saying "You think you're such a hot shot because you live a simple life, and you're pointing your fingers at *me?!*"

So, we didn't have any idea what poverty meant, and we still don't. I certainly don't think it means trying to be destitute. That doesn't prove anything. Nor does running around in a sack cloth and ashes or living in surroundings that aren't beautiful. That's not what it means at all. It means living simply. You can still recognize beauty and bring it into your living situation. You just don't get attached to it.

To me, it's all simple, but I'm not trying to preach. I used to. You get on a crusade when you're in your 20s and 30s. It might be a crusade to kill people in wars or to live in poverty. But if we grow, we get out of those phases, and we become something more authentic and helpful.

I don't know how long I'll be around, but I'd like to see what happens with our discussions around poverty.

## January 20, 2009

So many people are afraid of change, even with small things. They have to control the environment around them in a room, house or neighborhood. Any change that enters, throws them for a loop. It's about fear of the unknown. Because what you have, even if it's horrible, is something you can grasp and look at. You have some control over it.

But change, especially if it's drastic or abrupt, is so difficult for people. But if we can anticipate change, take it as it comes, roll with the punches, and welcome change... I know that in my life, things always turned out for the better, and brought on more beauty, goodness, and possibilities for new life.

## January 31, 2009

The unknown is the unknown, so why fear it? Why not live in the moment? Right now it's quarter after eight. Nine o'clock is unknown. It seems like a lot of folks are afraid of living, of taking chances, or of stepping out into the unknown and turning a corner, of letting go of something that's familiar, and embracing what's unfamiliar, and possibly making a fool of themselves by doing something different or being different. *"People might laugh at me or ostracize me or think badly of me."* Well, that's none of your business. That's their business. *"People might hurt me."* Well, take a chance and see if they do or they don't. That's living, and to live is to change.

Anyway, it was a really nice day today. Jane helped me with my cardboard coffin. Jane actually ordered the box. It was supposed to cost $20 and the saleswoman said she'd give it to us for $18, and then she never charged us anything. So we got it for free. It's pretty nice getting a free burial box. Some people pay $5000 or $10,000.

Jane also bought the acrylic paint to paint the box. Because to put it in the oven for cremation, you want to have paint that isn't volatile, or doesn't give off fumes that pollute the environment and acrylics don't. It will be done in a week or so, and it will be very nice. The funeral industry and all the myths that have grown up around it are antiquated and not helpful.

In caregiving, you're in it not only for the one you're caring for – you're also in it for yourself. First, because the patient allows you to care for them, and second, by what you do. Caregiving might be emptying a bedpan or changing sheets, or it can be listening or sharing things about yourself. It can also give you some meditation time if you're sitting in a chair while the patient sleeps.

I also know that caregiving can drive you crazy. If you don't have support, it's easy to lose your balance, and to become abusive to the one you're caring for. I've seen that happen. You can neglect your well being. If you don't take time for yourself, and you don't allow yourself to be nourished, it can end up being a stressful, tension filled time.

I don't have any regrets, and I can't remember sadness... because what has happened on the positive side has been so powerful. The love thing has put a blanket over any sadness or regrets I might have had.

Somebody was telling me that about 10 percent of people are born with an innate disposition toward joy. On the other side, about 10 percent are born with a tendency toward moroseness or melancholy. Then there are people who swing back and forth.

For me, a big part of disposition, is having a sense of humor. My Dad had a sense of humor and was a comic. He was good at mimicking and clowning and seeing humor in things. Maybe it's wrong, but I can see humor in everything. I think almost everything in life is a joke. It's not a mean joke, but life is so funny with its changes and turns and happenings... so I think humor is seeing things lightly. Not putting a heavy accent on things. It doesn't mean that we don't take life seriously when it's unjust, tragic, or sad. But the majority of things in life, ultimately, we should be able to laugh off. And boy, those people in Arizona... the Tohono O'odham and the Akimel O'odham, are just experts at this. They're joking and laughing all the time, and coming up with these quips and quotes and little words and joshing each other. It is so great to be around them. I learned humor from my Dad and it was reinforced with my 20 years on the reservations.

It's been my salvation to see the world in lightness. That's part of what's blessing me now. It's been so good and I'm so joy filled. I feel this is one reason I'm not dragging my feet about moving off to a different level of living, because I find it so exciting. It's like taking a trip. That's how I feel about this journey I'm getting ready for – packing up or unpacking. Let's put it that way.

I'm very leery of church men. I've always been. I wouldn't say I'm anti-cleric – I just have a healthy distrust of those in a position of power like priests. It's a dangerous game. It's dangerous enough when you're in a position of power in government; but when you start messing around with things of the spirit – that is really dangerous. Jesus said, "Few should be teachers." Not many should attempt to teach. Teachers in those days were rabbis. Maybe that's why I always prayed for a lack of vocations to the priesthood. There are too many teachers. And God knows how many hearts were broken and souls destroyed by too much teaching, and bad, false, self serving, controlling, power hungry, judgmental and misunderstanding of the fundamentals teaching. And piling high the burdens on others, that we are unwilling to carry ourselves.

Jesus said, what a sad thing to pile high on others' backs the things you refuse yourself to carry. Is it better to get a speck out of another's eye than to deal with that two by four in your own? Thank God I gave up on the Vatican a long time ago. It's really come to a head in the past ten years. Protestant people used to ask me, "Do you really believe in this and this?" Of course I did! This was when I was a kid. Sure it's right, it has to be right. It's what they teach us.

One of my caregivers was raised in a strict Mormon family, but he came to his senses. Part of it was the fact that he was gay. It just pushed him over the edge. They excommunicated him because he wasn't willing to give up his sexual orientation. They thought it was something he chose. His story isn't rare, and you don't have to be gay to have a story.

## December 12, 2009

Somebody asked me have I ever been in love. I said I hope I have, otherwise life wouldn't make sense. I can remember for sure being in romantic love twice, although I've also loved many people, places and things. With the romantic loves, one was puppy love and one was pit-bull love. Both were very informing and a great blessing.

The puppy love opened me up. It was new wine, and was full of beauty, surprises, and wonderful things. It was full of new life. I still have good memories of it. But it was puppy love. It got the whole thing started, but I needed more than that to keep it going.

The puppy love lasted a year. It never bloomed into true love. The bubbles went out of the wine. It wasn't that I didn't love the person. And it did awaken in me certain wonderful things and surprises and growth in my heart and emotions and in my spiritual life. It also instilled in me a template or a model to the physical type that was appealing to me. I guess that's what happens to us. It's such a strong impression on our hearts and minds, that we start looking for that type over and over again.

Many years later I was introduced to someone who was definitely not the physical type of that first person. The second was the direct opposite of what I thought I was looking for, and this is a wonderful thing about love. It can surprise you. I wasn't at all attracted to that second person, but as time went on, I realized that it was way beyond looks. It was something much deeper, stronger, inviting, and difficult. As time went on, I started to fall in love. At first it was puppy love, but that didn't last long. Then all of a sudden, a pit-bull jumped out. This was different than puppy love. It was a strong, demanding thing. It wasn't so much physical. It wasn't that I was turned off by the person, but the physical didn't matter so much.

All of a sudden I realized it was much deeper than that. I had to really work on giving of myself. I realized that love is about giving, and in giving we receive. It wasn't about receiving first and then I'll give something. It wasn't tit for tat. And it changed me entirely.

## May 10, 2009

Back in 1971 I read a book called *Star Seed Transmissions* by Ken Carey. Carey was a farmer in Southern Missouri. He lived with his wife and kids out in the country. One day he told his family he was going to go to one of the buildings in back because he had some important work to do. And he started to spend time in this little cabin. He began hearing voices that told him something, and he compiled all this stuff together in this book. It's called channeling.

I read the book back then, and it made a big impression on me. That was during a time when lot of people were channeling or whatever it means. A lot of folks made fun of it during those days, especially those who had all the answers like the high Church Catholics. As if people couldn't get messages. Well, the so called Bible was supposed to have come that way, so I don't know why other people couldn't hear messages.

For me, reading this book was very powerful. It made a big change in my spiritual life and my outlook on things. It's beautiful stuff that wasn't farfetched, and obviously, this man was some kind of Christian. It sounded like he was Catholic, but it didn't come through too strong. Maybe it's a little too strong for me at this point in my career. But it was interesting, good stuff, and that combined with other things that happened to me then... those were very powerful years with all the different changes. With the movement of the 60s and 70s, it seemed like the world was turning on its head. Especially, institution-wise, law-wise, and expectations of what should be.

In the late 70s and 80s I read another book by Ken Carey called *The Return of the Bird Tribes*. And this goes further than *Star Seed Transmissions*. It's a bigger collection of information that came to him. It's very believable. So that made an even bigger impression in my life and pushed me even further. I didn't base my entire spirituality on it, but it certainly filled in a lot of the spaces, and fleshed out a lot of the ideas that I myself was having.

About the end of the 80s the same kind of thing happened. Carey published another book called *Terra Christa: The Global Spiritual Awakening*. And that goes even further.

Over the years, I didn't forget about this stuff, but I kind of let it go. It's always been with me, but I didn't concentrate on it. Then one of the guys here was looking through a bag of junk in the house, and what should float like cream to the top – the books! I still have them. So I've been re-reading *Star Seed Transmissions*. I want to see if I have the same feelings or notions that I had in those days. With *The Star Seed Transmissions*, so far, I have even better feelings. I think this is because I have less of a fatal grip on the whole Christian thing. I was hanging on tight in those days because it was so important to me. Well, a lot has happened since then. So my notions have changed enough to give me a different slant on what Carey wrote. This is how reading can influence our lives. I know a lot of people who don't read anything.

## August 27, 2009

Edward Kennedy died yesterday. My friend Julio says it's good to die. When I questioned him about this, he said, "I didn't say dying is good. But to die is good."

I like that. It's influenced me a lot.

Every time I see a picture of the Kennedys, it reminds me a lot of the Purcell family. There are many similarities. Not money-wise and not political-wise. But the stuff that really counts – such as heart or generosity-wise. It's something about the Irish I think.

I was watching this film on the history channel – about what brought all the Irish here. The horrors of it all. It was blamed on the potato famine. But what was worse, England took all the produce from the country and because of this, about five million people died. When some got over here, they were the lowest on the totem pole and hated by everybody.

In our family, I wonder if that is what made us much like the Kennedys – to be concerned about the underdog and very much involved in helping the have nots, and on the side of the poor – of giving our lives to the *anawin*; the remnant.

Part of it certainly has to do with the social teaching of the Catholic Church. I'm not saying that everyone follows these teachings – even the popes. But the teachings of the Catholic Church really stick up for the little ones. That's why we started hospitals and schools in the history of the United States. Much of this was done by the Irish.

In my own case, a lot of it came from my parents' influence. Their ideas were so wonderful.

The railroad tracks used to be near our house, where there was a hobo town. A lot of people would ride the rails back then. They used to walk across the fields and come up to our house and knock on the door. Our mother would open the door and say, "Just sit in the yard and relax," and she'd fix them something to eat. If it was winter, she'd invite them in the house. She was very open minded and fearless.

My father was much the same way. He was very concerned with little people, working people, unions, and those on the side of justice and peace, and of what was right and good. He was never a soldier. My parents weren't military minded people. They weren't patriots or nationalists. They appreciated this country as much as anyone else, but they weren't war mongers. Very interesting and good folks. I'm so lucky that I had parents who were so generous and right minded.

## August 28, 2009

I was listening to the radio about Edward Kennedy's memorial. About 20-30,000 people walked by his coffin. They were interviewing those in line. One black lady from the South said that what she admired most about Kennedy was his lack of fear about doing the right thing. Being an older woman from the South, she saw what doing the right thing, and fighting for the right thing accomplished.

Kennedy had a lot to lose. Materially, he had anything he wanted. But if you do the right thing, as he knew from his brothers, Martin Luther King, Malcolm X, and all the other martyrs of the age – if you do the right thing, some will condemn you. It's all about fear.

If there was a Jesus, the real things he came to teach us were one: don't be afraid. Because fear will freeze you, and you won't be able to budge. And your life will go by and you won't have made a mark. Number two: wrap everything in love. Even if you're right in a disagreement, let it go. This doesn't mean you're a wimp and you back down on everything. You plow ahead. But you wrap everything in love, truth, respect, and peacefulness.

Ted Kennedy sure did this. He was friends with Republicans that hated him. That didn't mean he ran around with them or was their bed partner, but he was truthful, civil, and peaceful toward those who were not civil, peaceful, or honest and were hateful.

The thing that was most important to Kennedy was health care for everybody, and now this is coming to a head in the Senate and Congress. It's being fought both tooth and nail by people who are cutting off their noses to spite their face. They don't realize that they're in the same soup as everybody else. But maybe those politicians can afford private health care – and to hell with those who can't. Maybe that's what's fueling the fire. And sure enough, it works, because people all over are afraid.

It all starts with ignorance. A lack of knowledge or exposure to something. Ignorance leads to fear, fear leads to hate, hate leads to violence, and so it goes. Round and round.

I'm reading the book *The Return of the Bird Tribes* by Ken Carey. It's about channeling. Channeling doesn't mean you hear voices; it means something informs you of more than what you realized before.

The things Carey helps us realize is that human beings are stuck in some fear-filled era of our development. Our whole way of doing life is fear-based. And of course religions have a heyday with this kind of stuff. We have fear of not going to heaven, fear of hell, fear of people in other countries, other races, other tribes – fear of losing something, of death, of standing up for what's right, or of anything different. It's a very strange and horrible way of doing life.

Our notion of God is also fear-based. Tomorrow, two van loads of Pima Indians are coming to visit. They are people who seem to have an innate Bird Tribe lack of fear of being who they are. Not all of them, but many of them can live and let live in a way we outsiders have forgotten how to do.

Anybody who leaves their homeland and tries to save their asses, like the people in Central America and Mexico – imagine the fear that envelopes those people in those situations. Especially with the screwball antics of putting up huge fences and machine guns and minute men on the border. For what? Jails for what? Protecting what? Land that was stolen? People are not trying to take over – they're trying to retain some possibilities for their lives.

But no matter how high the fences, or how much fear fuels the fire on our side or their side – you cannot stop water from running. It will go uphill by going higher and higher, deeper and deeper, till it reaches a place where it has to flow down again.

So Jesus knew what he was talking about when he said we are all part of the divine, and it's all one. It's one huge being that pulsates. It's called G-O-D by some. The more you believe this, the less you will fear, because you have nothing to lose once you realize you've always been part of the divine. You just take on different forms at different times. Once you realize that, you know you have nothing to fear. You don't have to fall into addictions. You don't have to run or kill or hide. You can live in love. And you won't have to be afraid of change.

The brittle ones cannot bend. When the wind blows, they snap.

## August 29, 2009

Yesterday someone asked me, "Richard, if you hadn't become a Franciscan, what would you have been?" That was easy to answer. I would have been a farmer.

Another thing I would have liked to be is an actor. I remember in high school being in plays. I'm always interested in actors in movies. I would like to be an actor – speaking in different voices and different accents – a different person every time. That's exciting.

Sometimes people tell me I should have been an actor when I'm acting up. I think I got that from my father. He could put on different voices and accents and act different parts. I think that's great.

But here I am, a Franciscan. And I've also been a Franciscan farmer. Wherever I've lived, I've always had something growing, or tried to have animals around me.

I have a little dog named Plumita. She's 10 years old. She's a mix between a bichon frise and a North Island terrier. She's about 15 pounds and white and so cute! Oh, that face would just make you melt. And she's with me 24 hours a day. She's the best little nurse. She's always looking and listening. She's a tremendous creature – a very holy little creature.

I also have a cat named Pinto. He's black and white and he looks like he's wearing a tuxedo. He's got the most handsome face, and it looks like a Sphinx out of Egypt.

Plumita is always right there. She's snuggles right up to my head. Pinto keeps a little distance. He leaves when he wants to – goes out on the rooftops of housetops and stuff. But he's still very present. Plumita and Pinto sometimes get jealous of each other because they both have a job to do, just like the human caregivers around here. They also get jealous of each other. Sometimes it happens.

## November 20, 2009

I just celebrated by 71st birthday. Who knows if I'll get to be 72. I kind of hope not.

So many little children died on the reservation. Among poor people it happens all the time. It got me thinking about little children. It seems that kids – the ones that I've seen die – they seemed to die with more softness and ease than adults. I've often thought, "Why do they move on easier than a lot of adults?" I think it's because they're not so involved with themselves and their own lives, and trying to control things – trying to control the unknown. I've often thought that.

Panic and control are two big evils that cause trouble in our lives. I have quite a number of people in my life right now – well, I guess we all do – who are controlling types. I don't consider myself a controller. Maybe other people do. I don't try to control things, but maybe others see me that way. Maybe that's why I notice it so strongly in others, and it's so distasteful to me. I really resist it.

I think our culture puts a premium on control. Our heroes are controlling people. The business and corporate people – they're always in control. Those in authority… we hate them, but we allow them to control us. I've always believed we should question authority. It doesn't mean we don't respect those in authority, but we should question them. We should get up in their face. They think they're in control, but that's a myth. They're not in control at all.

Control just doesn't work. "Having it my way and I know what's best," causes horrible hurts in people.

People who are clergy are sometimes great controllers. People in the medical profession or politicians. They know what's best for us.

Kids aren't that way. Kids get out of control with tantrums and stuff, but that's different. So when it comes time for them to be transformed through dying, they do it in a much softer and easier way. At least that's what I've seen.

The alternative to control is surrender. That's how love grows… through surrender. But it sure as hell doesn't get much cultural support.

I guess I notice control more since I lost the use of my hands and arms. The legs weren't so bad when I couldn't walk anymore or move them. The loss of arms comes more slowly, but it shows the importance of thumbs and index fingers. Boy, without them, you're done for. There's no possibility of picking up anything, or writing or eating. That can really get to people.

It's not that people have to lose their thumbs or fingers – it's any kind of control. Controlling types are very scary to me.

I guess we all want to be in control. I think it comes out of fear. Because we don't want to suffer, or we don't want others to suffer.

What really is attractive to me is surrender. When we really love somebody, we don't control them. We don't love that person if we demand that they do it our way. If we get into a mood, or cop an attitude when they don't do what we expect them to do. It's not a pretty thing.

I see couples who stay together, but hate each other. Because one imprisons the other through controlling methods.

Surrender is the ticket. Surrender into the arms of the other and realize they are not our prisoner. Release 'em. Let them do what they have to do in their life, just so it isn't destructive to us, and love will keep going.

I've seen this in the Native American people. They have some kind of ability to welcome others into their lives, and not demand that they do life a certain way. Of course there are controllers in the native cultures – there are quite a few. But so many are easy going, not possessing, letting go, and surrendering people. It sure doesn't fit into the dominant US culture. We have to be people who take charge, and demand you do it our way. Capitalism is it, democracy is it... our brand of democracy. And if you don't do it our way, we will force it on you. That's what we're in in Afghanistan, and Iraq, and every other place we've touched down.

Surrender is not lying on the ground and letting people trample on us. It simply means not being in power over others and making demands on others. In other words, control.

## December 10, 2009

What a sad thing if somebody goes through their life and never allows themself to fall in love. Falling in love is part of me and has taught me life. It opened me to life. It taught and teaches me so many things.

I don't know how priests can talk to people about love, especially married love, committed love, without having experienced it. This chastity thing is really a horror. This business of keeping our knees together and guarding some dried up soul which is like a prune. Never having loved, never having suffered... it just doesn't make sense.

Sometimes people were put upon by priests who weren't lovers. People were used in a sexual way that was terrible. Very strange things happen to us if we don't open ourselves to love – to become flowers. We become tight buds, or maybe we just remain leaves on the vine with no flower or scent or beauty for the world.

## January 10, 2010

Water is such a wonderful meditation. Water is transformed, it isn't changed. It still stays water, but it's transformed from rain to oceans, and then it evaporates and turns to clouds, then rain, then rivers and streams. Then it flows to the ocean and becomes clouds and rain again. The ice melts and becomes vapor. I guess that's the way it is with us too. We go through these transformations, but it's the same us – the same one. Our bodies are water too. I think about 80 percent.

I like the way we use water as Catholic Christians. It's a tremendous meditation. We have holy water that we bless ourselves with. I think that's a great reminder that were made of water and will return to water. Then there's baptism, which is all about being transformed. Then we sprinkle water when we bless. That's very nice.

In prayer, we become one with water. We send our intentions up to the heavens. Then they come pouring down in rivers and streams of blessings when we are open to receiving them.

## January 17, 2010

Yesterday, we had a meeting between the Aurora Dawn Foundation and Dolores Street Community Services, which we're giving the house to. Dolores Street asked me, "How did you find people to populate the house?" Dolores Street has to go through this long process.

We just allowed people to come in, because we didn't take money from the government. We did have a list. When I got ALS, there were 52 people on the list. Poor things never had a chance of getting into the building. Who very often got into the house – was whoever showed up at the door. They were often people who were very sick physically and maybe in other ways. Probably triple diagnosis. Once they got bedded down and had a safe place and got some TLC, then they started to change

Very often somebody would die off in the morning, and in the afternoon while the bed was still warm, someone would come in the front door and ask if there was any space. I'd talk to them. Sometimes it would take several hours to try and check them out. Of course nobody tells the truth if they need a room. If I found out later that they were trouble, I'd get rid of them. Most often though, the ones who were invited in in that way, were angels in wolve's clothing. They had such beautiful qualities about them that weren't allowed to develop when they were under stress. But when they had a chance to relax and be themselves, they turned into angels.

That happened 98 percent of the time. The other 2 percent, I had to roll down the front steps and tell them to come back when they got their shit together. I learned a big lesson. I learned, at least for myself, that if a person showed up in front of my face at a certain time, he or she was there for a reason. Even if the reason at first, didn't look very appetizing. If it was something dangerous for me or other people, you use precaution. But most often, even if people are wrapped in barbed wire or glass shards, they are there for a reason

What it takes to get a blessing from that person is first of all, acceptance of who they are. The second thing is patience. Let people develop in whatever way they're supposed to grow. Maybe they grow crooked. Maybe they don't even come up from the ground for a long time and need a lot of sunshine and water. But pretty soon, a little bit comes peeping out.

Some of them never reach the top of the soil. That doesn't mean they're bad. Something is just wrong with the scene and it needs different stimulation. But patience is the number one virtue. Don't butt into other people's lives. Don't manipulate other people to suit your needs, or wants, or ideas of what works for you. When you damn up any flowing stream, you'll run into trouble. You'll flood the valley. You'll run out the inhabitants and have a big mess. If you let it flow, you'll have some good stuff.

In the Dead Sea, the water flows in, but there's no outlet. So the water becomes stagnant and salty with no fish. There are no trees or bushes around the periphery. It's dead. That's how it is if we dam up living water. It becomes stagnant.

The people from Dolores Street Community Services run a very different model. They're licensed and have staff. They have strict rules on who can enter and who can't. It has to be that way because they get money from Holy Mother the State. Thus, they need rules, regulations and bureaucracy. Ours was a Catholic Worker model which I learned from Dorothy Day. Both models are useful, but the one that is best, if you're the poor creature who needs a place to stay, is this one. Because it accepts people and it has no time limit. Most places have limits. Here, you can stay as long as you want.

Of course, you need challenges and direction, but not interference. Sometimes someone has to say, "Hey, you been here five years, and you haven't gotten out of bed." But usually, you just give the person time to resolve whatever made them homeless to begin with. It might have been a mental or emotional condition, or addiction or physical illness. It might have been divorce from family, or any kind of support group. Usually, that's because people are afraid of AIDS. I think this model for a small group worked best for me. Maybe for more people, you need a bureaucratic model.

## February 21, 2010

I have kept my Franciscan vow of obedience. Obedience doesn't mean that you turn your life over to some person in authority and do everything that person says. What it means is you listen, you discuss, and you bounce things off your brothers. They challenge you to do the right thing and live the right way. But ultimately, you listen to your own heart. It's called the primacy of conscience. Your conscience is who you owe your obedience to.

It's like if you kill somebody as a soldier. *"I did it because someone told me to."* Kill another person? Does our conscience tell us to kill another person?

A lot of us do things like that. *"My boss said... the Pope said... the Bible said..."* The Bible says lots of things. The Bible says don't kill, and on the next page it says kill them all. The Bible says love your neighbor, and on the next page it says stone your daughter. The Bible says turn the other cheek, and on the next page it says, if anybody wrongs you, do them 10 times worse. So I can't see living by the Bible. Sure, there are good things in the Bible... stories of love and that kind of stuff.

We've taken those words and turn them into our God – into our false idols. And this isn't about looking at the Bible as literature, poetry, possibly history... But as far as the way we treat the Bible; that it's literally true, and then the stuff we do with it... I just can't take it anymore.

I believe that we're here to alleviate the suffering of the creatures of the world, so that all might live in joy. It's very simple. It has nothing to do with heaven and hell, purgatory or limbo. It has nothing to do with power and glory, or sins on your soul. It's simply keeping it simple. For me, treating others fairly and following my own heart has paid off. I've always thought that we've complicated the business of living, but it doesn't have to be complicated.

## February 22, 2010

I was diagnosed with ALS in October of 2006. Many long-term ALS survivors croak during the third or fourth year. I've been staying in bed more lately. My skin hasn't broken down yet, thank goodness. Yesterday I got up at 4:00. Juan gave me a shower and then a friend, Jose, came to visit.

At dinner I only had one spoonful and I couldn't breathe, so I went back on the BiPAP. Then I had to go to the bathroom to see Mrs. Murphy.

When Jose put me back to bed, something happened. I absolutely could not breathe. The full face mask that I use at night – somebody put the straps on wrong. It was awful. The caregivers, Annie and Jose, didn't know what to do. I couldn't talk. I thought, this is it, I'm going out. I motioned for the morphine which was already drawn up. Annie shot it in my mouth. That woman was real good. She was very calm. She held the mask the best she could, but air kept escaping. After about five minutes, I motioned for more morphine. After a while, it started to work. It actually lessens your breathing, but it calms things down and relieves anxiety.

Pretty soon Angela, the head caregiver, showed up. Jose had called her. She got the masks set up correctly. I dozed off and woke up after an hour. Oh my god, that was an awful thing. As they say, we all want to go to heaven, but nobody wants to die. Well, I don't care about heaven, and I don't mind dying... It's just that lack of air is no fun. I was thinking about the people in Haiti who got buried under all that cement. Oh my Lord, the poor people...

I'm going to be grateful for every moment that I have an air to breathe – even though I'm on the breathing machine all day. I am more grateful now for the gift of air. Air is life. The Jewish people call air "*ruah*." It's also the word for spirit. The spirit is air and air is life.

Hopefully I'll just go to sleep in the night and not wake up in the morning, and I won't even know I can't breathe anymore. That would be nice.

## April 1, 2010

Four times a year at the San Damiano retreat house in Danville, we host gay, lesbian, bisexual and transgender folks and their family and friends. It's just a Talking Circle at it's a lot of fun. About a week ago was our most recent meeting, and I was the facilitator. We drove up the mountain and they plugged the breathing machine into the cigarette lighter in the van.

After they brought me into the room with a wheelchair, Rogelio wanted to put me into an easy chair. Rogelio picked me up, and he must've been distracted, because he forgot to hold onto my *pantalones*. All the people were sitting in the circle watching this performance. And the pants fell down. So there I was, he was holding me, and the pants were down around my ankles. My bare butt was hanging out and my legs, and oh, what a sight! I don't wear underwear anymore because it's too much trouble. Rogelio panicked and he twisted me to throw me into the chair, and then the front end was exposed. I laughed so hard. If I'd had pants on, I would have peed them. Poor Rogelio, he was so embarrassed. The rest of us got a kick out of it, at least I did. I guess the rest of them did – poor things, having to watch that performance.

On the Days of Dialogue, I always read from the book *How the Wild Things Pray* by William Cleary. It's a great book with all kinds of creatures – four leggeds, two leggeds, and some with fins or wings. And some have no legs at all, like eels or snakes. The book has a prayer and an action step for each animal. Last week we read about the fox.

The main emphasis of the reading was about how human types sometimes think they're better than others. Sometimes they elevate themselves to higher positions. The main victims in this diatribe were the clergy and the Vatican. The writer was talking about these high Roman collars, silk and gold, and riding around in a pope-mobile, looking out over the crowd, and blessing people while they cheered and screamed, "Here he is! Here he comes!"

But then the character riding in the pope-mobile spots in the crowd, Martin Luther King, Mother Theresa and Mahatma Gandhi... a whole line of humble, Godlike people that nobody paid attention to.

The little fox tried to teach us that the lower you are on the totem pole, the more blessed you are, and the more worthy you are of admiration. It got me thinking about the Old Testament and that famous prophet, Amos. He started this thing about putting the priests down. "Woe to you characters, you high priests who hang around the temple. You think you're such big shots, but you're loading burdens on people's backs that you don't carry yourself." I love the Book of Amos.

The New Testament is also filled with stuff like that, like where it says that in the Kingdom, or in the Reign of God, everything is level. No more big shots, no more haves and have nots. No more Jews and Gentiles. No titles. No professor, doctor, father, reverend, pastor, bishop... no registered nurse. Maybe even no sister or brother. We're getting that far in our evolution. Forget about this division of sexes. If we really believe in the scriptures, how can we be such fanatics on some things, and just completely ignore others? This one has been entirely ignored. Little people use titles and those types of tactics. Big people don't. I'm sure Mahatma Gandhi or Martin Luther King never said, "I'm so-and-so, or so-and-so..."

I've been running around with several titles. First man, as opposed to woman. Second, schooled, as opposed to unschooled. Another is Reverend Father. It gets me in the door of a lot of places.

But the best part of that Sunday meditation with foxy, was when my pants fell down. What a wonderful example that the emperor has no clothes. I was the emperor, because I was facilitating. I was the facilitator. That brought me down a peg or two. It was a great day.

## May 23, 2010

People often ask me, "Isn't it frustrating to not be able to move any part of your body?"

I don't feel it's frustrating. I just see it as part of the process of life. Some people's limbs are in good shape their whole life long. Some lose them when they're young, and some are born without limbs. I saw a video of a man who was born without arms and legs. He does just fine and is a happy guy. Well, I'm an old guy without the use of arms and legs, and I feel very happy.

I guess what I do miss though, is walking and dancing. My whole life long I loved to walk. Even when I moved to San Francisco. Instead of taking public transport, I would walk. Same with dancing. I started dancing in high school and really liked it. The Tohono O'odham are great dancers, and when I lived with them, I loved to dance.

One time, I'd been living there a couple of years, and I was learning the language. They had a feast day dance. It started at noon and went on all night. They decorated an outside dance floor with crepe paper, and they had a little tent and the people sat on benches. They danced the Waila, which is a kind of old time polka. It's very popular there. They'd go inside to the feast house, and then they'd come out and dance some more. They have ceremonial dancing too, which is very ritualistic, and another good kind of dancing.

Well, one day they had this feast at Covered Wells. It was all afternoon, and the music was playing and people were sitting on the benches. I couldn't contain myself any longer, so I asked a lady to dance. We started to swing around the dance floor, and then I sat back down. There were two old women sitting next to me. I'd never seen them before.

They must have been from another village or from Tucson. They were talking about me in Tohono O'odham.

"Who is that dirty old white man?" they asked. "He sure thinks he can dance. Did you see him dancing with that lady?"

I just sat there and listened, and then I said to them in their language, "You don't say!" I said some other things too in Tohono O'odham, asking them where they were from, and how they were doing. Oh my goodness! They were so surprised and discombobulated. They didn't say anything. Pretty soon they just picked up their sacks and left. I don't know whatever became of them, but maybe they learned a lesson. It's not nice to talk about a dirty old white man when you think he can't hear.

When I was in Brazil in 2006 with Julio, I noticed what a tremendous country that is for dancing. Down there, the people just love to dance. I was on crutches by then, but from the waste up I could still dance. And until recently, I could sit in a chair and wiggle the top. But I can't do that anymore. So walking and dancing are kinda nice. But I had 70 years, for God sake. That should be enough. Some people don't have any years.

As far as the arms, one thing I regret is not having done enough artwork – painting and sculpting – but that's beside the point. I do miss hugging. I come from an Irish Catholic culture where people didn't hug. That's just how it was. As a result, when I left home, I had no idea about hugging.

When I got to Santa Barbara with the Franciscans, in about my second or third year of theology... this was when the hippies were going full blast, and everyone started hugging. The friars decided to have sensitivity sessions, and brought in Esalen.[26] They brought in therapists to help us get in touch with our emotions. There were about 50 of us, and the therapists divided us into groups and had us talk. It really loosened us up. In fact, by the time we were through, about half of the seminarians left the friary.

That was a great time. It really brought life to the fraternity. One thing I learned then was how to hug. They didn't teach us how to hug, but our emotions opened up and we started hugging.

About a year later, we got to visit our families. We hadn't seen them in many years. I was all hyped up, but I was also scared because I knew when I got home, I was sure my Dad would extend his hand. And I wanted to hug him. I was in a quandary. So I went to one of my professors and I told him how I felt.

"Richard," he asked, "How old are you?"

I said, "26."

He said, "You're an adult. Your father never learned to hug. Nobody taught him. You're a man now, so you can teach him. You can teach him by giving him a hug."

"Oh my God!" I said. "I can't do that!"

"Well... it's up to you."

I was sweating all the way home. My Dad met me at the airport, and sure enough, extended his hand. And I hugged him! He put his two hands on my chest, and pushed me away. It wasn't offensive, just fearful.

Well, the next time I went home, he gave me a hug! He learned in that one lesson that it's safe to hug a man.

On my father's 80th birthday, the whole family got together. We had a Mass in our house, and after the readings, I told my Dad what I thought of him. They were all good things. Then I asked my brothers and sisters if they had something to say. As usual, in the old Purcell fashion, nobody said anything. It was the same holding back – not expressing emotions.

But pretty soon my Dad spoke up. He sat real straight and stiff. He kinda looked like a turkey. He said, "Well, there's one thing I know for sure – Dick taught me how to hug." Isn't that something? That's how powerful that thing was for him. That thing of hugging.

After I was ordained, I went to the reservations and started hugging. Those people weren't huggers either, but once I started hugging, it spread. They became huggers. Very interesting. Not everybody. Some people have had things that happen in their life that prevent them from hugging – traumas and stuff.

So that's what I miss about my arms and hands. Giving hugs.

Julio Moreno, one of Richard's caregivers, compiled an online memorial for Richard at:

http://www.legacy.com/guestbook/sfgate/guestbook.aspx?n=richard-purcell&pid=152878435&eid=sp_gbupdate

Gary Sponholtz, another member of the Circle of Care, has memorialized Richard in this photo and video website:

http://web.me.com/garyinrv/Richard_Purcell_ofm/Richards_World.html

The artist Lara Campos has painted a mural for Richard in Balmy Alley, between 24th and 25th Streets in San Francisco.

# NOTES

## Part I: Finding Richard

1 Vincent van Gogh, *1-Famous-Quotes.com*

## Part II: Documenting a Life

2 Willa Cather. 1-Famous-Quotes.com

3 The term "O'odham" means "people," and can be applied to both the Tohono O'odham and Akimel O'odham.

4 The Catholic Worker movement was founded in the 1930's by Dorothy Day to advance Catholic social teachings. Still alive, the movement focuses on nonviolence and caring for the poor through communal households, soup kitchens and farms.

5 Dorothy Day, *The Duty of Delight,* p. 636.

6 For years, the Aurora Dawn Foundation did serve women with AIDS. Although Marty's Place itself was set up for men only, the Aurora Dawn Foundation funded clothing vouchers, retreats, and a free breakfast program for women with HIV.

7 It is worth noting that none of the Aurora Dawn Board ever got paid for their services. Their time and efforts were all voluntary.

## Part III: Saying Goodbye

8 John O'Donohue, *Eternal Echoes: Celtic Reflections on our Yearning to Belong*, p. 19.

9 Swetha Sridharan, *Migration Information Source*, October, 2008.

10 Ceci Connally, *The Washington Post*, August 12, 2008

11 William Cleary, *How the Wild Things Pray,* p. 13

12 James Carroll, *Practicing Catholic*, p. 286.

13 Richard Adler and Jerry Ross, "Whatever Lola Wants (Lola Gets)," in *Damn Yankees* (Miami, FL: CCP Belwin, 1983): 76-81.

14 Walter L. Williams, *Spirit and the Flesh: Sexual Diversity in American Indian Culture*, p. 49

15 Ibid., p. 64

16 Spanish speaking Evangelistic Christians are regularly standing on 24th St. and Mission in San Francisco, preaching their views through bullhorns.

17 Richard was referring to the communion wafer, which indeed looks like something people feed to fish.

18 Frank MacEowen, *Mist-Filled Path: Celtic Wisdom for Exiles, Wanders and Seekers*, p. 138.

19 Ibid., p. 132

20 Francis of Assisi "Canticle of the Sun" in *Francis of Assisi: Performing the Gospel Life,* trans. Lawrence S. Cunningham (Grand Rapids MI: William B. Eerdmans Publishing Company, 2004), 99-100.

21 Hafiz, *The Gift: Poems by Hafiz The Great Sufi Master* p. 28

22 At the time of this writing, Most Holy Redeemer owns the Coming Home Hospice building. The church had started a hospice there in the 80s to care for many of the people in the city who were dying of AIDS. At the time Richard moved into Coming Home Hospice, the building was leased by California Pacific Medical Center.

23 Pema Chödrön, *Start Where You Are: A Guide to Compassionate Living*, p. 3

## Part IV. Documenting a Death

24 Sogyal Rinpoche, *The Tibetan Book of Living and Dying,* p. 11.

## Park V: Richard's Transcribed Journals

25 Martha Whitmore Hickman, *Healing After Loss: Daily Meditations for Working Through Grief,* December 19.

26 Esalen is a retreat center near Big Sur, California, which came out of the 60s' counterculture movements. Individual practitioners associated with Esalen have conducted experimental psychological seminars with different groups of people. According to Richard, the Franciscans also participated in some of these encounter groups.

# BIBLIOGRAPHY

Adler, Richard and Jerry Ross. "Whatever Lola Wants (Lola Gets)." In *Damn Yankees*. Miami, FL: CCP Belwin, 1983: 76-81.

Carey, Ken. *Star Seed Transmissions*. New York: HarperCollins, 1982

Carey, Ken. *Return of the Bird Tribes*. New York: HarperCollins, 1988

Carey, Ken. Terra *Christa: The Global Spiritual Awakening*. New York: HarperCollins, 1985

Carroll, James. *Practicing Catholic*. New York: Houghton Mifflin Harcourt, 2009

Chödrön, Pema. *Start Where You Are: A Guide to Compassionate Living*. Boston: Shambhala, 2001

Chopra, Deepak. Larry King. *Larry King Live*. Wendy Walker Whitworth, producer. October 29, 2009.

Cleary, William. *How the Wild Things Pray*. Leavenworth, KS: Peace Publishing, 1999.

Connolly, Ceci, "As nation treats gays better, asylum is elusive." *Washington Post*. 12 August 2008. 22 April 2008 http://www.washingtonpost.com/wp-dyn/content/article/2008/08/11/AR2008081102038.html

Cozzens, Donald. *The Changing Face of the Priesthood:* Collegeville, MN: The Order of St. Benedict Inc, 2000.

Cunningham, Lawrence S. *Francis of Assisi: Performing the Gospel Life:* Grand Rapids, MI: William Be Eerdmans Publishing Company, 2004.

Day, Dorothy. *The Duties of Delight: The Diaries of Dorothy Day.* Robert Ellsberg (Ed). Milwaukee, WI: Marquette University Press, 2008.

*Doubt*. DVD. Directed by John Patrick Shanley. 2008, Los Angeles, CA: Miramax, 2009.

Elie, Paul. *The Life You Save May be Your Own: An American Pilgrimage*. New York: Farrar, Straus & Giroux, 2008.

Hafiz. *The Gift: Poems by Hafiz the Great Sufi Master.* Translated by Daniel Ladinsky. New York: Penguin Putman, Inc., 1999

Hickman, Martha Whitmore. *Healing After Loss: Daily Meditations for Working through Grief.* New York: HarperCollins, 2002, December 19.

*In the Workshop of the Lord: Sister Mary Trinitas Morin, Her Life, Her Art.* Directed by D. Ayers. Gallery Trinitas, University of Great Falls, Montana. KRTV, 2004

Jones, Melissa. Following fracas, Indians to screen own missionaries. *The Catholic Reporter.* December 15, 1978.

Krasny, Michael. *Spiritual Envy: An Agnostic's Quest.* Novato, CA: New World Library, 2010.

MacEowen, Frank. *The Mist-Filled Path: Celtic Wisdom for Exiles, Wanderers and Seekers.* Novato, CA: New World Library, 2002.

Maté Gabor. *When the Body Says No: Understanding the Stress-Disease Connection.* Hoboken, NJ: John Wiley & Sons, 2003.

O'Donohue, John. *Eternal Echoes: Celtic Reflections on our Yearning to Belong.* New York: Cliff Street, 1999.

*Out. The Glenn Burke Story.* Produced by Doug Harris & Sean Madison. Comcast Sports Net: San Francisco, 2010.

Richo, David. *Shadow Dance: Liberating the Power and Creativity of your Dark Side.* Boston: Shambala Publications, 1999.

Rinpoche, Sogyal. *The Tibetan book of Living and Dying.* Edited by Patrick Gaffney and Andrew Harvey. San Francisco : Harper San Francisco, 1992.

Rinpoche, Sogyal. *Tibetan Wisdom for Living and Dying.* Boulder, CO: Sounds True, 2003

Sittser, Gerald. *A Grace Disguised: How the Soul Grows through Loss.* Grand Rapids: Zondervan, 2004.

Sridharan, Swetha. "The difficulties of US asylum claims based on sexual orientation." *Migration Information Source.* October 2008. http://www.migrationinformation.org/USfocus/display.cfm?ID=700

Vincent Van Gogh. 1-Famous-Quotes.com, Gledhill Enterprises, 2011. http://www.1-famous-quotes.com/quote/401364, accessed Mon Aug 29 22:42:17 2011.

White, Edmund. *City boy: My life in New York during the 1960's and '70s.* New York: Bloomsbury, 2009.

Willa Cather. 1-Famous-Quotes.com, Gledhill Enterprises, 2011. http://www.1-famous-quotes.com/quote/259940, accessed Fri Sep 2 21:37:34 2011.

Williams, Walter, L. *Spirit and the Flesh: Sexual Diversity in American Indian Culture.* Boston: Beacon Press, 1992.